THOMAS KYD

Oxford University Press, Ely House, London W.1

GLASGOW NEW YORK TORONTO MELBOURNE WELLINGTON
CAPE TOWN SALISBURY IBADAN NAIROBI LUSAKA ADDIS ABABA
BOMBAY CALCUTTA MADRAS KARACHI LAHORE DACCA
KUALA LUMPUR HONG KONG TOKYO

THOMAS KYD
Facts and Problems

by
ARTHUR FREEMAN

CLARENDON PRESS OXFORD
1967

© *Oxford University Press 1967*

PRINTED IN GREAT BRITAIN
BY W. & J. MACKAY & CO. LTD., CHATHAM, KENT

To the Memory of
WILLIAM A. JACKSON

PREFACE

CHRISTOPHER MARLOWE and Thomas Kyd are generally represented as the two premier English tragedians before Shakespeare, and the influence of Kyd upon Shakespeare's theatrical technique considered no less, by most, than Marlowe's upon Shakespearean verse. Yet while Marlowe's work has attracted appreciative criticism for centuries, and his plays retained a popularity on the stage in our own day, Kyd's have been relegated largely to the twin pigeon-holes of scholarship and neglect. Marlowe's quatercentennial birthday in 1964, widely observed, borrowed at least some of its light from the Stratford Jubilee of the same year; but no ceremony whatever attended the anniversary of Kyd's birth in 1958. Literature about Marlowe since 1900 will more than fill a five-foot shelf, whereas there is yet no book in English concerned wholly with Thomas Kyd and his work.

The comparative obscurity of Kyd is not entirely without reason, of course: one undoubted tragedy, a translation or two, and a scattering of attributions cannot compare, as extant *oeuvre*, with Marlowe's solid corpus of six plays, a long poem, and others shorter; with Kyd there is simply less to discuss, and much of it necessarily of conjectural authorship. Moreover, the appeal of Marlowe's poetry, finer by far at its maximum than Kyd's, has made its author quotable in small doses and hence memorable in particulars, where Kyd's writing demands either a long and sometimes tortuous immersion in the uneven text, or the advantage of staging that his plays have now ceased to command.

Has Kyd a claim to our consideration beyond his unquestioned originality, historical 'importance', and the theatrical debt owed him by Shakespeare and other eminent successors? Perhaps little; but perhaps more than has been usually granted. I have tried to estimate Kyd's achievement in our terms and our time as well as in his and Shakespeare's; I have tried to evaluate the plays themselves as well as their influence, and to bring together the surviving work and the personality into a coherent perspective. But some sort of scholarly consensus must precede critical investigation, and my first concern here has been factual, with matters of date, authorship, source, and stage history, with sifting traditional hypotheses and establishing whatever can be agreed upon summarily. My aim has been to provide a broad basis for the study of Kyd's works, and my approach relatively conservative. I have tried to be scrupulous in distinguishing between opinions and facts, and where footnotes are not given, anything stated factually should be either self-evident or verifiable in the obvious source.

The first two chapters cover Kyd's life, with emphasis on his environment, schooling, early company connexions and colleagues, his service with a 'noble lord', his scrape with the Government, subsequent imprisonment, and death. The third deals with the authorship, date, and sources of *The Spanish Tragedy*, and the fourth continues with a critical discussion of its style and structure, its theatricality, its printing history, stage history, echoes and parodies, and its critical and editorial career. The fifth chapter treats *Soliman and Perseda*, its attribution to Kyd, its date, sources, and reputation. The sixth chapter deals with Kyd's translations, fragments, lost plays, and apocrypha; here I give brief consideration to the translations, because much has been already done, and I slight the problems of *ur-Hamlet* and *ur-Andronicus*, because these are essentially Shakespearian questions and cannot be more than glozed over in a work of this scope. Two appendixes present (A) a transcript of the two letters from Kyd to Sir John Puckering in 1593, and (B) the summary of some Chancery documents concerning Francis Kyd.

My quotations from Kyd's works have been from the following texts: for *The Spanish Tragedy*, Philip Edwards's modern-spelling edition, for *Soliman and Perseda*, Boas's edition with some readings of J. J. Murray, as indicated, and for the remaining works, Boas or Appendix A. Line-references are in all cases to the edition cited, and quotations from other Elizabethan writers follow the editions listed in the bibliography.

I must record my gratitude to the attendants and officials of the Widener and Houghton Libraries at Harvard, the Newberry Library, the British Museum, the Bodleian, the Public Record Office, and the Guildhall Library; to the Society of Fellows of Harvard University for its continued munificence; and to the Graduate School of Boston University for a grant in aid of preparing the typescript. For assistance and criticism at many stages I am most indebted to Professors Herschel Baker, William Bond, Alfred Harbage, and Harry Levin, and for particular patience with my bibliographical uncertainties, and generosity with his time and understanding, to the late Professor Jackson.

CONTENTS

ABBREVIATIONS

BRS	British Record Society
CSPD	Calendar of State Papers Domestic
DNB	Dictionary of National Biography
HMC	Historical Manuscripts Commission
JEGP	Journal of English and Germanic Philology
MLN	Modern Language Notes
MLR	Modern Language Review
MLQ	Modern Language Quarterly
MP	Modern Philology
MSR	Malone Society Reprints
NED	New English Dictionary
NQ	Notes and Queries
PCRS	Publications of the Catholic Records Society
PMLA	Publications of the Modern Language Association
PQ	Philological Quarterly
RES	Review of English Studies
SEL	Studies in English Literature
SJ	Shakespeare Jahrbuch
SP	Studies in Philology
STC	Short-Title Catalogue of English Books before 1640

Orthographical Note

The titles of early printed works and quotations from them have been presented in original spelling, with the exceptions (a) that u/v and i/j have been normalized, and abbreviations expanded, and (b) that extremely familiar titles (e.g. *The Spanish Tragedy*) have been modernized. In quoting from manuscripts or transcripts of manuscripts, however, the practice of normalization and expansion of abbreviation has *not* been followed.

CHAPTER I

EARLY LIFE AND CIRCLE

THOMAS KYD was baptized in the Church of St. Mary Woolnoth, London, on 6 November 1558, eleven days before the accession of Queen Elizabeth at Westminster, six years before Shakespeare's birth at Stratford and Marlowe's at Canterbury. The registers of the parish record the event:

> November   Thomas, son of Francis Kidd, *Citizen*
> 6   *and Writer of the Courte Letter of*
>   *London.*[1]

He was buried on 15 August 1594, at thirty-six, about sixteen months after Marlowe; Shakespeare survived him by twenty-two years, and his Queen by nine.

Kyd's father, Francis, was a scrivener, a 'Writer of the Courte Letter', and at the time of his son's birth he had been a freeman of the Company of Scriveners about a year. He rose to the position of Warden of the Company in 1580, engaging several apprentices along the way; one of his apprentices, William Dunce, in turn gained admission to the Company in 1591.[2] A Chancery case of 1571 involving Francis is summarized in Appendix B.

Kyd's mother, Anna (or Anne, or Agnes), is named, in addition to her husband, as a legatee of Francis Coldocke, the publisher, in a will dated 1 February 1603 (20 Bolein). By the end of 1594 the elder Kyds had moved to the neighbouring parish of St. Mary Colchurch, as evidenced by the deed of renunciation filed by both on 30 December of the same year; and Anna was interred in the church cemetery there at the end of 1605:

[1] J. M. S. Brooke and A. W. C. Hallen, eds., *The Transcript of the Registers of the United Parishes of St. Mary Woolnoth and St. Mary Woolchurch Haw* (London, 1886), p. 9. The identification of the dramatist with this Thomas Kyd was first suggested by Gordon Goodwin, *NQ*, 8th ser., V (1894), 305–6, and may safely be endorsed. The surname is a rare one, and this and all subsequent records of Thomas, son of Francis Kyd, and his family square perfectly with what is otherwise known of the life-span and living conditions of the dramatist.

[2] See B. M. Wagner, *NQ*, CLV (1928), 420, citing Bodleian MS. Rawlinson D. 51, fols. 25^r–26^r.

December   Anne Kydd the wief of ffraunces Kydd
9   was buried the 9 daie of December 1605
            she lieth in the newe burieng place.[1]

No record of the death or remarriage of Francis Kyd has been discovered, despite his comparative eminence in the community, and
it is possible that he moved once again after 1605.

Other family records survive in the registers of St. Mary Woolnoth and St. Mary Colchurch: Thomas's younger sister Ann was
baptized on 24 September 1561. A servant of the Kyds, Prudence
Cooke, was buried on 2 September 1563. Francis held the office of
churchwarden at St. Mary Woolnoth's for a two-year term, 1575–6,
and in 1578 he drafted the will of a local well-to-do brewer, Richard
Pelter, by whom he was rewarded with the bequest of a robe in
addition to fee.[2] Another child, Thomas's brother William, died in
mid-1602 (Guildhall MS.):

June   William Kydd the sonne of ffrauncis Kydd
28   was buried the 28 daie of June 1602 in the newe
        burieng place.

These are all the early remains of Thomas Kyd and his family;
inference must fill out the picture of his youth.

As a scrivener, Francis Kyd was engaged in a profitable and
ancient trade, but one for which contemporary writers exhibited
little respect. '*Noverint*', or '*noverint*-maker', the cant terms for
scrivener (from the formal commencement of documents, '*Noverint
universi per praesentes*', i.e. 'know all men by these presents') were
distinctly derisive in the Elizabethan era: Nashe complains about an
'unskilfull pen-man or Noverint maker' who was supposedly producing unauthorized manuscript copies of *The Terrors of the Night*,
and Greene in his *Groatsworth of Wit* speaks bitterly of a man who
'was not . . . altogether unlettered, for he had good experience in
a *Noverint*, and by the universal tearmes therein contained, had
driven many a yoong Gentleman to seeke unknowen countries. . . .'
The author of *Histriomastix* laments, 'O age, when every Scriveners
boy shall dippe/Profaning quills into Thessaliaes spring.'[3] All such

---

[1] This and subsequent St. Mary Colchurch records are quoted from the
parish register, Guildhall MS. 4438; the leaves are unnumbered, but within
each category (baptisms, marriages, burials) the entries are chronological.

[2] Gordon Goodwin, *NQ*, 8th ser., V (1894), pp. 305–6, citing *Calendar of
Wills Proved in the Court of Hustings*, II, 693.

[3] *Histriomastix*, III, 197–8. See John Marston, *Plays*, ed. H. H. Wood
(London, 1939), III, 274.

popular odium is explained by the nature of the scriveners' business: originally a guild of scribes and letter-writers, they had gained a monopoly on engrossing charters, contracts, testaments, and official documents. By the early seventeenth century, moreover, they functioned not only as notaries and copyists, but also as money-lenders; Doll in Dekker's *Northward Ho!* (1607) refers to a 'scrivener' who has just 'put my father in minde of a bond, that wilbe forfit this night if the mony be not payd. . . .' And if usury were not enough, we can appreciate also that attorneys usually belonged to the Company and paid dues; and no profession was so execrated by Elizabethan writers as the lawyer's.

In Francis Kyd's time, however, scriveners were known formally as 'Writers of the Court Letter', and considered themselves a distinguished guild, or 'mystery'. They maintained high educational standards among themselves, as attests a mandate of 1497, whereby any scrivener's apprentice who had not a 'perfect congruity of grammar, which is the thing most necessary and expedient to every person exercising the science and faculty of the mystery' was to be sent to a grammar school until 'he be erudite in the books of genders, declensions, preterites and supines, equivix, and sinonimes', all this upon penalty of a heavy fine. Thus the Company had a tradition of literacy, and its members, like Francis Kyd, were sought after as churchwardens, and for other parish offices requiring a clear hand. Nor was Thomas Kyd the only scrivener's son to put his grammar to good use; John Milton's father was a member of the same Company.

From the entries in the Scriveners' Company records which concern Francis Kyd's apprentices, from his terms as churchwarden and as Company Warden, and from our knowledge of at least one household servant, we may safely infer that the Kyds were reasonably well-to-do. During Thomas's youth they lived in a thriving quarter of London. Their parish church, St. Mary Woolnoth, one of seven in the Ward of Langborn, was located near the western end of Lombard Street in what is now the banking district of the City. In Langborn, Stow (1598) says, there are 'seven Parish Churches . . . one Hall of a companie [the Pewterers'], diverse faire houses for merchants, and other monuments none'. Perhaps the Kyds occupied one of the 'faire houses' on Lombard Street near the church, for Lombard Street was by long tradition the street of scriveners, goldsmiths (whence today's banks), and, latterly, book-sellers. Inquisitions Post Mortem of 27 October 1575 and 15 April

1578 into the estate of Henry Gainsford, 'citizen and goldsmith of London', list Francis Kyd among the tenants of '11 messuages situate in Lumbardstrete'.[1]

Near by, if not adjacent to Francis Kyd's lodgings, would have been the establishment of a bookseller and publisher, Francis Coldocke, who in 1561 began his career on 'Lombard Street, over against the Cardinal's Hat', and remained there until affluence moved him to St. Paul's Churchyard, about 1570.[2] That Coldocke was a friend of the Kyds we know from his will, leaving separate token bequests of twenty shillings to both Francis and Anna; and, as we shall see, at least one of his publications was well known to Thomas. Another Lombard Street neighbour was the bookseller Thomas Hacket, who set up shop near Coldocke on Lombard Street about 1562, moved away before 1568,[3] and twenty-two years later, back at Lombard Street 'under the sign of the Popes head', published Tasso's *Padre di Famiglia*, 'translated by T. K.', as *The Housholders Philosophie*. Close quarters made for friction between the two booksellers, and in 1562 they were both fined by the Stationers' Company for giving each other 'unseemly words'.

Otherwise, despite 'monuments none', Lombard Street was a major artery, the access to the wholesale wool markets of London and a great street for taverns: the famous Bishop's Hat, and the Salutation were there; goldsmiths abounded, among whom, as we have seen, was Hugh Keale, who served with Francis Kyd as churchwarden of St. Mary Woolnoth in the year 1575. The 'one Simpson' who had Francis Bacon arrested for debt in 1598 was a Lombard Street goldsmith and moneylender.

Of Francis Kyd's known associates, Coldocke was perhaps locally the most distinguished. He entered his first book as a publisher in 1561, the year in which he engaged his first apprentice, and was received into the livery of the Stationers' Company on 29 June

---

[1] *BRS*, XXVI, 196, and XXXVI, 7. Gainsford's properties included 'The 4th part of 11 messuages situate in Lumbardstrete in the parish of St Mary Wolnoth in the Ward of langborne, London, now or late in the tenure of *Hugh Keale, Fulk Edwardes, Hugh Newbole, Ralph Smith, Francis Kidd, John Wilkyns, William Jones, George Newbole, James Allen, William Ingram* and *Richard Sharpe*' (quoting the later Inquisition, which is substantially the same as the earlier). Gainsford's share of these tenements was estimated worth seven pounds *per annum*.

[2] R. B. McKerrow, *A Dictionary of Printers and Booksellers, 1557–1640* (London, 1910), p. 72.

[3] E. G. Duff, *A Century of the English Book Trade, 1457–1557* (London, 1905), pp. 63–64.

1570. At about that time he transferred his quarters from Lombard Street to the centre of bookselling activity in London, St. Paul's Churchyard. He served as Junior Warden of the Stationers' Company in 1580-1; as Senior Warden in 1587-8-9; and as Master twice, in 1591-2, and 1595-6. By this time he was one of the largest and most important dealers in books in London, although his last-dated surviving publication is of 1590. He died between 3 September 1602 and 1 February 1603, when his will was proved, with bequests of twenty shillings to each of the elder Kyds.

Coldocke's 'list', in so far as it survives, was a respectable one; save one early ballad (1566), none of his books was particularly sensational. Thirty of his publications are now extant, a large proportion of which are sermons and theological treatises. Roger Ascham was perhaps his most popular author. *The Civill Warres of Fraunce*, by Jean de Serres (three parts, 1574), represented one of his more ambitious efforts; but the only book of Coldocke's we can be sure found its way into Thomas Kyd's hands was a slight production, Henry Wotton's *A Courtlie Controversie of Cupids Cautels* (1578), which evidently saw one edition only. One of its stories provided the source for the play-within-play of *The Spanish Tragedy*, and for the main plot of *Soliman and Perseda*. It would be natural to suppose that the young Thomas read through the immensely popular *Ethiopian Romance* of Heliodorus, the first three editions of which in English were published by Coldocke (1569, 1577, 1587) and perhaps also Peter Beverley's *Historie of Ariodanto and Jenevra* (1566), but we can only suppose.

A different sort of stationer, a specialist in broadside ballads and twopenny pamphlets about murders and disasters, was John Kyd, printer of *The Murder of John Brewen* (1592). Although 'Kyd' is an uncommon name, there is no reason to suppose, with Lee and the *DNB*, that John Kyd was a brother of the dramatist, or even a relative. There are no records pertaining to him in the registers of St. Mary Woolnoth or any adjacent churches, and since Thomas Kyd's authorship of *John Brewen* has now been largely discredited, there remains no documented business connexion to be pursued.

From what we know and can safely infer, then, Thomas Kyd passed his earliest years on or near Lombard Street in a lively commercial quarter of London, in a comfortable middle-class household, and in the company of a younger sister, a brother, and a servant or two.

Whether because Thomas lacked the 'perfect congruity of grammar' necessary to an apprentice, or because the education of an heir was a luxury he could now afford, Francis Kyd enrolled his son at Merchant Taylors' School on 26 October 1565. '26 Oct. Thomas Kydd, s. of *Francis*, scrivener',[1] the entry reads. Thomas would have been just seven at the time, and the schooling he was to receive would serve him for a short lifetime of literary accomplishment. For it was a remarkable school he had entered.

Merchant Taylors' School was younger than Thomas, having been founded on 24 September 1561, the very day of Ann Kyd's baptism. It was located in the parish of St. Lawrence Poultney, Ward of Downgate, on Suffolk Lane 'turning up to Candlewicke Streets' (Stow); its quarters were a mansion formerly owned by the Radcliffes. The walk would have been a short one for Thomas, who was expected to arrive in the morning 'at seaven of the clock both winter & summer, & tarry there untill eleaven, and returne againe at one of the clock, and departe at five';[2] he would very likely have passed his church, turned down St. Swithin's Lane, turned left on Candlewick Street (now Cannon Street) and continued toward the river-bank via Bush Lane. A passage-way led from Bush Lane to Suffolk Lane, and half-way between that and Thames Street lay the school. The walk now takes about ten minutes, and perhaps the proximity of the establishment partly determined Francis in his choice.

Admission requirements at Merchant Taylors' were not inconsiderable. Thomas at seven was two years younger than Edmund Spenser had been when he entered, but nevertheless he was obliged to know 'the catechism in English or Latyn', and be able to 'read perfectly & write competently'. Merchant Taylors' had a system of scholarships, full and partial, and there is an implicit distinction between the children whose names are followed by the names and qualities of their fathers, and those who are merely listed; hence we may be sure that Francis Kyd was not poor enough to qualify for complete remission of his son's tuition. He paid a 12*d.* fee at the time of registration (Stat. XXVI) and either 2*s.* 2*d.* per quarter as a 'poor parent' or, more plausibly, 5*s.* per quarter as a 'rich or meane man'. In its early days Merchant Taylors' was almost entirely

---

[1] Charles J. Robinson, *A Register of the Scholars Admitted into Merchant Taylors' School, 1562–1874* (Lewes, 1882), I, 9.

[2] Article XXVII of the Statutes: see F. W. M. Draper, *Four Centuries of Merchant Taylors' School* (London, 1961), p. 246.

populated by the children of tradesmen, save for the indigent scholars specially admitted at Mulcaster's discretion.

As a middle-class school, Merchant Taylors' was considerably less conservative than St. Paul's or Eton, and the original statutes of 1561 are notably liberal in temper and letter;[1] but the progressive atmosphere was due not only to the Company of Merchant Taylors, but specifically to the first headmaster, Richard Mulcaster. Mulcaster's place in the history of English education has been assessed frequently, and a good deal of his long life is known. He was an excellent Latinist and Greek scholar, a pupil of Sir John Cheke at King's College, Cambridge; a dedicated but irascible man, generous but severe with his students (Fuller); and a precursor, in his educational theory, of Montaigne and of Bacon. He believed in physical education ('Then must ye also have a special care, that the bodie be well appointed . . . The end of education and train is to help nature unto her perfection'),[2] although 'tennys-play' and other 'losse of tyme' were forbidden by the school statutes (XXX). He believed in the right of girls to a liberal education. He taught music and singing to his students, as we know from Sir James Whitlocke, and presented plays at Court—and presumably in Merchant Taylors' Hall—by which means, says Whitlocke, he taught his scholars 'good behaviour and audacity'. For all his humanistic emphasis on the classics he was able to say, 'I love Rome, but London better; I favour Italy, but England more; I honour Latin, but worship English.' Such was the man who, with the assisting ushers he himself chose, directed the education of Thomas Kyd.

The nature and duration of Kyd's education remains, however, a matter of restricted conjecture. F. S. Boas has very ingeniously shown where Kyd's knowledge of French and Italian betrays itself, and tabulated the classical authors he shows familiarity with. From the abundance of common Latin tags and occasional lapses of vocabulary and history we gain the impression of 'a clever schoolboy's reading, reinforced by later private study, rather than of a methodical university training'.[3] Boas's implied censure is both fair and unfair. It is true that Kyd's translation of Tasso is peppered with errors,

---

[1] See especially Articles XXV ('There shalbe taught in the said schoole children of all nations & countryes indifferently . . .'), and XXVIII, insisting on the constant use of the more expensive wax candles, rather than tallow, which smoked.

[2] Draper, p. 23, quoting *The Elementarie* (1582).

[3] F. S. Boas, ed., *The Works of Thomas Kyd* (corrected reissue, Oxford, 1955), xvii.

but no more so than most Elizabethan translations, and one hesitates to hold an author sternly to account for mistakes in a 'plaine and unpolished' version 'digested thus in haste', as the author himself characterizes it, to the extent of finding that it 'fully deserves Nashe's sneer'. *Cornelia* is in the main a faithful translation from Garnier's French, and most of the Latin errors in *The Spanish Tragedy* are probably the fault of a type-setter. Furthermore, while Kyd's ancient history and geography had their shaky moments, it is perhaps excessively strict to say that he 'blunders grossly' in his modern history (Boas, xix, followed by Edwards, p. 26) when he is simply recounting folk-tales which his commentators have been unable to find in Holinshed and Polydore Virgil.[1]

What Kyd did learn, apparently, was Latin, fluently enough to compose in at some length, French, and Italian, both of which languages he translated from, and possibly composed in. Perhaps he knew Greek, if Soliman's speeches in *The Spanish Tragedy* were really written originally in that language. Spanish he almost certainly did not know, however. None of his contemporaries or early critics refer to him as 'learned', we may note, and Dekker actually distinguishes between 'learned Watson', 'ingenious Achelow', and merely 'industrious Kyd'. It is perhaps just to say that his education, by its brevity, left him inclined to exhibit what he knew, and thus on occasion given to pedantry. It is easy to guess why Nashe, with his university education so casually—and arrogantly—worn, might find Kyd's schoolboy classicism a fair and slow-moving target for his own scorn.

Félix Carrère, among others, has permitted himself to imagine the young Kyd taking part in Mulcaster's theatricals, 'soit à la Cour, soit à l'école'.[2] The supposition is feasible, of course, although there are no records of performances by Mulcaster's boys until Shrove Tuesday, 1573, when Thomas may no longer have been at Merchant Taylors'; at any rate, it is scarcely providing evidence to point out that the play-within-play in *The Spanish Tragedy* shows 'une connaissance pratique de l'art dramatique'—a playwright, after all, might be expected to have acquired that independently. Mulcaster's boys performed at Court during Candlemas, 1573, when *Timoclea at the Siege of Thebes* was represented, with such notable lack of success that 'One Maske lykwyse prepared & brought thither in Redynesse' was 'not showen for the Tediusnesse of the playe that

---

[1] See Chapter III.
[2] Félix Carrère, *Le Théâtre de Thomas Kyd* (Toulouse, 1951), p. 15.

nighte'.[1] They were back again at Hampton Court the next Shrove Tuesday, and again in 1576. At Christmas, 1582, and Shrovetide, 1583, Mulcaster's troupe presented 'A historie of Ariodante and Genevora', presumably based on Peter Beverley's romance which Coldocke had published; but Thomas Kyd was by now twenty-four and long out of school.

How long did Kyd remain at Merchant Taylors' School? We possess no record of student departures, and we can only surmise. Spenser entered at the age of nine, and remained for about eight years; Robert Wilmot preceded Kyd by two years, and matriculated at Queen's College, Cambridge, in 1572, nine years after enrolling at Merchant Taylors'; Gregory Downhall or Downham seems to have spent ten or eleven years at school. Considering Kyd's age upon entrance, we may guess that if he pursued a full course at Merchant Taylors' his residence may have lasted from eight to ten years, or until 1573–5. Of course, he may have left or have been withdrawn at any time.

Under Mulcaster, Merchant Taylors' School became not only the largest school in England (with 250 students, as originally projected in the statutes) but one most distinguished by its graduates. Kyd's schoolfellows at Merchant Taylors' included Edmund Spenser (who was six years older and probably, if schoolboy tradition were served, had little to do with him), Lancelot Andrewes, only three years older than Kyd, and Matthew Gwynne, a future Latin poet and playwright, who entered in 1570. Robert Wilmot, entering in 1563 went on to Queen's College (B.A., 1576–7), was ordained deacon in 1578, and has been identified with the student of the Inner Temple who, with three others, 'compiled' the tragedy of *Tancred and Gismund* and presented it before the Queen (Venn, IV, 425). The identification seems most unlikely.[2] Nor is there any reason to equate, as T. W. Baldwin does,[3] Gregory Downhall or Downham, the future Sizar of Pembroke Hall, Cambridge, and Master in Chancery (Cooper, II, 61; R. Willis, *Mount Tabor*, 1639) with the 'C. Downhalus' who contributed a commendatory poem to Thomas Watson's

[1] A. Feuillerat, *Documents Relating to the Office of the Revels in the Time of Queen Elizabeth* (Louvain, 1908), p. 206.

[2] See E. K. Chambers, *The Elizabethan Stage* (Oxford, 1923), III, 514, indicating that the play was originally drafted by Inner Temple students as early as 1566.

[3] T. W. Baldwin, *On the Literary Genetics of Shakespeare's Plays* (Urbana, Ill., 1959), p. 178, presumably following David Horne, *The Life and Mino Works of George Peele* (New Haven, 1952), pp. 67–68.

Hekatompathia (1582). The initial is 'C', not 'G', and if there were any doubt of its typographical accuracy it is absolved by the same name, in the same form, appearing in Watson's slightly earlier Latin version of *Antigone*, again as a eulogist's. But if Kyd were still at Merchant Taylors' in 1571, he would certainly have made the acquaintance of the son of the Lord Mayor of London, Thomas Lodge, who was just Kyd's age and spending a year in the school before going up to Trinity College, Oxford. Few schools can boast a quartet of prospective writers like Spenser, Andrewes, Kyd, and Lodge, within the first decade of their existence. And to Richard Mulcaster, whose portrait hung in Andrewes's study while he laboured on the Great Bible of 1611, all these literary lights undoubtedly owed some of their coming brilliance.

Of Kyd's career between Merchant Taylors' School and about 1583, a span of perhaps eight or ten years, we know nothing for fact. A certain amount of negative evidence can be adduced, at least about university training, but most of the conjectures of Boas about Kyd's early professional activities have little to recommend them.

Despite the provision of forty-three tuition scholarships for Merchant Taylors' boys at St. John's College, Kyd's name does not appear at any time on the Oxford rolls; nor did he attend Cambridge, enter the Inns of Court, or visit Douai, like his play-writing colleague Thomas Watson. What of his classical reading we can reconstruct from quotations in the writings might all have been done at Merchant Taylors', and such extra-curricular works as Jasper Heywood's Seneca or Wotton's translation of Jacques Yver would have demanded little enough of midnight oil. There is no evidence whatever that Kyd was at any time abroad from England, although Boas has attempted to adduce the nature and extent of Kyd's travels from a pair of lines in *The Spanish Tragedy* and *Cornelia*. If only as examples of improper 'reading in', I think these inferences deserve a close look. In IV. i. of *The Spanish Tragedy* Hieronimo has rejected Balthazar's suggestion of a comedy, and insisted upon '*tragedia cothurnata*, fitting kings' for the Court performance he is preparing. He says:

> The Italian tragedians were so sharp of wit,
> That in one hour's meditation
> They would perform anything in action.
>
> (IV. i. 164–6)

Lorenzo adds:

> And well it may, for I have seen the like
> In Paris, 'mongst the French tragedians.
>
> (IV. i. 167–8)

Now Boas (p. 412) takes the first passage to refer to the Italian *Commedia dell' Arte* troupes, one of which performed in England at Windsor in 1577, and his interpretation has been widely followed. Commenting on the second passage, he writes, 'It is probable that [Kyd] visited France . . . the remark seems suggested by an experience of the author himself.' Here is a curious distinction: Kyd is supposed to have known about the Italian actors from their English visit, and about the French actors from his own travels. But were there 'French tragedians' who extemporized in Paris? The earliest company of French improvising actors we know of and the only one in existence at Kyd's time were *farceurs*,[1] and certainly no players of tragedies. For that matter, so were the Italians: among Scala's fifty scenarios for the famous Gelosi troupe there is only a single tragedy, and Catherine de Medici, the patroness of *commedia dell' arte* in France, was famous for her superstitious dislike of all tragedy.[2] Kyd is almost certainly retailing hearsay of both the French and Italian 'tragedians', and even if he were right, it would be a thin supposition that he need have travelled to Paris to be so.

Boas goes on to say that 'Kyd's journey could not have extended far south, or he would not have translated *dans le Loire* by 'at Loyre' (*Corn.*, IV. ii. 45)—meaning that Kyd apparently thought 'Loire' was the town rather than the river—and Carrère also picks up this 'error'. The passage in question is Caesar's speech of self-praise:

> The Gauls, that came to Tiber to carouse,
> Dyd liue to see my souldiers drinke at Loyre;
> And those braue Germains, true borne Martialists,
> Beheld swift Rheyn under-run mine Ensignes.

The first two lines correspond to Garnier's 'Les Gaulois qui iadis venoyent au Tybre boire/Ont veu boire sous moy les Rommains dans le Loire'. Now is it possible (*a*) that Kyd completely missed the point of the river-parallels, or (*b*) that his French was shaky enough to make *dans le* equivalent to 'at', when, if a town were meant, the preposition would have to be *à*? Is it not equally or more likely

---

[1] See I. A. Schwartz, *The Commedia dell' Arte and its Influence on French Comedy in the Seventeenth Century* (New York, n.d.), p. 50.

[2] Chambers, *Elizabethan Stage*, III, 14, quoting Brantôme.

that 'drink at' is a metrically padded irregular form of 'drink'? 'The' is not required before 'Loyre', inasmuch as 'Tiber' above, 'Rheyn', and 'Nilus' six lines below all go without articles.

Perhaps this is the time to raise the question of another geographical detail in *The Spanish Tragedy*: in III. xiv. the King of Spain salutes the Portuguese Viceroy as one who has 'so kingly crost the seas'. Boas assumes the scene is set in Madrid, and takes this line as evidence of Kyd's almost total ignorance of Spanish geography; Edwards[1] calls it 'an amusing howler' and implies that Kyd momentarily thought of Portugal as an island. But Kyd's error is more subtle than that, surely: Madrid is nowhere mentioned in the play, and the setting might as well be Seville, the sixteenth-century 'Spanish capitol of Spanish Spain', and a traditional seat of Court. Although Philip II was notoriously loath to leave Castille, he is known to have passed time in Seville in 1570; the trip from Lisbon to Seville would quite likely have been made partially by sea, coasting to Cadiz. I do not mean to suggest that Kyd was right, but that his geographical errors were hardly more enormous than endowing Bohemia with a sea coast.

Other guesses about Kyd's activities in his early twenties are scarcely more convincing. From the few scraps of legal jargon in *The Spanish Tragedy* and *Soliman and Perseda* we can infer no more than that Thomas was his father's son. Sarrazin's fancy that Kyd may have turned schoolmaster for a time, which Boas seems also to affect, has no foundation beyond a 'didactic vein' in his works. Perhaps the only plausible surmise is that for some period Kyd was engaged, perhaps as an apprentice, in his father's trade; for here at least we have a shred of evidence. Kyd's handwriting, as it survives in two letters of 1593-4 to Sir John Puckering, is remarkably clear and formal: it is perhaps the finest secretary hand among all those represented in Greg's *English Literary Autographs*, and Greg himself thinks it shows the training of a scrivener.[2] Since we cannot permit ourselves to use Nashe's putative attack on Kyd in the preface to *Menaphon* for evidence, that allusion to those who 'leave the trade of *Noverint* whereto they were borne' must not be taken as substantiation of the last conjecture; but the fact that Kyd attended grammar school and not college does suggest, in the light of the Scriveners' requirements for apprentices, that his father may have taught him his own trade when preliminary schooling was over.

[1] Philip Edwards, ed., *The Spanish Tragedy* (London, 1959), p. 91.
[2] Sir W. W. Greg, *English Literary Autographs* (Oxford, 1925), I, XV.

One of the few early allusions to Thomas Kyd by name occurs in a passage of Thomas Dekker's pamphlet, *A Knights Conjuring* (1607). The setting is the Elysian Fields, in a laurel grove where the dead poets are consorting, severally grouped. First there is Spenser, seated with his spiritual father Chaucer, and,

In another companie sat Learned Watson, industrious Kyd, ingenious Atchlow, and (tho hee had beene a player, molded out of their pennes) yet because he had bene their louer, and a register to the Muses, inimitable Bentley: these were likewise carowsing to one another at the holy well, some of them singing Paeans to Apollo, som of them hymnes to the rest of the goddes. . . .[1]

In a third group are Marlowe, Greene, and Peele, who 'had got vnder the shades of a large vyne', and they are being joined by late arrivals Nashe and Chettle. While the passage in question has been known for a long time, it was not until 1926 that T. W. Baldwin noted the date of John Bentley's death,[2] and was able to relate it to Kyd's career. While Baldwin overextended himself in drawing inferences from the passage,[3] his first point is telling: Dekker says that Bentley, the famous actor of the early eighties, was 'molded' from the pens of Kyd, Watson, and Atchlow: i.e. that these three poets wrote the plays he acted in. If Kyd wrote parts for Bentley, he must have done so before 19 August 1585, when the thirty-two-year-old actor was buried at St. Peter's Cornhill in London. And if Bentley was a 'louer' of all three poets, we may assume, I think, that they all knew each other. Dekker's grouping of the four does, of course, suggest a clique, and since these are the earliest literary associates of Kyd we can trace any report of, a glance at them may be in order.

'Inimitable Bentley' is numbered among the best-known actors who preceded Alleyn and Burbage. Along with Knell and Richard Tarleton he was a mainstay of the powerful Queen's Company, at least from its re-formation in 1583 to his own premature death two years later. His fame as a player is attested by Nashe, in *Pierce Penilesse*,[4] and by Heywood in *An Apology for Actors*,[5] as well as by

[1] Thomas Dekker, *A Knight's Conjuring*, ed. by E. F. Rimbault (London, 1842), pp. 75–76.
[2] T. W. Baldwin, 'Nathaniel Field and Robert Wilson', *MLN*, LXI (1926), 32–34.
[3] T. W. Baldwin, 'Thomas Kyd's Early Company Connections', *PQ*, VI (1927), 311–13. See Edwards, xxv–xxvi.
[4] Nashe, *Works*, ed. McKerrow, I, 215.
[5] Thomas Heywood, *An Apology for Actors* (1612; rptd. London, 1841), p. 43.

Dekker; and though a mere 'register to the Muses', he has been supposed, on slender evidence, the author of seven indifferent poems preserved in the Lysons MS. at Folger Library.[1] Presumably he acted before 1583, but nothing is known of him before that date, when his name appears in a City record as a Queen's Man.[2] We can assume that he was born about 1553, for the record of his burial gives his age as 'yers 32'. There has been preserved one anecdote about a fray in Norwich, in June 1583, when Bentley, two other actors, and a servingman were involved in a street fight. Another servingman was killed, but no subsequent court records have been unearthed.[3]

Perhaps Bentley's temper led him to the same end as Marlowe's, for he died young and not in time of plague. In 1931 G. E. Bentley first published the actor's will, dated 12 August 1585, from the transcript in Somerset House.[4] The original will is also in Somerset House, but there are no significant variations between copies; the will shows that John Bentley left a wife but evidently no children, and a rather tidy estate. There are two hundred pounds in specific legacies and the 'residue' to his wife Joan. Others mentioned by name are his mother Elizabeth, his brother Steven, and two 'trusty friends', Robert Scotte of Shoreditch and a brother-in-law, Henry Haughton, saddler. The will was written out by Richard Gall and witnessed by John Lantham and Elizabeth Maye. None of these names seems to link up with Kyd's circle, but the *Wills Index* of the Prerogative Court of Canterbury describes the deceased as 'servaunt to the Queene, All Saints, Lombardstreet, London'. And we are back again among the neighbours of the scrivener.

Bentley's burial came a week after his will, and the register of St. Peter's Cornhill records his interment on 19 August: 'Thursday John Bentley one of ye Queens players, pit in ye north ile. yers 32.' The will was proved on the same day.

'Ingenious Atchlow' is the Tudor poet Thomas Achelley, famous in his own time, and now almost totally forgotten. Even his name is

---

[1] See W. H. Bond, 'The Cornwallis-Lysons Manuscript and the Poems of John Bentley', *Joseph Quincy Adams Memorial Studies* (Washington, Folger Library, 1948), pp. 683–93. Dr. Bond disputes Ritson's attribution of these poems, signed 'J. bentley' and 'Jon Bentley', to the actor, on palaeographical grounds.

[2] *Eliz. Stage*, II, 105–6.

[3] See Edwin Nungezer, *A Dictionary of Actors* (New Haven, 1929), p. 44, quoting Halliwell-Phillipps.

[4] G. E. Bentley, 'The Wills of Two Elizabethan Actors', *MP*, XXIX (1931), 110–14.

shrouded with uncertainty: contemporary forms of it include Acheley, Achelley, Achelly, Achely, Achilley, Achellye, Atchlow, Atchelow, and Achlow. Nowadays we should probably settle on 'Achelley', as that is the spelling the poet himself chose on three occasions (on one other it was 'Acheley', but the book in question was not his own). Achelley's birth date is unknown. There is no record of him at Oxford, Cambridge, at the Inns of Court, or at Westminster, Paul's or Mulcaster's school; although Nashe characterizes him as 'deep witted', he was evidently self-taught. Possibly he had means of his own, as in 1587 he went surety for thirty pounds lent to George Peele.[1]

His earliest extant work is a diminutive prayer book, *The Key of Knowledge, contayning sundry Godly Prayers and Meditations* (STC 85a), a pious and uninteresting collection of prayers and aphorisms published, without date or entry, by William Seres. There is, however, an almanac preceding the main body of text, running 1572–88; thus it has been assumed that *The Key* appeared in 1571 or early 1572. Only a single copy of it survives, now preserved in the library at Lambeth Palace.

The dedicatee is 'The Right Honorable . . . Lady Elizabeth Russell', probably identifiable as the second daughter of Francis, second Earl of Bedford, who married the Earl of Bath in 1583 and lived unhappily thereafter (Gibbs, *Complete Peerage*, II, 18). Lest she be thought too young for a dedication in 1572, we may note that her younger sister Margaret married in 1577; Lady Elizabeth was evidently for some time a spinster.[2]

In the preface to *The Key*, Achelley mentions in passing 'those fewe ragged verses, whiche, aboute two yeares paste I presumed to tender unto your [i.e. Lady Elizabeth's] discreete iudgement', but they have not survived. Presumably they were among his earliest attempts at poetry, and thus we may fix the beginning of Achelley's career in the 'drab' heyday of Turberville, Churchyard, Gascoigne, Googe, and the miscellanies.

---

[1] See Horne, *Life of Peele*, pp. 82–83.

[2] F. B. Williams, *Index of Dedications and Commendatory Verses* (London, 1962), p. 161, identifies her as the widow of Thomas Hoby (*née* Elizabeth Cooke) who had a reputation as a patroness of letters before her marriage to John 'Lord Russell', second son of Francis, fourth Earl of Bedford. But Elizabeth Hoby's marriage to Russell and acquisition of a new name did not take place until 23 December 1574. If she were indeed the dedicatee, why does *The Key* begin with an almanac already three years out of date? The almanac is not, incidentally, inconjugate with the text: it occupies the first six leaves of a gathering of eight (sig. B), the last two of which contain the beginning of the dedication itself.

The year following his *Key of Knowledge*, Achelley presented the manuscript of a Latin poem to Alexander Nowell, the Dean of St. Paul's, and a great patron of education in England. *Cupidinis et Psychis Nuptiae* consists of 232 hexameter elegiacs, treating the story of Cupid and Psyche up to Psyche's reconciliation with Venus; its source is evidently Apuleius, but its inspiration most probably Ovidian. As an Anglo-classical verse-narrative with erotic overtones earlier than Lodge's *Glaucus and Scilla* or Marlowe's *Hero and Leander*, it deserves attention, and perhaps translation; it has never been published.[1] The four-page dedication praises Nowell's generosity toward scholars, but gives no indication that Achelley himself had benefited thereby.

Achelley's next appearance in print seems to have been in 1576, with *A Most Lamentable and Tragicall Historie conteyning the Outragious and Horrible Tyrannie which a Spanish Gentlewoman named Violenta Executed upon her Lover Didaco . . . newly translated into English meter by T. A.*, printed by John Charlewood for Thomas Butter (*STC* 87). Like *The Key of Knowledge*, this little octavo is excessively rare, only one nearly complete copy (Edmund Malone's, now at the Bodleian) being now known. There are two leaves missing from the dedication, however, and we must consult a fragmentary copy in the Newberry Library to find these: between the two, fortunately, the whole dedication and text can be reconstructed. *Violenta and Didaco* is a narrative poem in split fourteeners— 'poulter-meter'—a crude but vigorous verse, and by no means artistically worthless. Although the title-page represents it as 'newly translated', and its ultimate source is Bandello, it should not be considered a translation; furthermore, its immediate source is probably not Bandello but Painter's *Palace of Pleasure*.[2] The dedication is to Sir Thomas Gresham, the 'merchant prince' of Elizabeth's early reign, who had recently gone into retirement from public affairs. Achelley was unacquainted with the statesman personally,[3] and perhaps casting about for a new patron.

For our purposes, perhaps the most interesting feature of *Violenta and Didaco* is the hispanophilia, both overt and implicit, it contains. It appears that Achelley thought highly of the country

---

[1] MS originally in the Tollemache collection (probably from the early seventeenth century onward; calendared in the H. M. C. *First Report* of 1840), and sold at Sotheby's 14 June 1965 (lot 30).

[2] Collier, *Rarest Books*, I, 4.

[3] See *Violenta*, A4ᵛ (Newberry): 'presuming (although unknowen to you) to present the same unto your worship . . .'

where his poem and Kyd's later tragedy were set, for he speaks in the dedication of 'Spaine . . . where God is knowen and honoured, mutiall amitie frequented, and all kinde of good order and civilitie observed . . .' (A2ᵛ). Now in 1576 England and Spain were on reasonably good terms, but enthusiasm like Achelley's was by no means universal. There is a wide rift between Achelley's cosmopolitanism and the common Englishman's traditional distrust of foreigners, all the more interesting for Kyd's similar attitude, taken in later years when it was distinctly less popular. For there is a certain amount of undeniable hispanophilia implicit in *The Spanish Tragedy*, despite its lack of a truly Spanish setting and details, and English precedents for such are scarce indeed.

Thomas Achelley next appears as a puffer of Thomas Watson's *Hekatompathia, or passionate centurie of love* (1582), with a quite pleasant twelve-line poem 'To the Author'. Now Achelley's verse is more fluent and delicate than before, and he has made the transition to iambic pentameter with a craftsman's facility. His fellow puffers are George Buc, John Lyly, 'C. Downhalus', George Peele, and Matthew Roydon—a distinguished group—but Kyd was not among them. We can be sure Kyd read the collection, though, for a few lines of Watson's verse find their way into II. i. of *The Spanish Tragedy*, without benefit of citation.

Nothing more, beyond fragments, of Achelley's undoubted work has come down to us. A poem which is definitely not by Achelley has been persistently attributed to him, namely *The Massacre of Money*, 'by T. A.', a young man's 'first fruits' of *c.* 1602. In 1600 Robert Allott's anthology of short poems, *nugae*, and verse *sententiae* from contemporary writers, *England's Parnassus*, published thirteen passages assigned to Achelley. Of these, two are actually by Thomas Lodge, one by Thomas Churchyard, one possibly altered from Daniel, and one similarly close to *Soliman and Perseda*.[1] The remaining ten, all decasyllabic, appear to be fragments of lost poems or plays, evidence of a body of work by Achelley which has perished. Plays seem the more likely origin, I think, considering the subject-matter and versification.

Another anthology of the same year, *Bel-vedere, or the Garden of the Muses*, numbers Achelley among its contributors, but in this curious compilation none of the 4,482 quotations is signed. Charles Crawford actually identified no less than 2,380 of them,[2] but found

[1] Charles Crawford, ed., *England's Parnassus* (Oxford, 1913), p. 422.
[2] *Englische studien*, XLIII (1910–11), 198–228.

none from Achelley; Kyd was a substantial contributor to *Belvedere*, with forty-nine quotations identified by Crawford.

From *Bel-vedere* we learn that Achelley was dead in 1600, for the preface lists him among a group who, 'being deceased, have left divers extant labours, and many more held back from his publishing'. Moreover, since the alternative list of 'Moderne and extant Poets, that have liv'd together' includes such writers as Kyd (d. 1594), Watson (d. 1592), and Marlowe (d. 1593), we may gather that the 'deceased' group consisted of poets of an earlier period. Indeed, the four others listed in addition to Achelley ('Thomas Atchlow'), Norton, Gascoigne, Kindlemarsh (=Kinwelmershe), and Whetstone, died in 1584, 1577, ?1580, and ?1587 respectively,[1] leading us to estimate Achelley's date of death no later than the early nineties.[2] He was alive, evidently, in 1589, when Nashe speaks of him, in his preface to Greene's *Menaphon*, as 'extant about London', and goes on to group him with Roydon and Peele and praise his 'deepe witted schollership . . . more than once or twise manifested . . . in places of credite'.[3] The only other contemporary reference to Achelley I know of is by Meres (*Palladis Tamia*, 1598), where he is grouped with Roydon, Watson, Kyd, Greene, and Peele, in a parallel with the Italian poets Dante, Boccaccio, Petrarch, Tasso, Celiano, and Ariosto, and apparently matched against Boccaccio, as Kyd is against Tasso.[4] We may note that the trio of Peele, Roydon, and Achelley, whom Nashe associates in 1589, all contributed commendatory verses to Watson's poems of 1582, and are reunited with Watson by Meres in 1598. And Thomas Kyd is alongside Achelley and Watson here, as he is nine years later in *A Knight's Conjuring*, our starting-point. There is strong indication, I think, of a clique.

Of Thomas Watson far more has been discovered, and hence less need be said. A biographical sketch was prepared by Edward Arber as an introduction to his 1870 reprint of Watson's poems, and a full article was contributed by Sir Sidney Lee to the *DNB*. More recently Mark Eccles (*Christopher Marlowe in London*, 1934) has unearthed a wealth of information about the poet in the London Chancery records and elsewhere; and Watson's position in the history of the English sonnet has been reassessed from time to time by twentieth-century critics.

---

[1] *Eliz. Stage*, III, 456, 320, 394, 512.
[2] Thus the identification of Achelley with a Thomas Asheley mentioned in a legal document of 1599 (Horne, *Peele*, p. 67) is unlikely.
[3] Nashe, *Works*, III, 323.
[4] G. G. Smith, *Elizabethan Critical Essays* (Oxford, 1904), II, 319.

His birth date is unknown, despite Arber's confident guess of 1557; he seems, however, to have been a university student in the seventies and hence slightly older than Kyd. Professor Eccles has found evidence of an extended visit to France and Italy, from at least 1573 to 1577 or later, the main purpose of which appears to have been study. Watson attended Oxford, most likely between 1577 and 1579, but took no degree. He was married, as Eccles discovered, 1585, to Anne Swift. In 1579 he was apparently living in Westminster, and evidently by 1587 in St. Helen's, Bishopsgate, where he became involved in a curious case of fraud.[1]

Aside from Dekker's testimony that Watson was a playwright, we have that of Meres, who lists Watson among 'our best for tragedie'. His only surviving play, however, is a Latin translation of *Antigone*, published in 1581. If Watson wrote for the Queen's Company with Kyd and Achelley, no extant play bears his name; indeed, he was best known to his contemporaries as a Latinist, perhaps the foremost Latin poet of his nation and day. In addition to *Antigone* we have his best-known work, *Amyntas*, a pastoral poem also in Latin, and a Latin translation of Coluthus, as well as a Latin elegy (*Meliboeus*, 1590), another Latin pastoral (*Amintae Gaudia*, 1593), and a Latin tract on memory (?1585). But Watson could write English verse, as his *Hekatompathia* (1582) and *Tears of Fancy* (1593), as well as an English version of *Meliboeus* show, and among his eulogists recurring praise of his wittiness indicates he was a man of varied talents. William Cornwallis, who had employed Watson as a tutor to his son, wrote after his death that he 'could devise twenty fictions and knaveryes in a play which was his daily practyse and his living'.[2] Watson was dead by 1593,[3] but if his play-writing helped 'mold' John Bentley, he was at work for the Queen's Company before 1585.

Sir Sidney Lee has given a canon of Watson's works in his biographical article, listing ten books and some scattered commendatory poems. We may note that while *STC* attributes *Compendium Memoriae Localis* to a different Thomas Watson, a look at the dedication will return it to the poet's canon.[4] There are two autograph

---

[1] Eccles, pp. 145–61. Yet the identification of the charlatan Thomas Watson with the poet Watson is somewhat tenuous. Eccles attempts it on pp. 158–9; but for another Watson in St. Helen's Bishopsgate see *CSPD*, May 11, 1594 entry.

[2] *The Athenaeum*, 23 August 1890, p. 256. Eccles, p. 7.

[3] In the prologue to George Peele's *The Honour of the Garter* (1593), Watson is 'worthy many epitaphs'.

[4] *Compendium* was dedicated to Henry Noel, the dedicatee of *Amyntas*; and in the epistle Watson three times mentions his own pastoral by name.

manuscripts, of the *Compendium* and of part of *Hekatompathia*, in the British Museum; and the unpublished autograph manuscript of Watson's translation of Bernard Palissy, *Dialogue . . . concerning Waters and Fountains*, cited by Eccles (p. 161), is now at Harvard (M.S. Eng 707) and still unpublished. A play, *Thorney Abbey*, first printed as late as 1661, was attributed to Watson by Oliphant on the strength of initials alone;[1] but *Thorney Abbey* is patently and deliberately imitated from *Macbeth* (*c.* 1606), and hence Oliphant's suggestion may be discarded. There is better reason to consider Watson's authorship of the Elvetham *Entertainment* (1591), printed by R. W. Bond, as Lyly's (*Works*, I, 522 ff.). One poem in the *Entertainment* is certainly by Watson,[2] and another shows traces of his style.[3]

Watson's reputation in his own time was considerable. In addition to the citations by Dekker and Meres we have complimentary references to him by Spenser,[4] Lodge, Nashe, Peele, the *Returne from Parnassus*, and W. Cavell, who in 1594 allows Shakespeare the honour of being 'Watsons heyre'.[5] Since his own time, however, Watson's reputation and substantial works have fallen into neglect, redeemed only by bibliographical rarity, and finally, in the late nineteenth century, by the inevitable attentions of antiquarian scholarship. It is difficult to reconstruct artificially, even in the academies, the climate of taste which made his ponderous verse admirable to his discerning contemporaries. Even in his hackwork and adaptations Kyd seems nowadays more enduring and valuable.

Although Professor Eccles has shown that Watson knew Christopher Marlowe well enough to take up arms for him,[6] the contemporary testimonies of Nashe, Meres, and Dekker link Watson with Achelley, and latterly with Kyd. It may, however, be straining these casual

---

[1] See E. H. C. Oliphant, 'Elizabethan Problems of Authorship', *MP*, VIII (1911), 411–59; esp. pp. 437–9.

[2] The poem reprinted in *England's Helicon* (1600) and ascribed there to Watson (see Watson, *Works*, ed. Arber, p. 17) was actually published in Watson's lifetime in *The Honorable entertainment given to the Queene's Majestie . . . at Elvetham in Hampshire* (1591); see Bond's Lyly, I, 433.

[3] The echo poem (Nichols, *Progresses of Queen Elizabeth*, III, 113) seems not unlike Watson's echo poems in *Hekatompathia* and *Tears of Fancie*; and it contains the phrase 'second sun' as a term of praise for a woman, which may be found in *Hekatompathia*, XXXV, XXXIX, XLIV, XLV, and LXXVIII.

[4] See William Ringler, 'Watson and Spenser', *MLN*, LXIX (1954), 484–7.

[5] In *Polymanteia* (1595). See Watson, *Works*, p. 16.

[6] Eccles, pp. 9–31.

allusions to imagine a tight literary clique or society; at any rate, we should be sparing of our inferences. T. W. Baldwin[1] aligns Watson with Sidney, Francis Walsingham, the Earl of Oxford, and other 'courtly reformers', posits an opposition of 'Marlowe and his crew of rebel angels', and describes 'Kyd's dilemma' as a choice between the two factions. But Marlowe's friendship with Watson poses an unanswerable objection to such an hypothetical reconstruction of literary society in the eighties. Baldwin is on safer ground when he reads into the Dekker passage the implication that Kyd-Watson-Achelley as a group *precede* historically Marlowe-Greene-Peele-Nashe-Chettle, a valuable inference, but little upon which to base a dating argument for *The Spanish Tragedy*. Still, we may wish to remember that Dekker seems to think of Kyd as earlier than Marlowe. Dekker seems also to be distinguishing between a relatively sober and dedicated group of writers—Kyd's—gathered about 'the holy well', singing 'paeans' and 'hymns', and a somewhat more rowdy assemblage, who 'had got under the shades of a large vyne' (why 'vyne' if not in opposition to the 'holy well'?), 'laughing' at the bitter railing of late-arrival Nashe. Perhaps Watson spanned the two camps; Kyd, certainly, who was later to profess himself shocked at the levity and irreverence of Marlowe, belonged more to the first.

About the company of actors with which Kyd probably began his play-writing career we have some unusually specific data. The formation of the Queen's Company can be dated about 10 March 1583, when the Master of the Revels drew travelling expenses connected with being sent for 'to choose out a companie of players for her maiestie'.[2] By the fifteenth of June the Company were actually playing, for a brawl (mentioned above) occurred at Norwich during their performance there, and involved Bentley, Singer, and Tarleton.

An extremely useful City record[3] of 26 November in the same year gives us the names of twelve members, probably all the players, of the Company, viz.: Robert Wilson, John Dutton, Richard Tarlton, John Laneham, John Bentley, Thobye Mylles, John Towne, John Synger, Leonell Cooke, John Garland, John Adams, William Johnson. From other records we can make certain observations about the group Tilney had chosen for Her Majesty.

---

[1] T. W. Baldwin, *Literary Genetics*, p. 179.
[2] *Eliz. Stage*, II, 104.
[3] Ibid., II, 106.

To begin with, it was an experienced company: at least six, and possibly seven, of the twelve had been playing since the early or mid-seventies, with established companies. Five at least of them— Singer, Adams, Tarleton, Bentley, and Wilson—either had or went on to acquire considerable reputations as actors, and Tarleton and Wilson were probably already stars. At least three existing companies had been drawn on for material: Sussex's, Warwick's-Oxford's, and the Earl of Leicester's, which contributed Laneham, Johnson, and Wilson. It is possible that Leicester's Men were entirely subsumed by the new and stellar organization, as little more is heard of them;[1] and Leicester himself might have been unwilling to protest, what with Elizabeth still contemplating an alliance with the Duc d'Alençon, and Leicester himself devoting every effort to blocking the match. Naturally the new company began at once to dominate the Court calendar, and one may assume that they required a good deal of fresh 'book'. Kyd, Achelley, Watson, probably Robert Wilson, and possibly George Peele would have provided it.

We can make further inferences about the organization of the Company. It was somewhat top-heavy with comic talent perhaps, with Tarleton the leading clown, Wilson certainly another,[2] Adams a third,[3] and Singer, who may possibly have been only a boy in 1583, a potential fourth.[4] The 'straight' lead actor was probably Bentley, and there is good reason to believe that William Knell took

[1] Ibid., II, 89, suggests that later provincial mention of Leicester's Men may attach to a newly formed group, or to 'the relics of the old company'. The complete disappearance of the Company (once a most popular one) from Court records underlines the former possibility.

[2] Edmund Howes in 1615 couples Wilson with Tarleton, for 'quicke delicate refined extemporall wit', but perhaps is retailing his description from Meres (1598), who also speaks of Wilson's 'extemporall witte'. But Gabriel Harvey mentions as early as in 1579 the two clowns together, while reprehending Spenser for 'thrustinge me thus on the stage to make tryall of my extemporall faculty, and to play Wylsons or Tarletons parte'. See Nungezer, pp. 394–5.

[3] Nungezer, p. 1, quoting the well-known passage from the induction to *Bartholemew Fair*, where Adams and Tarleton are represented performing slapstick; but the strong possibility that Adams played the part of Oberon in *James IV* (see Greene, *Plays*, ed. Collins, II, 153, and n.) may serve as an example of the versatility required by Elizabethan companies of their actors— and another good reason not to base theories of dramatic proprietorship on the supposed make-up of companies (see below, *re* Baldwin).

[4] Many references to Singer as a clown show that his forte by *c.* 1600 was comedy: see Nungezer, 327–9. He was dead by 1612, but the sequence of baptisms of his children (1597, 1599, 1600, 1601, 1603) suggests a newly-wed; on the other hand, he may have been involved in a debt for 'certen playebookes' as early as 1571, and was old enough to help murder a man in Norwich in 1583 (*Eliz. Stage*, II, 105).

his place in the Company after Bentley's death in 1585.[1] About Towne, Cooke, Johnson, and Garland we know very little, save that they were all still with the Queen's Company in 1588. Garland may have been a boy; and Towne was still acting in 1597. It is possible that Tobias Mills was considerably older than the rest.[2] John Dutton and John Laneham, along with Dutton's brother Lawrence, who joined the group at a later date, appear to have had something to do with managing the men.[3]

The twelve names given may not be a complete list of the Queen's Company, but we know that the City authorities desired to know specifically who and how many there were.[4] J. T. Murray was evidently unacquainted with the list when he asserted as 'practically certain' that James Burbage was a member as well, and there is no evidence whatever for such a contention.[5]

The Queen's Company divided its time between London in the winter, the Court on holidays, and the provinces during the warm

---

[1] An undated letter of 'W.P.' to Edward Alleyn refers to a wager, between W.P. and another, that Alleyn could excel both Bentley and Knell in any of their own parts in 'any one playe, that either Bentley or Knell plaide'. (*Henslowe Papers*, p. 32; see the extraordinary conclusions drawn by Baldwin, *Genetics*, p. 248.) From this, as well as a reference to Bentley's playing 'the Duke' during the Norwich affair, and Dekker's laudatory allusion (see above, Ch. 1), I think we may infer that Bentley (and Knell) played parts similar to Alleyn's, i.e. leading roles. Now, Knell is not mentioned as a Queen's Man in the lists of either 1583 or 1588 (he is supposed to have died by 1588—see Nungezer, pp. 228–9), but we know from *Tarlton's Jests*, 1611, that he played Henry the Fifth in *The Famous Victories of Henry V*—a leading part—in company with Tarleton. In W.P.'s letter, as well as in *Pierce Penilesse* (Nashe, *Works*, I, 215), Knell is compared to Bentley and to Alleyn. Bentley died in 1585; Knell was not with the company in 1583, but was before 1588 and Tarleton's death. May we then hypothesize that Knell replaced Bentley after 1585, and that both were 'stars' in the modern sense? *The Famous Victories* may, of course, have also been played by Bentley with Tarleton, but other considerations suggest that it is no earlier than 1585.

[2] Mills was buried 11 July 1585, and had sons baptized 3 January 1584 and 5 September 1585, after his own death (Nungezer, p. 251). But there is little reason not to identify him with the player of the same name who *fl.* before 1552 (Collier, *History of English Dramatic Poetry*, I, 139), which Chambers (*Eliz. Stage*, II, 330) seems unwilling to do.

[3] See J. T. Murray, *English Dramatic Companies* (London, 1910), II, 375, and M. S. Steele, *Plays & Masques at Court* (New Haven, 1926), pp. 99–100; Nungezer, pp. 123, 125.

[4] See *Eliz. Stage*, II, 106, and the document printed in full by the Malone Society, *Collections*, I, 168 ff., and in *Eliz. Stage*, IV, 298 ff. The City authorities were perturbed at a plurality of groups calling themselves the Queen's, taking advantage of permissions to play granted specifically to one company.

[5] Murray, pp. 7, 32 ff. See *Eliz. Stage*, II, 305–6, and J. Q. Adams, *Shakespearean Playhouses* (Cambridge, Mass., 1917), p. 67.

months, playing in London at the Bull, the Bell, the Bel Savage, the Theatre, and possibly the Curtain. Nine of the original twelve members were still with the Company in 1588, Bentley and Mills having died in 1585, and Wilson being no longer mentioned. Knell, who probably replaced Bentley, may have died by 1588 and been in turn replaced by John Hemings, but the argument for this is somewhat speculative.[1] Lawrence Dutton had joined his brother John with the Queen's Company by 1589.[2]

As for Thomas Kyd, there is no evidence to set a term on his activities with the Company, except his own statement about being in the service of a Lord (which would not necessarily exclude him from another enterprise) by 1587-8, and the argument, advanced below, that *The Spanish Tragedy* was not a Queen's play. What part Kyd may have had in creating the repertory for the Company is again purely speculative, for it is impossible to assign any of the extant plays known to have been performed by the Queen's Company to the years before Bentley's death. T. W. Baldwin has attempted such a disposition of dates,[3] basing his arguments largely on a 'two-comedian' theory which, as we have suggested above, is valueless, given three and perhaps four actors who might take a comic part when given it. Among the following titles, however, of lost plays performed by the Queen's Company before Bentley's death in 1585, we may have the earliest dramatic attempts of young Kyd, or the compositions of his colleagues in the same organization: *A pastorall of Phillyda & Choryn, The history of Felix and Philomena, Five Plays in One, Three Plays in One. The Famous Victories of Henry V (pace* Baldwin) probably dates from 1585 or later.

---

[1] See Nungezer, p. 180.
[2] See ibid., p. 125, and Murray, II, 375.
[3] Baldwin, *Genetics*, pp. 200-13.

CHAPTER II

LATER LIFE

AT the time of John Bentley's death, in 1585, Kyd was twenty-seven and apparently a practising dramatist. We have, however, no contemporary record or testimony of the playwright in the prime of his life and in order to gain some idea of his activities in the succeeding decade we must skip to the unhappy events of spring 1593. For it is only by these that Kyd's intervening years are illuminated—dimly at best, but by his own testimony.

By the beginning of 1593 the euphoria of an unexpected sea victory over Spain had abated; London faced one of its heaviest seasons of plague, and the restless population turned its attention to unemployment. The readiest scapegoat was the foreigner, whose numbers had risen sharply in recent years, seemingly sheltered by a lenient government policy toward immigration and alien hiring. The latent xenophobia of the English commoner burst out in form of public protest, and the expression of protest, naturally enough, was scurrilous. On 22 April 1593 the first written or printed 'libels', 'latelie published by some disordered and factious persons in and about the cittie of London', came to the hands of the Privy Council, who instructed Sir Julius Caesar, Sir Henry Killigrew, Sir Thomas Wilkes, and others, to 'examine by secrete meanes who maie be authors of the saide libelles, and . . . what the intencions are of the publishers thereof . . . wherewith you shall ymediately acquainte us. . . .'[1] John Strype prints one such popular petition, a bitter attack on Belgian, French, and Dutch nationals resident in London, accompanied by threats against them in the name of the workers: 'For there shall be many a sore stripe . . . all prentices and journeymen will down with the Flemings and Strangers.'[2] The minorities were given until 9 July to quit the realm.

Evidently this libel, like the following ones, was set out at large in the City. The walls of the Dutch Churchyard might have

[1] *Acts of the Privy Council of England*, ed. J. R. Dasent, N.S., XXIV (1592–3) (London, 1901), 200–1.
[2] John Strype, *Annals of the Reformation* (London. 1725–31), IV, 167.

accommodated it, as a menacing ballad was discovered posted there on 5 May, beginning:

> You, strangers, that inhabit in this land,
> Note this same writing, do it understand.
> Conceive it well, for safeguard of your lives,
> Your goods, your children, and your dearest wives.[1]

On 11 May the Privy Council lost its patience. Noting that 'there have bin of late diver lewd and malicious libells set up within the citie of London, among the which there is some set uppon the wal of the Dutch churchyard that doth excead the rest in lewdnes', they instructed their officers 'to make search and aprehend everie person so to be suspected [of writing or publishing the libels] . . . to make like search in anie the chambers, studies, chestes, or other like places for al manner of writings or papers that may geve you light for the discoverie of the libellers . . . And after you shal have examined the persons, if you shal finde them dulie to be suspected and they shal refuze to confesse the truth, you shal by aucthoritie hereof put them to the torture in Bridewel, and by th'extremetie thereof . . . draw them to discover their knowledge concerning the said libells. We praie you herein to use your uttermost travel and endevour. . . .'[2] Earlier and milder protests to the Lord Mayor of London, whose sympathies may have been with the citizenry, had gone unheeded; no arrests had occurred. Now the Privy Council took matters into its own hands.

One of the first victims of their zeal was Thomas Kyd, as we learn from an intriguing fragment preserved in Harleian MS. 6848, fols. 187–9. The nature of these papers is explained at the end, where we find the following endorsement:

> 12 May 1593
> vile hereticall Conceiptes
> denyinge the deity of Jhesus
> Christe o[r] Savio[r] fownd
> emongst the pap[r]s of Thos
> Kydd prisoner

In a different ink and possibly a different hand is added, presumably on a later occasion:

[1] Ibid., IV, 168.

[2] *Acts of the Privy Council*, XXIV, 222. The *Acts* transcript varies in many details from Boas's (lxvii), the most serious of which is the reading 'malicious' (*Acts*) for 'mutinous' (Boas).

wch he affirmethe that he
had from Marlowe

Kyd, then, was a prisoner on 12 May 1593:[1] that he was originally investigated and apprehended in connexion with the libels is made clear in his first letter to Puckering, but it is also evident that these 'vile hereticall Conceiptes' became the greater reason for his detention.

The fragmentary disputation contained in the papers presented Elizabethan scholars with a problem unsolved until 1923. W. D. Briggs[2] then showed that they were, in fact, parts of an early sixteenth-century Theistic or proto-Unitarian treatise, which is quoted more fully, for purposes of confutation, in John Proctor's *The Fal of the Late Arrian* (1549); hence rather outdated and certainly, as examination shows, not 'atheistic' arguments. The original author has been tentatively identified as John Assheton,[3] a parish priest of Henry VIII's reign who was allowed to recant similar heresies in 1549. Nevertheless these arguments, found among Kyd's papers, caused serious trouble. Evidently Kyd went along with the official estimate of their vileness, or more likely he did not know the source of the copy, for while he is at pains to disown possession of the manuscript and call it Marlowe's, he never identifies its printed origin—which might, after all, have been an acceptable defence. It remains to be said that in spite of Tannenbaum's assiduous argument to the contrary[4] these papers are almost certainly *not* in Kyd's handwriting,[5] nor in any which can be identified.

'W^{ch} he affirmethe that he had from Marlowe' poses another problem. In Kyd's first letter to Puckering, written after Marlowe's death on 30 May, this charge is made—or perhaps elaborated. Tannenbaum's contention that the 'cautious wording' of the addition suggests Marlowe was then still living is unconvincing: the added note might simply be the docketer's record of the gist of Kyd's protest to Puckering. Nor does the change of ink help prove

---

[1] Not 'arrested on 12 May', as most writers say. That Kyd was arrested between 11 and 12 May is an inference.

[2] 'On a Document concerning Christopher Marlowe', *SP*, XX (1920), 153–9.

[3] G. T. Buckley, 'Who was the Late Arrian?' *MLN*, XLIX (1934), 500–3.

[4] S. A. Tannenbaum, *The Booke of Sir Thomas Moore* (New York, 1927), pp. 43–47.

[5] Cf. Greg, *English Literary Autographs*, I, XV. It is worth noting that the fragments *are* in a professional hand—a copyist's—but not Kyd's.

that the interval between notes was only 'a few days'.[1] Still, we have
the telling fact that Marlowe was called in shortly after Kyd's arrest
(18 May) and examined by the Privy Council. He was released on
20 May, although instructed to 'give his daily attendaunce to their
Lordships untill he shallbe lycensed to the contrary'.[2] Ten days
later he was dead at Deptford, of a stab in the eye.

Does Marlowe's arrest mean that Kyd informed on him? Possibly,
for Kyd was aware that someone had informed on *him*—'some outcast *Ismael* . . . incensd yor L^{ps} to suspect me . . .'—and he
harbours no affection for the dead Marlowe. But the common biographical charge against Kyd of personal treachery deserves re-
examination, if not dismissal. And from what we know of Marlowe's
connexions with Walsingham and the witch-hunting English Secret
Service, his quick dismissal by the Privy Council need not surprise
us.

How long Kyd remained a prisoner we cannot tell. By the time of
his letter to Sir John Puckering, Keeper of the Great Seal of England
and effectual head of the Privy Council, he was evidently free, for he
speaks at the beginning of 'my last being wth yor L^p to entreate some
speaches from yo^u in my favor to my Lorde'—an expedition he could
not have made from Bridewell. The letter, which forms fols. 218–19
of Harleian MS. 6849, is undated; but it refers to Marlowe as
'deade' and is hence after 30 May 1593.[3] I have appended a transcript of the letter, after Boas, with Tannenbaum's readings and
Baldwin's crucial correction, for it is a most important document for
the study of both Kyd and Marlowe. From the letter we learn something of Kyd's past, both immediate and more distant. He speaks of
'the late commission^{rs}' to whom he gave 'some instance . . . of my
religion & life', and of 'my paines and vndeserved tortures', which,
'felt by some, would have ingendred more impatience . . . wch it
shall never do wth me'. This last pathetic token of humility shows
that the agents of the Privy Council had availed themselves of their
warrant and subjected Kyd to the 'extremetie . . . at such times
and as often as [they] shal think fit', thus probably hastening his
wretched end with such 'privie broken passions' as the ruined poet
speaks of in his dedication to *Cornelia*.

[1] Tannenbaum, *The Assassination of Christopher Marlowe* (Hamden, Conn.,
1928), p. 21.
[2] *Acts of the Privy Council*, XXIV, 224.
[3] Baldwin, *Genetics*, p. 177, unaccountably states that the letter is of 'May,
1593'. Its early limit is, of course, May 30, but it might have been written at
any time after that.

Kyd's experience in Bridewell or Newgate can be reconstructed approximately from the accounts of other unfortunates of the period. 'A taste of the rack' could permanently debilitate a victim, as it did Anne Askew, who in the reign of Henry VIII had to be carried in a chair from Newgate to Smithfield 'because she could not walk on her feet by means of her great torments'.[1] We know nothing of the character of William Deyos, Keeper of Newgate during Kyd's incarceration, but if he was at all similar to his predecessors Crowder and the notorious Alexander, no kindness could be expected of him. Compulsory bribery would have drained Kyd's purse rapidly, and thereafter even the simplest amenities would be hard to come by. And meanwhile the wheels of justice moved slowly indeed: six months, nine examinations, and four appearances in court did not suffice to condemn or exonerate George Barkworth in 1598.[2] And to Keeper Puckering came the petitions, many from prisoners like Henry Ashe and Michael Genison, 'long since committed . . . where they remain [in Newgate] to their great shame and utter undoing, and are likely to continue, unless he extend his mercy'.[3] It should not be difficult to imagine Kyd's apprehension and despair, jailed as he was for a capital crime, ignorant of his accuser (although perhaps suspecting Marlowe), deprived of the protection of his patron, and most likely innocent to boot. Under the circumstances his bitterness against the man whose purported literary property had brought on such calamities can be understood.

A good part of Kyd's letter to Puckering concerns 'this Marlowe', who, dead as he then was, could neither retaliate for the accusations, nor deny them, nor suffer for them. The 'fragments of a disputation' which 'vnaskt [Kyd] did deliuer up' to the investigating commission are averred to be Marlowe's papers, 'shufled wth some of myne (vnknown to me) by some occasion of o^r wrytinge in one chamber twoe yeares synce'. Kyd goes on to explain this circumstance of proximity, for, he says, Marlowe was nominally employed by Kyd's own patron; but only, Kyd adds, 'in writing for his plaie^{r}s, ffor never cold my L. endure his name, or sight, when he had heard of his conditions. . . .' Marlowe, in addition to being an irreligious reprobate, was 'intemp[er]ate & of a cruel hart, the verie contraries to w^{ch}', Kyd

[1] Arthur Griffiths, *The Chronicles of Newgate* (London, 1884), I, 78 (quoting Foxe).
[2] Ibid., I, 91–92; see also Catholic Records Society, *Collections*, II, *passim*, for evidence of long preliminary imprisonments.
[3] Griffiths, I, 91.

declares pitifully, 'my greatest enemies will saie by me'. He goes on
to apologize for being forced 'to taxe or to opbraide the deade *Quia
mortui non mordent*', explaining that he must, in order 'to cleere my
self of being thought an *Atheist*'. The latter charge hangs heavy on
Kyd, and he dares recommend that Puckering interrogate the friends
of the late Marlowe, '*Harriot, Warner, Royden*, and some stationers
in Paules churchyard', 'ffor more assurance that I was not of that
vile opinion'.

In 1921 a Rhodes Scholar at Exeter College, Oxford, Mr. Ford
K. Brown, discovered among the Harleian MSS. another communication of Kyd's to Puckering, unsigned and unaddressed, but
certainly in the same hand as the foregoing.[1] It is undated, and
probably fragmentary, but since it goes on to enumerate and specify
charges against Marlowe, it has generally been assumed to have
followed the longer letter (Appendix A). Kyd says apologetically that
he is less capable of particularizing 'marlowes monstrous opinions'
than 'them that kept him greater company' might be, but nevertheless he will set down what he can, 'in discharg of dutie both towrds
god yor l^{ps} & the world'. Kyd's charges against the dead poet are
carefully itemized: he would 'iest at the devine scriptures gybe at
praie^{r}s, & stryve in argum^t to frustrate & confute what hath byn
spoke or wrytt by prophets & such holie meñ'. Marlowe 'wold
report St John to be o^r savio^r Christes Alexis', i.e. homosexual bedfellow. Marlowe ridiculed Kyd's intention 'to wryte a poem of S^t
paules conversion', holding that Paul was 'a Jugler'. Marlowe thought
the Prodigal Child's portion was slight indeed, only 'fower nobles',
because he 'held his purse so neere the bottom in all pictures', and
Kyd explains that Marlowe failed to comprehend that the story was
a parable. Marlowe thought that most miracles 'might have aswell
been don by observation of men'. Furthermore, Marlowe's 'rashnes
in attempting soden pryvie iniuries to men' prevented others from
restraining him and his blasphemies. In conversation Marlowe was
always pressing 'men of quallitie' to quit England, and 'go vnto the
k of Scotts', whither, Kyd believes, Matthew Roydon has already
gone—and where Marlowe himself told him at last meeting he
meant to go, 'if he had liud'.

The circumstances of this second communication have been
called into some doubt. Carrère imagines the following sequence of
events: Puckering receives the first letter, with its plea for reinstate-
ment with Kyd's patron; he seizes his chance to find out more of

[1] *Times Literary Supplement*, June 2, 1921.

Marlowe's group, ordering Kyd to furnish more details of the heretical opinions of Marlowe and his fellows; possibly he promises to intervene with Kyd's Lord as a price for the information; Kyd provides what is asked for. Tannenbaum, on the other hand,[1] thinks that this second fragment 'was almost certainly written during Kyd's incarceration, and therefore before the letter to Puckering', a bewildering contention. A conservative reading of the unsigned fragment tends, I think, to suggest that it is not a reply to a demand, as Carrère thinks (or why 'thus much have J thought good breiflie to discover'?), but a spontaneous offer of information—quite useless, as it happens. My own feeling is that it represents a second try: considering its specificity, where the other letter merely hints at Marlowe's heresies, I think it must follow the longer plea. If Puckering ignored Kyd's supplication (as the dedication to *Cornelia* suggests), Kyd might have sent another one, salting the second attempt with scandalous details that he imagined would interest the Privy Council. The disorganized and inconsequent state of these accusations, as well as the deterioration of hand and prose style, suggest the desperation of impoverished waiting. By the tone of them they are not admissions wrung out of a reluctant prisoner by threats or promises, but testimony given up voluntarily, even eagerly. And the charge concerning the Prodigal Child is so innocuous, comparatively, it suggests a man racking his memory for all the scandal it contained. That much also weighs against our considering these charges fabrications.

What of Kyd's accusations—are they trustworthy? And even if so, are they (as Marlowe's biographers tell us) cowardly and invidious? As to their truthfulness, we have the independent 'note' of Richard Baines, a Walsingham spy like Robert Pooley, preserved among the Harleian MSS., which corroborates one of Kyd's charges specifically, and most of the others by implication. Boas first printed the original note, but was sufficiently embarrassed by the nature of some of the charges to bowdlerize the manuscript severely: in one of the cut passages Baines gives it as Marlowe's opinion that 'St John the Evangelist was bedfellow to Christ . . . and that he used him as the sinners of Sodoma'.[2] Marlowe also 'affirmeth that Moyses was but a Jugler', a pejorative which Kyd has him applying to St. Paul. The whole tenor of Baines's note is in agreement with Kyd's second communiqué, which may lead us to think of a single source,

---

[1] Tannenbaum, *Assassination*, pp. 24–25.
[2] C. F. Tucker Brooke, *The Life of Marlowe* (London, 1930), p. 99.

and that most plausibly Marlowe himself.[1] As for the cowardliness involved in Kyd's accusations, three considerations need be borne in mind: (1) Marlowe was dead; (2) Kyd may well have thought Marlowe informed on him, or was at least responsible for his imprisonment—for Marlowe certainly did not come forward to claim possession of the incriminating papers; (3) Marlowe was quite possibly, as Dr. Hotson has shown, an *agent provocateur* or spy of the 'English Machiavelli', Sir Francis Walsingham,[2] and if Kyd knew or suspected this, any amount of post-mortem backbiting might seem justifiable. Furthermore, we see that Kyd specifically does not testify against any living person save Roydon, who has fled the country: his citation of '*Harriot, Warner, Roydon*' is palliated with 'whom I in no sort can accuse', although he declares himself equally unwilling to shield them. And the calumnies and heresies which he reports of Marlowe may seem to be disguising, with their virulence, their virtual uselessness. Perhaps Kyd thought he was throwing dust in Puckering's eyes; but to all indications the Lord Keeper was unimpressed. More documentation and naming names, and less loyalist rhetoric, might have forstalled Kyd's 'bitter times and privie broken passions', and it is sadly to his credit in history that he gave none, or had none to give.

The identity of Kyd's patron, 'my Lord . . . whom I have servd almost these vj yeres nowe, in credit vntill nowe', has remained obscure. To cast what light we can we must look forward a year to the publication of *Cornelia*, and gather up the pertinent details of Kyd's first letter to Puckering.

Pompey the Great, his Faire Cornelias Tragedie, Kyd's translation from the French of Robert Garnier, was registered on 26 January 1594—about nine months after his arrest—and published first in the same year. It is dedicated 'To the vertuously noble, and rightly honoured lady, the Countesse of Sussex'. In the remarkable epistle Kyd speaks of 'afflictions of the minde', 'misery', and the 'bitter times and privie broken passions' which are now his lot, and attend on the making of this book. He deprecates his own effort as no more than the stuff to beguile 'the passing of a Winters weeke' with, but

---

[1] Baines's testimony is generally credited. See Paul H. Kocher, *Christopher Marlowe* (Chapel Hill, 1946), pp. 33 ff.

[2] Leslie Hotson, *The Death of Christopher Marlowe* (London, 1925), pp. 64, 67.

promises to take more pains the following summer with a translation of Garnier's *Porcie*. The allusions to his wretched estate assure us that the aftermath of imprisonment was grim for Kyd, and the pleading tone of the epistle suggests that the restoration to grace which he had begged Puckering to effect had not come about. And the terms with which Kyd addresses the Countess may lead us to an hypothesis about Kyd's patron during the six years of his service.

Among the conventional praises of her Ladyship's wit, beauty, and virtue, Kyd takes to refer to her 'honourable favours past', which he will not itemize, because he considers it 'Pharasaical' to do so. He calls the Countess 'a Patronesse so well accomplished', and concludes by assuring her that he will 'ever spend one howre of the day in some kind service to your Honour, and another of the night in wishing you all happiness'. All these phrases, especially the 'service' and 'honourable favours past', indicate that Kyd was personally acquainted with the Countess, and that he had been in a position to receive her favours earlier—presumably before his imprisonment. Boas comments that 'Kyd may be merely alluding to some tokens of good will which she extended to him as to other men of letters, including Greene, who dedicated to her his *Philomela*'. But the fact is that the 'other men of letters' who dedicated books to the Countess at this period did *not* know her personally, by their own testimony, and Kyd, by his, did. Greene presented her *Philomela* in 1592 because he was 'humbly devoted to the Right honourable Lord Fitzwalters your husband', but the Countess herself he knew by repute only. Likewise the publisher William Bailey, who dedicated a book of lute music to her in 1596, writes of 'your Honourable Ladyship, whom I have heard so well reported of. . . '. And the only other surviving dedication to Bridget, Countes of Sussex, is a scrap of doggerel as late as 1613, Humphrey King's *Half-Pennyworth of Wit*. Evidently, then, she was not a notable literary patroness, or the centre of a circle of writers, as Boas and Carrère suggest. And more important, in the light of her 'honourable favours past', at the time of Kyd's dedication she was only nineteen years old.

Now, if Kyd had known Bridget before his imprisonment, and had been in a position to receive favours from her, he must have had some connexion with the house of Sussex. Bridget married Robert Radcliffe during or before 1592, at the tender age of sixteen or seventeen.[1] Even to know a bride of age, Kyd must needs have

[1] G. H. White, ed., *The Complete Peerage* (London, 1953), XII, 526 and note.

frequented her house, which he most logically might have done if he were in the employment of the family. Boas, noting that the *Cornelia* dedication gives us our only knowledge of a connexion between Kyd and a noble house, proposes as Kyd's patron Robert Radcliffe, the husband of Bridget, and finds in the dedication a roundabout effort to win back the grace Kyd once enjoyed. But Robert Radcliffe was only two years older than his wife,[1] and Kyd's six years of service began in 1587-8—when the future Earl was only fourteen. Even if Kyd were the young Lord's tutor, he was salaried by someone else.

The father of Robert Radcliffe, namely Henry, fourth Earl of Sussex, springs naturally to mind. If Kyd were in Henry's employ, either as secretary or a boy's tutor (as Thomas Watson in his maturity became), he might have had opportunity to know and serve young Bridget, who would have entered the house at least a year before Kyd's disgrace. From the nearly hysterical tone of Kyd's first letter to Puckering, where he represents himself as 'vtterlie vndon w^{th}out herein be somewhat donn for my recoverie', it is clear that Kyd's connexion with his Lord transcended nominal patronage— that he was, in fact, wholly dependent on him, or actually employed. When the letters to Puckering had no effect, the jobless secretary or tutor endured his 'bitter times', and then returned to his former livelihood, the pen. *Cornelia* could be turned, he hoped, to double advantage.

To return to the young Countess and the other Radcliffes, we may observe that Bridget gained her title only six weeks before *Cornelia* was registered. The Radcliffes had had a winter of deaths: Henry's wife Honor, Countess of Sussex, died shortly before 9 November 1593. Henry himself followed her by a month, on 14 December. The new Earl and Countess were thereupon installed, and *Cornelia* came to be registered on 26 January following. Now, either Kyd's composition followed on Henry's death and was intended as a belated accession present to Bridget or the intended dedication was changed after 14 December. In either case, Kyd was abreast of conditions among the Radcliffes, and if his Lord and former patron had, in fact, been Henry, we can understand the family concerns which may have prevented him from giving much consideration to a disgraced secretary's complainings. And we can imagine Kyd—in a plague year which forbade theatrical activity— looking hopefully toward a new régime in the family he had earlier

[1] Ibid., XII, 526 note (e), correcting the error in *DNB* and elsewhere.

served, a chance of restitution through the very young Countess.

Let us further consider how well Henry, fourth Earl of Sussex, fits the picture of Kyd's patron we can reconstruct from the Puckering letter. The first piece of determining information Kyd has left us is that his Lord maintained a company of players, and Marlowe wrote for them some time in 1591. Since we cannot be sure, with Carrère, that Marlowe wrote for only three troupes, such a qualification appears to exclude all but a maximum of eleven noblemen of the period. The Earl of Sussex is one; likewise, Lord Strange (Ferdinando Stanley), and Charles Howard, the Lord Admiral since 1584. Beyond the stage connexion nothing specific is to be learned from Kyd's letter, but we are left with notions of three qualities the obscure patron had: piety, timidity, and comparative lack of importance. Piety we learn from the slur on Marlowe, that such a man would not have 'quadred' with 'the forme of devyne praiers vsed duelie in his L^{ps} house', and from Kyd's emphasis on the avowedly unfounded charge of 'atheisme'. Timidity and relative unimportance we can only infer from the apologetic remark about 'my Lorde, whoe (though I thinke he rest not doubtfull of myne innocence) hath yet in his discreeter judgm^t feared to offende in his reteyning me'. Likewise Kyd's Lord 'holdes yor hono^{rs} & the state in that dewe reverence, as he wold no waie move the leste suspicion of his loves and cares both toward hir sacred Matie yor L^{ps} and the lawes. . . .' Now, these are significant qualifications of the personality of Kyd's patron, and they have not had their share of consideration. Robert Radcliffe, for example, from what we know of his life was scarcely pious,[1] nor, as Tannenbaum remarks, was the Earl of Pembroke a godly man.[2] We know nothing for or against Henry Radcliffe in point of piety, but of his stature in the realm we know a little. In 1589 Henry petitioned the Queen, somewhat pitiably, for release from a crushing debt: he owed the Crown the annuity of £500 per year, and possessed an income of only £450! If the Queen would not excuse him his obligation, he was beggared.[3] The details of Henry's escape from bankruptcy are obscure, but such a man would have good reason to be deferential to 'hir sacred Matie yor L^{ps} and the lawes'. Furthermore, although an Earl, Henry was not among the twenty-four jurors at Mary Stuart's trial in 1586; he was not on the Privy

---

[1] See *Diary of John Manningham*, ed. John Bruce (Camden Society, 1868), pp. 60–61.

[2] Tannenbaum, *Moore*, p. 40n.

[3] Lodge, *Illustrations*, II, 319.

Council at any time, and he is rarely mentioned in official correspondence of the period. During the war with Spain he held down at Plymouth a rather minor provincial administration; on the whole he seems not to have been a powerful or important Elizabethan. Ferdinando Stanley, on the other hand, was pursuing a luminous if brief career in 1593, and had a father among the 'Lordships' Kyd addresses on the Privy Council. It is difficult to imagine Lord Strange as deferential as Kyd represents him; nor the Lord Admiral, also a member of the Privy Council. It is quite possible to imagine Henry Radcliffe so.

Carrère dismisses the Earls of Sussex, father and son, on the sole grounds that Henry's Company, mentioned only in the 'tournées provinciales', was too unimportant for Marlowe to have written plays for it. In such an opinion he is evidently following Fleay,[1] who considered the provincial companies effectively ignominious, and expressed the same doubt of Marlowe's participation. J. T. Murray, however, in opposing Fleay, calls the Company 'of considerable importance',[2] and points to a series of London appearances in 1592-4; W. W. Greg and E. K. Chambers also find no difficulty in conjecturing Marlowe's association with Radcliffe's Company.[3] Furthermore, the Earl of Sussex's Men 'reentered the charmed circle of London' (Chambers) with a Court performance as early as 2 January 1592, over a year before Kyd's arrest. If Kyd either wrote his letter to Puckering in the winter of 1593-4 or was purposely exaggerating the time lapse in his acquaintance with Marlowe (as seems plausible), the 1592 appearance would account for the London-based Marlowe's connexion with the Sussex troupe. At any rate, the partly provincial career of the Company does not in the least weigh against Marlowe's possible association, or Kyd's, with the Earl of Sussex himself.

Thus we are left with a likely candidate for the office of Thomas Kyd's patron in Henry Radcliffe, fourth Earl of Sussex. It remains to be said that Ferdinando Stanley has been advanced as an alternate candidate, originally by S. A. Tannenbaum,[4] and subsequently by Carrère. Lord Strange, the assumptive Earl of Derby, is an attractive figure, and fits some of the characteristics of Kyd's Lord as we have numbered them: he was pious, and patronized a company of

[1] F. G. Fleay, *A Biographical Chronicle of the English Drama* (London, 1891), II, 299.

[2] *English Dramatic Companies, 1558-1642* (Boston, 1910), I, 304.

[3] Greg, ed., *Henslowe's Diary*, II, 79n. Chambers, *Eliz. Stage*, II, 94.

[4] *Sir Thomas Moore*, pp. 39-42.

players—for whom Marlowe undoubtedly wrote at one time. But (as above) he seems in 1593 too important for the role of deferential nobleman Kyd had cast him in: would Kyd have used a phrase like 'loves and cares towards . . . yor L^{ps}', or 'holdes yor hono^{rs} & the state in that dewe reverence', of one whose own father was among 'yor L^{ps}' and 'yor hono^{rs}'? Moreover, in 1587–8, when Kyd's service commenced, Lord Strange was acting as the Mayor of Liverpool, living in that city, his London and literary renown beginning only in 1589, when he was called to Court. Finally, there is no evidence beyond purest conjecture to associate Kyd with Lord Strange, whereas with the house of Sussex we have the *Cornelia* epistle.

Charles Howard, Lord Admiral, and Henry Herbert, Earl of Pembroke, the other noblemen for whose companies Marlowe is known to have written, can effectively be eliminated as claimants.[1] Robert Radcliffe, the choice of Boas, and Greg following Boas,[2] was too young in 1587. We cannot be certain of the identity of Kyd's patron, of course, but among possibilities Henry Radcliffe appears the most likely.

In 1585 Kyd was apparently writing plays for the Queen's Company. In 1587–8 he entered the service of a Lord, possibly the Earl of Sussex, possibly as a secretary or tutor. At any rate, we know he had the leisure to contemplate a poem on the conversion of St. Paul, and speak with perceptible condescension of the trade of play-writing; although we have no real reason to assume, with Baldwin, that he ever finally severed his connexion with the stage.

The remaining dates in Kyd's life tie in so closely with authorship and dating arguments presented in later chapters that it will only be necessary to mention them here, reserving discussion. In 1586 Kyd may have written part of a leaflet of verses published on the occasion of Elizabeth's escape from the Tychborne Conspiracy. *The Spanish Tragedy* was probably written before 1587. In 1588 appeared a translation of Tasso's *Padre di Famiglia* which can safely be attributed to Kyd. In 1589 Thomas Nashe published a preface to Greene's romance *Menaphon*, in which he may be attacking Kyd specifically as well as the general tradition of Senecan English drama. Late in 1591 the two greatest pre-Shakespearean tragedians, Kyd and Christopher Marlowe, were sharing a room and possibly even writing

---

[1] See Carrère, pp. 21–22.
[2] Greg, *Henslowe's Diary* (London, 1908), II, 79n.

together. On 14 March 1592 Henslowe records the first known performance of *The Spanish Tragedy*, although the play was probably at least five years old. In November of the same year *Soliman and Perseda* was registered for publication.

Exhausted, perhaps, by the 'bitter times and privie broken passions', Kyd died in the year *Cornelia* appeared. The parish register of St. Mary Colchurch records his burial on 15 August:

> August   Thomas Kydd the sonne of ffrauncis Kydd
> 15   was buryed the 15 day of August 1594.

We may note that Kyd's family, who now resided in that parish, were probably responsible for his burial; no more than a half-dozen or so each year were accommodated by the small churchyard. Church and cemeteries (note that Kyd's mother and brother were placed in 'the newe burieng place', which was begun after Thomas's death) were destroyed in the Great Fire, and no trace of the original grave now remains.

In 1899 Josef Schick drew attention to a document of the following 30 December, preserved in the *Archdeaconry of London Probate and Administration Act Book*,[1] consisting of a formal Latin renunciation of the administration of Thomas Kyd's estate, presented by Anna Kyd in the name of her husband Francis. Thomas is represented as *defuncti*, and, *dum vixit*, a parishioner of St. Mary Colchurch, where he may plausibly have returned, in his difficulties, to live with his parents. Now Boas (lxxvii) has read into this rather common form of legal disowner a kind of posthumous 'paternal repudiation': 'It would seem . . . that Kyd's family were anxious to dissociate themselves completely from his memory.' Such an inference is unnecessary, for the consideration could merely have been debt, and Kyd's parents simply attempting to escape their dead son's creditors. Furthermore, if Thomas died intestate, the petition of renunciation might have had another intent: that of speeding up the settlement of estate through Chancery. Without a will and without formal disclaimer of the right to administer a close relative's estate, the court's determination could take years. A scrivener would know that.

But it is true that the renunciation has a forlorn ring, like the *Cornelia* epistle and the letters to Puckering before it. Kyd's last years lie under a cloud of misfortune and rejection, and his death, at

---

[1] J. Schick, 'Thomas Kyds Todesjahr', *Jahrbuch der Deutschen Shakespeare-Gessellschaft*, XXXV (1899), 277–80.

thirty-six, was certainly premature. 'Utterlie undon' by an unfair process of investigation, he apparently found no more restitution than his own Hieronimo, for whom 'Justice is exiled from the earth'. He was evidently unmarried and finally poor; in all he presents a sad figure to the biographer, a sober, industrious man, more sinned against than sinning, at times humourless (although Jonson styles him 'sporting'), professedly pious, meticulous in his handwriting as in his syntax, self-schooled, and a trifle pedantic. Humble, perhaps, but never, in his dedications, a groveller. Ingenious always, but rarely brilliant, and above all to be known through his works, for it is his works which redeem him from the inglorious roles of school-boy, scrivener, hack, secretary, tutor, suspect, prisoner, petitioner, and victim. His life is at best a dim glass to read by, and his plays scarcely require it. With *The Spanish Tragedy* alone, Kyd enters the foremost rank of Elizabethan writers prior to Shakespeare, and it would be appropriate to render him in our time at least the justice of recognition which his own denied him.

Nearly all indications of Kyd's contemporary renown derive from *The Spanish Tragedy*, scraps and passages of which are among the most quoted in English literary history. But references to Kyd personally are few, no more than two of which—one doubtful—fall before his death. In the chapters dealing with each of Kyd's works I shall indicate some of the contemporary reactions to them, in the form of parody, adaptation, allusion, and quotation, but here only the early references to Thomas Kyd by name—or, in the case of Nashe's famous attack, by analogue—need be recorded.

More attention has been lavished on a paragraph of invective in Nashe's preface to Robert Greene's *Menaphon* (registered 23 August 1589) than on anything else in Nashe or perhaps even in Kyd. The analysis has been so diverse and so thorough that little new can be added; it is enough to pick and choose among the interpretations as judiciously as possible. Nashe has been coursing the contemporary literary scene, and pauses to consider the effects of hard times on practising hacks, dramatists in particular:

I'le . . . talke a little in friendship with a few of our triviall translators. It is a common practise now a daies amongst a sort of shifting companions, that runne through every arte and thrive by none, to leave the trade of *Noverint* whereto they were borne, and busie themselves with the in-devors of Art, that could scarcelie latinize their necke-verse if they should have neede; yet English *Seneca* read by candle light yeeldes manie good sentences, as *Bloud is a begger*, and so foorth: and if you intreate him faire in a frostie morning, hee will affoord you whole *Hamlets*, I should say handfulls of tragical speaches. But ô griefe! *tempus edax rerum*, what's that will last alwaies? The sea exhaled by droppes will in continuance be drie, and *Seneca* let bloud line by line and page by page, at length must needes die to our stage; which makes his famisht followers to imitate the Kidde in *Aesop*, who enamored with the Foxes newfangles, forsooke all hopes of life to leape into a new occupation; and these men renowncing all possibilities of credit or estimation, to intermeddle with Italian translations: wherein how poorelie they have plodded, (as those that are neither provenzall men, nor are able to distinguish of Articles) let all indifferent Gentlemen that have travailed in that tongue, discerne by their twopenie pamphlets: & no mervaile though their home-born mediocritie be such in this matter; for what can be hoped of those, that thrust *Elisium* into hell, and have not learned so long as they have lived in the spheares, the just measure of the Horizon without an hexameter. Sufficeth them to bodge up a blanke verse with ifs and ands, & other while for recreation after their candle stuffe, having starched their beardes most curiouslie, to make a peripateticall path into the inner parts of the Citie, & spend two or three howers in turning over French *Doudie*, where they attract more infection in one minute, than they can do eloquence all dayes of their life, by conversing with anie Authors of like argument.[1]

Boas, after Fleay,[2] expresses the extreme Kydian interpretation of this passage: the 'sort of shifting companions' is actually a rhetorical expression for 'one man', and the man is Kyd, by training a '*Noverint*'. Boas goes on to identify each of the specific slurs with 'errors' in *The Spanish Tragedy*, and draw by implication that Kyd was the author of the pre-Shakespearean *Hamlet*.

With the proper conservatism of an editor of Nashe, R. B. McKerrow took the contrary position: Nashe was 'speaking not of one writer, but of a group—probably, but not certainly, of dramatists. He did know of a Hamlet play, but the passage throws no light upon its authorship. There is no reason for supposing either Kyd or *The Spanish Tragedy* to be referred to.'[3] McKerrow's enormous prestige and undeniable familiarity with all facets of Nashe's work carried this opinion far. W. W. Greg accepted it;[4] Chambers ac-

---

[1] Robert Greene, *Menaphon* (London, 1589), sig. **3ʳ⁻ᵛ. McKerrow's text follows the 1610 edition.
[2] Boas, xxviii–xxix; Fleay, *Biographical Chronicle*, II, 32–33.
[3] Nashe, *Works*, IV, 451.
[4] Ibid., V, supplement, 68.

cepted it with reservations,[1] and Philip Edwards, the most recent editor of *The Spanish Tragedy*, endorsed it completely.[2] Meanwhile, J. W. Cunliffe[3] felt there was a reference to Kyd, but considered it indecisive, and G. I. Duthie[4] saw no connexion between the allusions to Kyd (if they were, in fact, allusions) and the pre-Shakespearian *Hamlet* also mentioned. Duthie's account is the fullest and fairest of all.

I hesitate to add my ink to so much already spent, but a cursory explication of the whole passage seems necessary. To begin with, the plural usage: Nashe may be referring to a whole group of writers ('sort' = 'group'), as he says, but again he may not, or he may be keeping 'them' in mind as he particularizes the offences of one writer. For example, in Nashe's *Anatomie of Absurditie*, aspersion is cast on writers (plural) who are 'pretending . . . to anatomize abuses and stubbe up sin by the rootes'.[5] Here Nashe is certainly referring to Philip Stubbes, the Puritan author of *The Anatomie of Abuses*, and even if there *is* a plurality of followers of Stubbes, the specific sneer is at Stubbes himself. Furthermore, there is some question of the number of dramatists available to Nashe for subjects: save Kyd, and Anthony Munday, and eliminating the writers Nashe speaks favourably of in the same preface, there is no one we know of who could fill the description Nashe gives.

About '*Noverint*' we must recall that Nashe was in the habit of damning scriveners,[6] but nevertheless Duthie's attempt to minimize Kyd's connexion with the profession is unconvincing. Nashe *does* say 'the trade of *Noverint*, whereto they were borne', and Kyd *was* born to that trade. Nashe says the 'companions' are so illiterate or unschooled they could scarcely fulfil the Latin requirements for a murder pardon (as Ben Jonson did), and yet they draw inspiration from 'English Seneca', presumably the translations by Jaspar Heywood and others (1560–81), finding such phrases as 'Bloud is a beggar' during their bouts with the midnight oil. *Hamlet*, for example, is the result of their efforts. (We may observe that if one takes Nashe entirely at his word, with McKerrow, he might expect to find the phrase 'Bloud is a beggar' somewhere in Heywood's Seneca;

---

[1] *Eliz. Stage*, IV, 234; Chambers, *William Shakespeare* (Oxford, 1930), II, 412.
[2] Edwards, xxiii.
[3] *Early English Classical Tragedies* (Oxford, 1912), xcv–xcvii.
[4] *The Bad Quarto of Hamlet* (Cambridge, 1941), pp. 55–76.
[5] Nashe, *Works*, I, 20.
[6] Ibid., I, 240, 341.

but it occurs nowhere. Nor should we be surprised, if we allow the satirist the latitude of his genre, to find the same writers he reproaches for illiteracy here castigated a few lines below for excessive classicism, or at least the pretence of it.)

In considering the problem of the *ur-Hamlet* one well might urge that there is good reason quite beyond this passage for attributing the early *Hamlet* to Kyd, and if those arguments are acceptable, they can return and lend weight to the association of Kyd with this passage. But I must agree with Duthie that a reversed order of logic is questionable, and I would not wish to use Nashe's preface alone to establish the authorship of Shakespeare's source.

Now, Nashe says that the Senecan drama is beginning to fall out of favour with theatre-goers, 'to die to our stage', and that Seneca's 'famisht followers' must seek sustenance elsewhere. In doing so, they 'imitate the Kidde in *Aesop*'. Koeppel[1] first showed that the fable Nashe cites is not really in Aesop at all, but in Spenser's May eclogue of *The Shepheardes Calender*; and yet, as McKerrow pointed out, Nashe made any number of similar errors of citation. More recently a Danish scholar, V. Østerberg, submitted a very sophisticated argument about this fable[2] which J. D. Wilson found telling,[3] and Duthie 'of great cogency'. Østerberg argued that the fable is irrelevant to the point Nashe is trying to make, that the parallels break down under examination, and that the probable reason Nashe chose to involve this far-fetched analogy in his diatribe was that 'he particularly desired a pun on the name of Thomas Kyd'. We have good reason to think of a pun, surely, when Greene can speak of *Tamburlaine* as 'bred of *Merlin's* race', or inveigh against the upstart crow who considers himself 'the only Shake-scene in a country', when Ralegh and Henry Noel exchange punning couplets on each other's names, and *Willobie his Avisa* undergoes six printings on the strength of its initials and innuendoes. The details of Østerberg's argument may seem less sure—Edwards finds them 'most unconvincing'—but they come as close as anyone's to proving direct allusion to Kyd. It is not difficult to imagine the mental process by which Nashe himself may have arrived at the idea for his pun-*cum*-fable (see below).

Against Østerberg we must revive two parallelisms noted by

---

[1] *Englische Studien*, XVIII, 130.
[2] *Studier over Hamlet-Teksterne* (Copenhagen, 1920), paraphrased by J. Dover Wilson, *RES*, XVIII (1942), 385–94.
[3] J. Dover Wilson, ed., *Hamlet* (Cambridge, 1934), xviii–xix.

McKerrow: one, a reference to 'the Glow-worme mentioned in *Aesop's* Fables', two pages earlier in the preface to *Menaphon;* and the second, a complaint made by Nashe (epistle to the second impression of *Pierce Penilesse*), that 'In one place of my Booke, *Pierce Penilesse* saith but to the Knight of the Post, *I pray how might I call you,* & they say I meant one *Howe,* a Knave of that trade, that I never heard of before.'[1] But if we consider the 'Stubbe' reference against the 'Glow-worme', we realize that Nashe could be allusive or not, as the occasion suited; it is true, as McKerrow says, that there happens to have been no writer named Glow-worme, but, in fact, there *was* a writer named Kyd, and Nashe and his audience certainly knew of him. Cannot we imagine Nashe, having just used an illustration from Aesop (the glow-worm), searching his memory for another one here, thinking of Kyd himself and the animal name, thinking of Spenser's kid (perhaps forgetting where he read of it), and abandoning the search for an entirely applicable fable in favour of a witty allusion? Writing in haste, he simply mis-cites his mis-applied analogy. The second passage quoted ('Howe') cuts both ways in McKerrow's argument: true, Nashe denies that he meant 'one *Howe*', but the fact is that 'they' thought he did—in other words, that Nashe was *suspected* of a punning allusion. Surely the suspicion was not entirely unfounded, as Philip Stubbes knew. Furthermore, McKerrow seems to have missed the point of Nashe's 'complaint' altogether: what Nashe is really doing, of course, is to bring Howe and his discreditable profession to everyone's attention, under the pretence of disowning the earlier pun. Whether or not he originally intended the pun, now he has made sure that we notice it; this is an ancient comic technique, particularly popular among the Eliza-bethans.

Finally, one must concede that Nashe's citation of 'the Kidde in *Aesop*', taken alone, is insufficient to attach the whole passage and its reproaches to Thomas Kyd. But if the specific jeers which precede and follow the citation can be linked with any certainty to Kyd, the strength of the association increases to the point of plausibility, and even probability. We have already observed that 'triviall trans-lators' who 'intermeddle with Italian translations' might well be taken to include the translator of Tasso, and that Kyd certainly was born to the profession of *Noverint.* We know that Kyd read his Seneca very closely, perhaps more so than any other surviving popular dramatist whose reading came out in his writing. And

[1] Nashe, *Works,* I, 154.

several of the obscurer points Nashe makes can be explained by reference to *The Spanish Tragedy;* here, however, the scholarly dispute thickens.

The specific accusations which follow the 'Kidde in *Aesop*' have, as I mentioned above, been identified with 'errors' in *The Spanish Tragedy* by Boas, as well as Sarrazin, Schick, and Fleay.[1] 'Those that thrust *Elisium* into hell' is taken by Schick and Boas as an allusion to Andrea's famous prologue, *Spanish Tragedy*, I. i., where the 'faire Elizian greene' is represented as a region of the underworld beyond the Acheron. Boas admits that Kyd's description of the topography of Hell is taken from Virgil, and McKerrow cannot see why Nashe should take it upon himself to ridicule any description founded on such classical authority. Duthie and Edwards agree: 'Why should Nashe object to Kyd's modelling his lower world upon Vergil's account, when upon Vergil was founded for many centuries the whole Christian conception of the afterworld?'[2] McKerrow points out in passing, as well, the line from *Doctor Faustus*, where Faustus claims to 'confound hell in Elisium', and a delineation of the underworld similar to Andrea's in *Locrine*, IV., iv.

All these arguments have cogency, but if they are admitted, just what *is* Nashe ridiculing? 'Ignorance of the classics' or 'identifying irreconcilable opposites', as Duthie suggests, seem vague. Marlowe's line specifically means that Faustus, following Virgil, thinks of his Christian Hell as containing a Paradise, and that he is deluding himself thereby—which is why 'The word "damnation" terrifies [him] not'—hence Faustus is not 'thrusting' Elisium into Hell, but carrying on from the original confusion. 'Thrusts' seems to imply that someone has placed Elisium in Hell, presumably in a literary context; it seems to contain at least one secondary meaning, namely that he has botched the job, discrediting and possibly mistranslating the classical original. McKerrow and his followers all assume, furthermore, that Nashe knew and revered his Virgil as well as they do; it is, of course, just possible that Nashe forgot the appropriate lines from *Aeneid* VI, or that he was unimpressed by their cultural importance. Considering that he immediately proceeds to deprecate excessive classicism, the argument that Virgil is beyond satire seems fairly shaky. Now, if Nashe is indeed referring to a literary example of Elisium in Hell, the description in *The Spanish Tragedy* will attract our attention: it certainly precedes the example from *Locrine*

---

[1] Ibid., IV, 449–50, V, supplement, 67; Boas, xxviii–xxix.
[2] Edwards, p. 7; Duthie, p. 61.

(which is patently based upon it), and the passage which contains it was among the most famous and 'purple' of the whole play. And let us remember that Nashe is writing for an audience who will recognize and appreciate his witty gibes, and that 'thrust *Elisium* into hell' would mean very little without an immediate referent. I would agree with Boas that the phrase probably alludes to *Spanish Tragedy*, I. i., or at least to a very similar description of the under-world which has perished.

The famished followers of Seneca 'have not learned', says Nashe, 'so long as they have lived in the spheares, the just measure of the Horizon without an hexameter'. Here Boas overextends his argu-ments, and claims a reference to *Spanish Tragedy*, I. i again, this time as a sneer at Kyd's slavish copying of Virgil's details in the topography of Hell. McKerrow quite reasonably asks what 'Horizon' has to do with Hell, and finds the meaning of the phrase itself obscure: 'we must, I think, confess that the correct explanation of the charge—as of the last—is yet to be found'. McKerrow also rejects the notion that the composition of English verses in classical metre is being hit at; Duthie agrees, and suggests two possible interpretations: (1) that Nashe's enemies 'could not give the right quantity of the word without the scansion to guide them', and (2) that 'these men are very ignorant—even their pronounciation is weak; in order to remember the correct pronounciation of the word "horizon" they have to run over in their heads a line of verse which contains it'. Now even if these alternative solutions seem un-satisfactory, as I think they do, Boas's interpretation is surely not right. In his effort to tie everything in with *The Spanish Tragedy* he ignores the possibility of allusion to other plays—perhaps even Kyd's—which are now lost. It seems to me, however, that Nashe's charge, whatever its specific referent may be, means generally that the writers under attack resort overmuch to classical copying: that 'so long as they have lived in the spheares', i.e. despite their residence in the real world, they cannot speak of its dimensions without resort-ing to classical authority—for which 'hexameter' stands. 'Without' means, I think, 'outside of', rather than '*sans*'. No specific allusion to Kyd has been shown, but all the general charges possibly involved do fit him.

'To bodge up a blanke verse with ifs and ands' was taken by Sarrazin[1] as a reference to *Spanish Tragedy*, II. i. and III. xiii., where, successively, four lines begin with 'And' and three with 'If'.

---

[1] *Thomas Kyd und sein Kreis* (Berlin, 1892), p. 101.

This is a far-fetched suggestion, and no one has taken it seriously. More plausibly, Boas proposed an allusion to II. i. 77, where Lorenzo cries, 'What, villain, ifs and ands?' Commenting on this, McKerrow becomes extremely pedantic, allowing Nashe no latitude whatever for his satire. He takes 'bodge up', to mean 'pad out', and 'ifs and ands' to be representative of 'small unnecessary words, in order to eke out the metre'. Duthie rather mechanically agrees, but let us look back at the charge: 'bodge', allied to 'botch', means 'to patch clumsily' (*NED*), and is obviously just an insult, not an analytical description of a method of versifying. Furthermore, as poets will testify, one does not *pad out* lines with conjunctions like 'ifs and ands', but with adjectives, adverbs, and irregular accents. The crucial phrase here is 'blanke verse', which Nashe evidently wanted to specify, and 'ifs and ands' the afterthought, merely what the blank verse is 'bodged up' with. As I would construe it, Nashe says that these wretched writers think it sufficient to fling together a blank verse, blank perhaps because rhyme demands at least ingenuity, employing expressions quite as unpoetical as, say, 'ifs and ands'. Sarrazin evidently misunderstood the phrase, which, of course, means 'ifs and *ifs*', but Boas's suggestion seems quite acceptable, if the citation was intended—as surely it was—to be recognized. The scene containing Lorenzo's line was notorious enough to be parodied years later by Ben Jonson (*Poetaster*, III. i), and the line itself has the ring of a 'familiar quotation'.[1] If Nashe were angling for a phrase to bring another smile to the lips of theatre-goers, this one would do.

The last specific allusion is to 'turning over French *Doudie*', in the 'inner parts of the Citie'. Here begins a brouhaha of scholarship: Schick[2] thinks there is some French play called 'Dowdy', more or less, and that it is being shown at some noble house in the City. Fleay thinks a brothel is involved, and that *Doudie* is some sort of coinage for a harlot. MacCallum also suggests a light lady. Cunliffe[3] says *Doudie* is 'evidently an author and not, as some have supposed, a woman of ill fame'. Duthie goes along with MacCullum, but Edwards[4] construes *Doudie* as 'smut'. Now, the word 'dudie' or 'doody' (a corruption of 'duty', itself a euphemism) is still current in English usage, although not in the dictionaries: it means, simply,

[1] Cf., from the Shakespearean *True Tragedy of Richard III*, 'If, villain, feed'st thou me with ifs and ands?'
[2] See Duthie, pp. 62–65.
[3] *Early English Classical Tragedies*, xcvii.
[4] Edwards, xxiii.

excrement. 'The inner parts of the Citie' ought to be Paul's Church-yard[1] (not Shoreditch, certainly), where our author spends 'two or three howers' leafing through (as McKerrow says, 'turning over' could only refer to a book) lewd French publications. Nashe immediately proceeds to carry the figure over into whoring and 'infection', via the *double-entendres* of 'inner parts' and 'French [= pox]', but the original meaning of the phrase is clearly literary. Boas seems to have understood this, but his effort to link everything to *The Spanish Tragedy* led him to propose Garnier as the ribald French writer in question; which, considering Garnier's substance, is implausible. Jacques Yver, or Belleforest, whose italianate tales include the model of *Hamlet*, would be a better choice; but a specific identification is unnecessary.

I have nothing further to add to the wealth of scholarship expended on this passage save the observation that nowhere in all Nashe's work does he refer to Kyd by name, or again to a 'Kidde in *Aesop*', while he devotes paragraphs of encomia to Greene, Watson, Roydon, Achelley, and even Marlowe. Considering the encyclopedic nature of the survey of literature contained in this preface to *Menaphon*, the possibilities of allusion to Kyd seem strong. Baldwin's offhand suggestion[2] of Anthony Munday, rather than Kyd, for the main subject of attack, can be discarded. J. W. Cunliffe's interesting point might close the discussion: 'It is, of course, not necessary for the identification that Nashe's taunts should be well founded, but merely that they should be as near the truth as this unscrupulous pamphleteer was in the habit of sailing.'[3]

If Kyd is the subject of Nashe's attack, or even a member of a group of writers (perhaps including Munday) unloved by the university wits, we may be justified in imagining a presumptive socio-artistic split in the eighties between the self-educated artisans of the drama like Kyd and Shakespeare and the college men like Nashe, Marlowe, and Greene. But any extrapolation is dangerous, for one must remember that the affections of Nashe and Greene changed with the wind: Greene's attitude towards Marlowe is a good example of mobile loyalty. Any attempt to place Kyd among the unschooled literary journeymen of London, apart from those discriminating intellectuals of Oxford and Cambridge, must also ignore Kyd's unambiguous statement that Marlowe lived with him

---

[1] See Nashe, *Works*, V, supplement, 68.
[2] *Genetics*, pp. 19–24.
[3] *Early English Classical Tragedies*, xcvii.

in 1591. Nashe's attack has great interest in relation to the *ur-Hamlet*, to the date of *The Spanish Tragedy*, to the state of Elizabethan Grub Street, and to the fluctuations of theatrical fashion; but its relevance to Kyd's life and personal allegiances is in the end not much better than slight. We would *like* the passage to concern Kyd, and it probably does, but finally it tells us little about him.

In 1598, four years after his death, Kyd was listed by Meres (*Palladis Tamia*) among 'our best for Tragedie', and alongside Watson and Achelley in a passage already cited. Two anthologies of 1600, *Bel-vedere* and Robert Allott's *England's Parnassus*, mention him by name and represent his poetry; Ben Jonson makes his well-known allusion to 'Sporting Kyd' in the Shakespeare folio of 1623. In the same generation of poets, we have Dekker's description of Kyd in *A Knights Conjuring* (1607) as 'industrious', and Heywood's in *The Hierarchie of the Blessed Angells* (1635), where it is 'famous *Kid*', who by the English custom 'was call'd but *Tom*'.[1]

Heywood's disclosure sounds like hearsay, as Dekker's may be. It is a pity to base so much inference on so little record, but I hope we have milked dry whatever record there is. Admitting the tenuousness of any possible biography of our shadowy playwright, we shall pass from Kyd's personality to what is at least largely substance, Kyd's works.

---

[1] *The Hierarchie of the Blessed Angells* (London, 1635) sig. S1ᵛ.

CHAPTER III

THE SPANISH TRAGEDY:
AUTHORSHIP, SOURCES, AND DATE

I. *Authorship*

It is characteristic of the career of Thomas Kyd that his major surviving work remained unattributed to him during his own era. *The Spanish Tragedy* as printed in 1592, 1594, and subsequently, names no author,[1] and until 1773 no editor or theatrical historian had discovered one. Thomas Hawkins (*The Origin of the English Drama*, Oxford, 1773) in designating Kyd pointed to a passage of Thomas Heywood's *Apology for Actors* (1612); Heywood is speaking of plays sponsored by Roman emperors, and quotes accordingly (E3ʳ):

Therefore M. Kid, in his Spanish Tragedy, upon occasion presenting itselfe, thus writes.

> Why, Nero thought it no disparagement,
> And kings and emperours have tane delight
> To make experience of their wits in playes.

Beyond this offhand attribution by a member of a later generation, we have no external evidence whatever of Kyd's authorship; by so slender a thread hangs his chief claim to memory. But a reading of *Cornelia*, which names Kyd on the title-page of its second edition, leaves little doubt of one common composer, and between Hawkins and the present day no one has attempted to abstract *The Spanish Tragedy* from Kyd's minimal canon.

One well may wonder if Kyd sought obscurity. Besides *The Spanish Tragedy*, nothing in print bore Kyd's name until after his death: *The Householder's Philosophy* and *Verses of Prayse and Joie* are subscribed merely 'T.K.', as is the only edition of *Cornelia* printed in the poet's lifetime. *Soliman and Perseda* is anonymous, and the attribution to Kyd rests entirely on internal evidence. Of the poems or plays from which Allot's fragments (see Chapter VI) are printed, nothing more than those *sententiae* survives.

---

[1] But see Chapter IV for a mid-seventeenth-century bookseller's attribution of the play to 'Thos. Kyte'.

II. *Sources*

One of the most remarkable characteristics of *The Spanish Tragedy* is its lack of reliance on a simple narrative source. Despite the most assiduous search over a considerable period, none has turned up, although several minor sources and distinguishable influences have been identified. And it remains unlikely that any general basis for the story will ever be discovered.

Boas (xxxi) writes: 'For though no source of the story of Hieronimo has hitherto been found, it is probably drawn from some lost romance which preceded the play. It is antecedently improbable that an English dramatist would invent a plot concerned so entirely with incidents in the southern peninsula.' Yet we may disagree: since Boas's edition another quite likely partial source has come to light, and by now it is clear that Kyd drew on so many uncorrelated writings in forging his play that the frame-story itself is nearly lost in accretions and extraneous details. If the 'lost romance' were discovered, it would have to be the bare bones of Kyd's plot alone, minus the historical setting, the character of Lorenzo as Kyd has portrayed him, the incident of Pedringano's entrapment, and the play-within-play—leaving, at most, another partial source. As for the improbability of Kyd's inventing a plot located in Spain, we shall see that the Spanish setting is based on history so recent as practically to exclude the possibility of a tale grounded in it, and we shall suggest that Kyd knew little or no Spanish, and scarcely more about Spain itself.

The genre of Kyd's plot is more Italian than Spanish: it belongs to a style of narrative epitomized by Bandello, and taken through the French into England via translations of collections of tales by Pettie, Painter, Wotton, and others. Spanish stories of this era place less emphasis on intrigue and complexity of action; they are shorter and simpler, stressing themes of loyalty, friendship, hatred, revenge, etc., almost to the extent of reducing tale to anecdote. Kyd's involved plot adapts a style of story-telling which his colleague Achelley employed in *Violenta and Didaco*, a style which, for the Elizabethan period, 'romantic' has come to denote. But Kyd's manner of spinning out the plot reveals nothing less than genius for altering, intensifying, blending, and augmenting story lines only hinted at by known precedents. In the absence of any further known sources, we must credit him with powers of invention unparalleled among the dramatists of his time.

What follows is a summary of known sources for *The Spanish*

Tragedy, with a few new suggestions, and a general estimate of formal, stylistic, and thematic influences which may have acted upon the play.

A curious analogue to the situation with which the main action begins may be seen in the third history of Henry Wotton's translation of Jacques Yver, *A Courtlie Controversie of Cupids Cautels*, published in 1578 by Francis Kyd's acquaintance Coldocke. As is well known, this book provided Kyd with the plot of the play-within-play in *The Spanish Tragedy*, and it is not unreasonable to suppose that the dramatist read further than the initial history of Solyman and Persida.

In the third history (T1ʳ ff.), set in and around Mantua, a young Prince, Adilon, is in love with Clarinda, the daughter of Francisco Gonzaga. Clarinda encourages him slightly. During the siege of Milan, however, a French Prince, 'the younge Lorde of *Alegre*', is taken prisoner by Don Ferdinando Gonzaga, Clarinda's brother. The prisoner is carried off to Ferdinando's castle and is treated with utmost consideration; Ferdinando becomes his personal friend and eventually his sponsor at the Court of Mantua. Inevitably, the Lord of Alegre meets Clarinda, and falls in love with her.

So far we have an almost perfect analogue of the relationship of Horatio, Bel-imperia, Lorenzo, and the captive Prince Balthazar. In Wotton's tale, however, Clarinda reciprocates the love of her alien suitor (we must remember that Jacques Yver was French) and the action erupts into a spate of poisonings, culminating in the deaths of most of the main characters. It is not improbable, I think, that Kyd found the germ of his plot in this tale, and altered its outcome to extend and complicate the dramatic possibilities. The same compositional technique in *Soliman and Perseda* has been pointed out by Sarrazin:[1] a close adherence at first to the source's situation and early action, with imaginative variation exercised in later acts.

Josef Schick first identified what he took to be a nearly contemporary historical framework of the plot of Kyd's play.[2] Don Andrea's allusion to 'the late conflict' between Portugal and Spain in which he met death places the action, or more precisely the composition, subsequent to the Hispano-Portuguese wars of 1578 to 1580–2, culminating in Spain's constitutional conquest of late 1580. Further,

---

[1] Gregor Sarrazin, *Thomas Kyd und sein Kreis* (Berlin, 1892), pp. 40–41.
[2] Schick, ed., *The Spanish Tragedy* (London, 1898), vi.

he argued, the description of the battle which occupies part of I. ii. suggests the actual Battle of Alcantara, where on 24 August 1580 the Duke of Alva routed an inferior Portuguese contingent captained by Antonio, Prior of Crato; and the mention of 'Tersera' (I. iii. 82) may have been occasioned by the great naval battle fought around Terceira in the Azores between the Spanish and a semi-mercenary allied fleet supporting the pretension of Antonio to the vacated Portuguese throne (July–August 1582).

Boas endorsed Schick's view, but Philip Edwards[1] has not. Edwards is primarily concerned to deny the dating argument which would make a factor of Kyd's failure to mention the Armada, and as a result he rather arbitrarily discards all attempts to connect *The Spanish Tragedy* with actual history, or history as it was reported by Kyd's contemporaries. But in emphasizing minor differences between what is mentioned in *The Spanish Tragedy* and what had happened shortly before in the Iberian peninsula, Edwards unjustly minimizes the similarities. The relevant facts are these:

The Spanish Tragedy speaks of 'the late conflict with Portingale' (I. i. 15) in which Spain has achieved 'Victory . . . and that with little loss' (I. ii. 6). The political situation which underlies these events supposes Portugal, as a tributary subject of Spain, in revolt. Portugal is governed by a 'Viceroy'.

Prior to 1580 Portugal had never been conquered by Spain, despite the considerable efforts of Philip II's ancestors; and we may fairly say that the situation described in *The Spanish Tragedy* depends on that historical precedent. Now Edwards declares that 'there was no war between Spain and Portugal after the institution of a viceroy by Philip', but Elizabethans would demur. The action at Terceira and indeed the continued resistance of Antonio of Crato, who specifically had sought (and perhaps received)[2] English aid, would stand, in an Elizabethan's estimate, for Portugal's own struggle. None would be less willing than the English to acknowledge the pacification of Portugal, or the illegitimacy of Antonio's claim to the crown.[3]

---

[1] Edwards, xxiii–xxiv.

[2] See R. B. Merriman, *The Rise of the Spanish Empire* (New York, 1934), IV, 397.

[3] For example, the title of the first account of the Azores battle, printed in London in 1582, 'A discourse of that which happened in the battell fought between the two Navies of *Spaine* and *Portugall* at the Islands of *Azores*' [*STC* 1103], indicates that Antonio's mercenary fleet was considered a navy of Portugal.

Philip II's institution of the office of Viceroy in Portugal did, in fact, follow Spanish practices in Naples, Sicily, Sardinia, and the New World, and while the Viceroy was, as Edwards points out, a nephew of Philip himself, he was also native Portuguese. It is perhaps less plausible to connect the battle narrated by the Spanish General in I. ii. with the débâcle at Alcantara, if only because the General locates his battle on the border of Spain and Portugal (I. ii. 22–23), while the actual event took place just outside Lisbon; and the General's narrative makes a far less uneven match of it than historically it was. Besides, literary sources, may contribute to Kyd's description.[1]

Alexandro, the Portuguese Lord falsely accused in I. iii. is described by the Viceroy as 'Terceira's lord' who 'hadst some hope to wear this diadem' (I. iii. 82–83). It is difficult to imagine the name of the second-largest island in the Portuguese Azores as having much currency before the notable battle there of July–August 1582, when the cruelty of the Marquis of Santa Cruz ordained a general slaughter of prisoners, and the back of Antonio's resistance was broken. In London, two accounts came off the press: *A discourse of that which happened in the battell fought between the two Navies of Spaine and Portugall at the Ilands of Azores. Anno Dom. 1582* [STC 1103] and *Relation of the expongeable attempt and conquest of the ylande of Tercera . . . done in An. 1583* [STC 1104, ent. 16 oc. 1583]. In the earlier report Terceira is not mentioned by name at all, which may give some idea of the obscurity of that island; while in the latter it occurs by name in the title, and on sigs. A3r, A3v, and A4r.

If Kyd did not learn of Terceira from a printed account of the battle, he may have picked up a description from his old schoolmate, Thomas Lodge, who almost certainly visited the island in 1585.[2] At any rate, one must assume that 'Terceira' evoked for an Elizabethan audience the famous last stage of Portuguese subjection by a country in whose affairs all had a quickening concern.

Another echo of the historical wars occurs in III. xiv. 6–7. Speaking of the Portuguese, the King of Spain states:

> For as we now are, so sometimes were these,
> Kings and commanders of the western Indies.

These lines have puzzled commentators. Edwards notes, 'Kyd is

[1] See p. 67.
[2] Sarrazin, p. 51; see also N. B. Paradise, *Thomas Lodge* (New Haven, 1931), pp. 35–37.

far from accurate; Portuguese imperialism had been directed towards India, Africa, and the East. Either Kyd was thinking of Brazil, or he simply confused the East and West Indies', and Boas remarks, 'Another of Kyd's historical blunders . . . the lines may be a confused reference to the capture of the Azores by the Spanish fleet in 1582.' Actually, the error is not Kyd's, but his critics'. 'Indies' in Elizabethan usage meant mainland as well as islands,[1] and one of the most viable prizes of the Spanish victory was Portuguese Brazil. In *The Spanish Masquerado* (1589) Greene writes: The *Indies* beeing first sought out by the Portugall, and lately conquered and possessed by the King of *Spaine*, yeldeth him all his treasure',[2] and goes on to describe Drake's depredations—obviously in the American 'Indies'.

Antonio, Prior of Crato, explains in 1585 that 'Emanuell [King of Portugal] . . . conquered and annexed to his crowne, a good part aswell of the East and West Indies'.[3] Even Mexico was 'Indies', as a title of 1578 indicates: *The Conquest of the Weast India by Cortes* [*STC* 16807].

The temptation to censure Kyd's learning has been seized on all to eagerly. Plausibly, Kyd is again alluding to the turn of events which put all of Portugal's colonies in the hands of Spain; and what with English attention to the New World and near carelessness of Asia, it is understandable that Kyd's Spanish King would emphasize his American acquisitions. There are a few other points of possible historical influence which no one has yet pointed to: the King in *The Spanish Tragedy* has no Queen, and Philip II's fourth and last wife, Anne of Austria, had died as recently as 1580. Furthermore, Kyd's King has no children, and this presents a possible instance of faulty international reportage: the recognized heir of Philip's crown, Diego, died in 1582 at the age of only seven, the latest in a long line of bereavements for the Prudent King. Conestaggio (1585) mentions the death, but says nothing of a lone surviving heir, subsequently Philip III, who was at the time a mere infant. Did the Elizabethans think Philip II's dynasty was doomed? Lastly, the characters in *The Spanish Tragedy* bear predominantly Italian names, save Don Cyprian, the Duke of Castile. Perhaps Kyd picked this name from narratives of the Terceira battle, for the Governor of the island and close friend of Antonio of Crato was Cipriao de

---

[1] See *NED*, s.v. 'Indies'; Merriman, IV, 379–80, 384–6, 388–9.
[2] Robert Greene, *Works*, ed. Grossart, V. 281.
[3] *The Explanation of the . . . Right and Tytle* (1585), A1ʳ.

Figueiredo, whose name is anglicized in 1591 as 'Don Cyprian Figeredo Vasconsalus'.[1]

In I. iv. Hieronimo presents a pageant to the Court, the substance of which is chosen to glorify English exploits in Spain. Dramatically, the scene is a well-contrived parallel to the fatal playlet which Hieronimo will stage in unhappier times; but in addition the fact that among the English successes no mention, or even passing hint, of the amazing triumph in northern waters in 1588 is offered has served some scholars for an argument to place the play before 1588. We will reserve our discussion of this point for a little later, but it is in order here to vindicate Kyd of a few more critical aspersions. Hieronimo speaks of 'English Robert, Earl of Gloucester,/Who when King Stephen bore sway in Albion,/Arriv'd with five and twenty thousand men/In Portingale, and by success of war/Enforc'd the king, then but a Saracen,/To bear the yoke of English monarchy' (I. iv. 141–6). Boas comments, 'Kyd's history is here curiously inaccurate. There is no reason to suppose that Robert of Gloucester was ever in Portugal', and Edwards reiterates, 'It is a problem to know where Kyd got his rosy account of English triumphs in Iberian lands', and goes on to quote Boas. Now, to begin with, it is Hieronimo and not Kyd who is spinning the tale, and it is a pageant, not a lecture which he is presenting; the ultimate audience were intended to be playgoers, not historians. But beyond dramaturgic arguments, we may also submit that a tradition of popular or oral history exists alongside of the soberer versions preserved in chronicles. American schoolboys in our century believe that both World Wars were won chiefly, if not solely, by American forces. In Elizabethan times a tradition of Robert of Gloucester in Portugal was current, and Kyd's history is not 'mainly fanciful' (Boas), but merely popular: Anthony Wadeson collected a payment of twenty shillings from Henslowe in 1601 in earnest of 'A Boocke called the life of the humeros earlle of gloster wᵗʰ his conquest of portingalle'.[2]

Subsequently Hieronimo evokes 'Brave John of Gaunt, the Duke of Lancaster', who 'with a puissant army came to Spain,/And took our King of Castile prisoner' (I. iv. 164–7), and here Edwards reports, 'I have found nothing in the full accounts of Holinshed, Froissart, or Polydore Vergil to warrant Kyd's account.' One must turn, again, to a less-austere source: Christopher Ockland's *Anglorum*

---

[1] See G. B., *A Fig for the Spaniard* (London, 1591), sig. C3ʳ.
[2] R. A. Foakes and R. T. Rickert, eds., *Henslowe's Diary* (Cambridge, 1961), p. 171.

Proelia, a standard secondary-school textbook (done into English by John Sharrock in 1585 as *The Valiant Actes and Victorious Battailes of the English Nation* [*STC* 18777]), cheerfully records an expedition to Spain in which John of Gaunt subdues the nation, exacts a heavy yearly tribute, and marries off his two daughters to the Spanish and the Portuguese Kings.[1] When Shakespeare refers (*3 Henry VI*, III. iii. 81–82) to 'great John of Gaunt,/Which did subdue the greater part of Spain', it is somewhat too neat to suggest, as Edwards does, that 'Shakespeare may have been thinking of *The Spanish Tragedy*'. And another lost play commissioned by Henslowe is cited by P. A. Daniel: *The Conquest of Spayne by John a Gant*.[2]

It is absurd to condemn Kyd on the one hand for excessive pedantry and simultaneously to assail him for not following the strictest lines of historical accuracy in his dramatic adaptations. We should be able to recognize Kyd's use of a tradition or a recent series of events without requiring him to parrot the details authoritatively from the best authors. In putting the recent history of Spain and Portugal and the heroic folk history of England to work, Kyd shows a fine sense of selection, imagination, and ability to conflate separated details with dramatic possibilities into a fluent and homogeneous whole. That he puts history to use should be self-evident; that he uses it cleverly may be admired.

The character of Lorenzo in *The Spanish Tragedy* deserves individual examination. He is of a type commonly designated 'Machiavellian villain', and historically—presuming that Kyd's play precedes Marlowe's *Jew of Malta*—he is the first of his kind on the Elizabethan stage. But his pedigree is mixed.

Edward Meyer and subsequently Mario Praz have discussed in depth the use and misuse made of Machiavelli by the Elizabethan dramatists, and the growth out of all proportions or meaning of the term 'Machiavellian'. Of the sly, contriving, devious, and ego-centric malefactor, perhaps first associated with Machiavelli by the French polemicist Gentillet, Lorenzo is practically a prototype; and Nashe's Devil (*Pierce Penilesse*, 1592) might be Lorenzo himself when he specifies, as part of his 'Machiavilisme', the art of disposing of accomplices:

. . . such as I have imployed in any murther or stratagem to set them privilie together by the eares, to stab each other mutually, for feare of

---

[1] Christopher Ockland, *The Valiant Actes* (London, 1585), sig. B3ʳ.
[2] Edwards, p. 26, n.; *Henslowe's Diary*, pp. 167, 168, 294.

bewraying me; or, if that faile, to hire them to humor one another in such courses as may bring them both to the gallowes. . . .[1]

For Nashe the prototype is not Machiavelli's Prince, but Aretino's hero-villains, and for the dramatists, as Praz suggests, Giraldi Cintio may have provided models. 'Pure' villains like Iago and Aaron (in *Titus Andronicus*) are comparatively rarer on the Elizabethan stage than characters merely tinted with italianate policy; among the latter may be numbered Hamlet, Webster's malcontented instruments, Tourneur's and Marston's heroes, and Kyd's Hieronimo himself. We can isolate characteristics of ingenuity, deviousness, and quasi-aesthetic delight in the complexity of plot and stratagem to associate with the Machiavellian type in Elizabethan drama, by which standards even comic intriguers like Diccon the Bedlam, in *Gammer Gurton's Needle*, would claim a place, but naked malice must be another determinant. Lorenzo shares with Barabas and Aaron an essentially incomprehensible and shameless pleasure in doing harm, although Lorenzo's character is more subtly shaped than either of the others'. Lorenzo bends his malice to practical ends, obscure as they may seem (why, for example, is he so anxious to forward Balthazar's suit?), where Barabas walks indiscriminately abroad at night to poison wells—for no apparent profit to himself. Lorenzo, simply, is more politician, in the modern sense, than psychopath. And in creating his character Kyd may well have had recourse to contemporary examples of practising politicians.

In Kyd's time any prominent statesman was subject to accusations of 'Machiavellian' practice in carrying out the duties of his office, and doubtless most statesmen merited such a description. In Spain, with the apparent consent of the King, Antonio Perez engineered the murder of an unco-operative courtier, Juan Escovedo, and found himself trapped by his even more politic accomplice Philip II. In France, the Duke of Guise gathered a formidable reputation for poisoning and assassination; while in England, Secretaries Walsingham and Burleigh drew fire on the same account. But for Elizabeth's personal favourite, Robert Dudley, Earl of Leicester, a concentrated opposition managed a whole book of slanderous tales and defamatory imputations. After Scott's *Kenilworth*, and to the present day, Leicester has not altogether lived down the contents of *A Copie of a Leter* (1584).

For our purposes, the most important feature of the banned

---

[1] Nashe, *Works*, I, 220.

tract is the story of one Gates, a thief, employed by Leicester about various business. Fredson Bowers[1] and T. W. Baldwin[2] have pointed out the remarkable similarity between Leicester's device to throttle Gates and Lorenzo's method of disposing of Pedringano. Gates, in the Leicester calumny, is assured of Leicester's protection even after capture, and placated by the Earl with promise of a pardon. When at last no pardon is forthcoming Gates realizes he has been deceived, and places a full account of his activities and of Leicester's complicity in the hands of an unnamed gentleman. Gates, like Pedringano, is hanged, and Leicester, like Lorenzo, escapes even censure.

The libels which were gathered into the first printing of *A Copie of a Leter* cannot be exactly dated, but the earliest text in print seems to have been about 1584. The book was suppressed by special proclamation, and what copies of it circulated in England were undoubtedly printed abroad. Manuscript copies both before and after 1584 survive, with considerable variation in the text.

That Kyd had access to some version of the Leicester slanders seems probable, and that his contemporaries recognized Kyd's use of the very material seems possible. About 1604,[3] Thomas Rogers of Bryanston (Dorset) composed a very long poem in the manner of *A Mirror for Magistrates*, entitled *Leicester's Ghost*. A truncated version of the poem was appended to the 1641 reprint of the Leicester scandals (*Leicester's Commonwealth*) and, as Fredson Bowers first pointed out, a few lines of the poem link the source-story with Kyd's Pedringano episode beyond doubt:

> Of pardons, I did put him still in hope
> When hee of felony was guilty found . . .
> For his reprivall (like a crafty Fox)
> I sent no pardon, but an empty Box.[4]

Now, we may wish to suppose that Rogers found this detail in some now lost manuscript version of the slanders, to which Kyd likewise had access, but the possibility also remains that Rogers recognized the quasi-historical Leicester in Kyd's Lorenzo, and appropriated a

---

[1] Fredson Bowers, 'Kyd's Pedringano: sources and parallels', *Harvard Studies and Notes in Philology and Literature*, XIII (1931), 241–9.

[2] T. W. Baldwin, *Genetics*, pp. 185–98.

[3] Edwards, xlix, 'of unknown date'; but see F. B. Williams, 'Leicester's Ghost', *Harvard Studies and Notes*, XVIII (1935), 272, and 'Thomas Rogers of Bryanston', *Harvard Studies and Notes*, XVI (1934), 253–67, where the approximate date and authorship are established.

[4] Bowers, 'Kyd's Pedringano', p. 249.

bit of business originated by Kyd for a new character of the Earl. This latter possibility is reinforced by F. B. Williams's observations of other (and numerous) contemporary literary borrowings in Rogers's poem. Further, some other, hitherto unnoted, details may strengthen the connexion between Kyd's Lorenzo and *A Copie*'s Robert Dudley, viz.: Lorenzo is the unworthy son of a noble father. In *A Copie of a Leter*, Leicester's father was 'verie wise, valyant, magnanimous, liberal, and assured friendlie . . . of all which vertues, my Lord his sonne, hath neither shew nor shadow . . . being craftie and subtile to deceive, & ingenious to wickednes'.[1] Lorenzo controls all access to the King's ear, and is able to fob off even the Knight Marshal, Hieronimo, when the latter craves justice. The same is said of Leicester (p. 48): 'Nothing can passe but by his admission . . . no bill, no supplication, no complainte, no sute, no speach, . . . but by his good lyking.'

Elsewhere in *A Copie of a Leter* (p. 59) we hear of the mutual dislike of Leicester and Sussex. If Kyd were in the employment of the latter, or even angling for such a situation, his choice of Leicester as a prototype for a villain would take on added propriety. Whether suggestive or not, we read also in *A Copie* (p. 10) of 'the late contention' between Portugal and Spain, and of John of Gaunt's Spanish expedition (pp. 126, 130), with its traditionally triumphant outcome.

Kyd was not alone, perhaps, in patterning his villainous courtier on Robert Dudley. It will be recalled that Webster's Bracciano, in *The White Devil*, has his wife poisoned by a physician named Doctor Julio. Surely it is more than a coincidence that the Italian physician, employed by Leicester (who himself supposedly murdered his wife Amy) as a poisoner according to *A Copie* (p. 29), bears precisely the same name.

Another 'first' for *The Spanish Tragedy* is Kyd's use of a play-within-play; and, like the pattern of villainy exemplified by Lorenzo, this innovation proved most popular. The idea of a sub-action contained in the primary drama, however, is in a general sense antique; it is Kyd's elaboration and dramatic use of the notion which gives his own playlet the importance in theatrical history it has come to possess.

As early as the *Hippolytus* of Euripides a Prologue contrives to separate levels of dramatic action. Aphrodite, who takes no part in the story, tells us who she is, and describes Hippolytus. She explains what has happened before the time of the scene, and what will

---

[1] *A Copie of a Leter* (N.p., 1584), p. 196.

occur in the course of the action. In conclusion, she announces that
the hero is approaching, and leaves the stage to him.

Now, while Aphrodite's prologue is at most faintly suggestive of
later play-within-play and play-without-play complications, and is,
of course, an exterior 'frame', rather than action inserted (as with
Kyd's playlet), what may have been Euripides' innovation bears
noting. There is nothing like it in the extant plays of Sophocles or
Aeschylus; while in *The Trojan Women* a similar induction shows us
Poseidon and Athene discussing what is about to ensue; and in
Hecuba, the Ghost of Polydorus narrates his return from Hades as a
prologue.

Seneca takes over the Euripidean prologue in his *Hercules Furens*,
where an angry Juno predicts the madness and despair of the hero.
Again, it is Seneca[1] who provides the transition between gods and
ghosts, as in the most famous of his tragedies, *Thyestes*, the framing
prologue is shared by Tantalus and a Fury, the former agreeing to
witness the acting-out of a revenge. Among later Senecan playwrights, ghosts speak their fore-pieces with increasing frequency
(for example, the shade of Antony in Jodelle's *Cléopatre Captive*,
the Ghost of Selina in Giraldi Cintio's *Orbecche*, and the Ghost of
Gorlois in *The Misfortunes of Arthur*), while in Kyd's play, and more
so in *Hamlet*, these formerly aloof figures have come so far as to
mingle in the primary action they once introduced.

Lesser examples of split-level action established by the speakers
in prologues and inductions may be seen in England as early as
Fulgens and Lucrece (1497), where 'A' and 'B' are found in the
opening scene discussing the topic of the action about to be staged,
and in *Cambyses* (1561-9), where the Prologue 'sees the players
coming in'. In *Soliman and Perseda*, three abstract deities discuss
the action on the stage at intervals, and quarrel about its control.
And, of course, *The Spanish Tragedy* is itself framed in the same
manner, with Revenge and the Ghost of Andrea actually present
during the play, and available for occasional comment.

The Spanish Tragedy, with its framing characters and its inserted
elements, at several points devolves into play-within-play-within-
play; the Elizabethan audience could watch the supernatural
audience watching the courtly audience watching Hieronimo's

---

[1] It is generally assumed that most Elizabethan playwrights were unfamiliar
with the Greek theatre, and that such English devices as ghosts derive from
Seneca, not Euripides. But having noted the ghost-prologue in *Hecuba*, we may
also note Sidney's allusion to that very play in the *Defence of Poesy* (see G. G.
Smith, *Elizabethan Critical Essays*, I, 198-9), specifically mentioning the ghost.

tragedy, or his pageant of knights and escutcheons. Perhaps we may see the genesis of the idea for the innermost play in the original and ancient concept of an outer play; and while *The Spanish Tragedy* includes the former while preserving the latter, in later Elizabethan theatre we can observe a merging of these devices into a less artificial way of complicating the plot. Peele's *The Old Wives' Tale*, nearly contemporary with *The Spanish Tragedy*, encloses a fantastic romance within a naturalistic frame, and points the way to Beaumont's theatrically preoccupied masterpiece, *The Knight of the Burning Pestle*—in many ways the ultimate play-within-play. Here the paradox is that one cannot distinguish between play and enclosure or frame-story, as the time of the competing actions is about equal, and the actors of each half are acutely conscious of the action of the others. A vanishing point of 'withinness' is reached, three hundred years before Pirandello.

But Hieronimo's drama draws from another tradition as well, that of interior complication, or insertion. J. W. Cunliffe has traced the origins of the Elizabethan dumb show, as it appears first in *Gorbuduc*, and subsequently in a number of Senecan plays including *The Spanish Tragedy*, to the Italian *intermedii* of the late fifteenth and sixteenth centuries.[1] *Intermedii*, diverting *entr'actes*, were appended to each act of an Italian version of the *Menaechmi*, early in the sixteenth century, and although ordinarily these entertainments allegorized or summed up the prior action (in the manner of a Senecan act-ending chorus), Ariosto's *I Suppositi* (1509) contained entirely irrelevant *intermedii*; and by 1582 it was complained that the comedies were being written for the *intermedii*, rather than the reverse—a situation with which the Elizabethan use of comic relief may occasionally bear comparison. But these Italian devices, we must remind ourselves, were more in the nature of diversion than integral parts of the plays they figured in, and, as 'relief', they came at the ends, rather than the beginnings, of acts. Examples of the *intermedii* Englished may be seen in Greene's *James IV*, at the ends of Acts I, II, and IV.

Gorboduc's dumb shows precede the performance of each act,

---

[1] See J. W. Cunliffe, 'Italian Prototypes of the Masque and Dumbshow', *PMLA*, XXII (1907), 140–56, 'The Influence of the Italian on early Elizabethan Drama', *MP*, IV (1907), 597–604, and the reiteration in his *Early English Classical Tragedies* (Oxford, 1912). But Cunliffe takes scant account of either a native English tradition, or the possibility of influence by French 'tableaux vivants'. An interesting exposition of the native tradition is given by H. A. Watt, ed., *Gorboduc* (Madison, Wis., 1910), pp. 78–82.

as do the dumb shows in *Gismond of Salerne*, *Locrine*, and *The Misfortunes of Arthur*; and it seems likely that the dumb show in *The Spanish Tragedy* should be placed at the beginning of Act IV, rather than at the end of Act III. All these inserted actions relate closely to the main action, with greater fidelity than the *intermedii* did, and represent at least one aspect of the play-within-play as it was employed before Kyd, But it may be an overstatement to say, with Watt (p. 90), that 'later it [the dumb show] developed into the play within the play'. For as early as *Fulgens and Lucrece* (1497) a legitimate play-within-play was enacted on the English stage.[1]

The play-within-play in *Fulgens and Lucrece*, however, bears little dramatic relevance to the main plot of the play. In *The Spanish Tragedy*, Kyd contrived to combine the dramaturgic possibilities of an inner action, as revealed by such disparate efforts as Medwall's and Seneca's, with the idea of reflective secondary action, as it is exemplified in the *intermedii*, the Tudor dumb shows, and, to some extent, by some sub-plots.[2] The imaginative leap from a diversionary action with fireworks or 'wild men', or a play-within-play staged merely for the sake of variety, to a tightly functional microcosmic performance—wherein the conscience of a king might be caught, or a tardy justice be achieved—is an extraordinary one. Here again, his handling of only faintly suggestive sources assures us that 'Kyd's originality in ordering his material is more remarkable than his powers as a copyist'.[3]

The specific source of Hieronimo's tragedy is to be found in the first tale of Henry Wotton's translation from Jacques Yver, published as *A Courtlie Controversie of Cupids Cautels* in 1578 by Francis Coldocke. Kyd's use of this tale has been studied, with an eye to proving Kyd's authorship of *Soliman and Perseda*, by Gregor Sarrazin. Within the minimal space of his playlet, however, Kyd exercised no particular licence in dramatizing the story. As for the device of murder-on-stage, we may recall that Hieronimo himself, with sublime irony, signals his own recollection of Nero's practice:

---

[1] I think it unlikely that Munday's *John a Kent and John a Cumber* preceded *The Spanish Tragedy*, but see Arthur Brown, 'The Play within a Play', *Essays and Studies*, 1960, p. 37 and n., where the possibility is raised. Saving *Fulgens and Lucrece*, Kyd's play-within-play is probably the earliest on record.

[2] For an excellent discussion of the relation of the play-within-play to the concept of *theatrum mundi*, see Jean Jacquot, ' "Le Théâtre du Monde" de Shakespeare à Calderon', *Revue de Littérature Comparée*, XXXI, 3 (1957), 341 ff.

[3] Edwards, xlix.

> Why, Nero thought it no disparagement,
> And kings and emperors have ta'en delight
> To make experience of their wits in plays!
>
> (IV. i. 86–88)

Hieronimo's hint falls on the deaf ears of Balthazar and Lorenzo, but in the same passage by which Kyd is identified as the author of *The Spanish Tragedy*, Thomas Heywood caught the clear allusion to Nero's practice of personally slaughtering condemned criminals on the stage:

> It was the manner of their Emperours, in those days, in their publicke Tragedies to choose out the fittest amongst such, as for capital offences were condemned to dye, and imploy them in such parts as were to be kil'd in the Tragedy.[1]

Julius Caesar, furthermore, while playing the role of the hero in *Hercules Furens*,

> . . . was so extremely caryed away with the violence of his practised fury, and by the perfect shape of the madnesse of Hercules, to which he had fashioned all his active spirits, that he slew him [a servant playing the part of Lychas] dead at his foot.[2]

In the published text of *The Spanish Tragedy* a note precedes the play-within-play:

> Gentlemen, this play of Hieronimo in sundry languages, was thought good to be set down in English more largely, for the easier understanding to every public reader,
>
> (IV. iv. 10, ff.)

and earlier, Hieronimo has assigned the actors each a different tongue:

> Each one of us must act his part
> In unknown languages,
> That it may breed the more variety.
> As you, my Lord, in Latin, I in Greek,
> You in Italian, and for because I know
> That Bel-imperia hath practised the French,
> In courtly French shall all her phrases be.
>
> (IV. i. 172–8)

---

[1] Heywood, *Apology*, sig. E3ʳ.

[2] An actual event of 1587 might have contributed a suggestion to Kyd of the murder-on-stage in the guise of playing: the Admiral's Men, 'having a devyse in ther playe to tye one of their fellowes to a poste and so shoote him to deathe', one of the pieces turned out to be loaded, swerved, and killed two members of the audience (*Eliz. Stage*, II, 135). See also *Huntington Library Bulletin*, no. 11 (April, 1937), 153–5, concerning a similar accident at Westminster School in 1623.

Balthazar rather understandably objects:

> But this will be a mere confusion,
> And hardly shall we all be understood.

Nevertheless, Hieronimo insists, 'It must be so.' And at the conclusion of the fatal action, Hieronimo says: 'Now break we off our sundry languages/And thus conclude I in our vulgar tongue.'

Now the play-within-play in 'sundry languages' has not come down to us, and there has been considerable resistance to the idea that such a device was ever actually used. Edwards (xx) finds himself dubious of the 'complaisance among the audience if, in the theatre, they had been asked to endure sixty lines in languages they could not understand'. But no one questions the actual use of Hieronimo's fourteen-line speech in Latin (II. v.), or the Italian and Latin scraps scattered throughout the play; and it may be observed that Kyd evidently did know Latin, French, and Italian, and quite possibly through his elementary schooling, Greek, so it is unnecessary to suppose that the playlet was merely a dumb masque 'accompanied, for the sake of "drama", with a few well-chosen lines of gibberish.'[1]

However, Biesterfeldt's suggestion that the original playlet was shorter ('set down in English more *largely*'), and indeed multilingual, and was subsequently replaced, perhaps by popular demand, with the surviving English version, seems reasonable, and does serve to explain certain peculiarities of plot in the last act.[2] If, indeed, Hieronimo's play was originally macaronic, there are a few identifiable precedents for such drama. As early as the famous French farce *Maître Pierre Pathelin* (*c.* 1465) we have a scene partially enacted in 'divers langaiges', a scene which stuck in the French imagination for centuries.[3] Among classical examples of partially macaronic drama we have *The Birds* of Aristophanes, with its 'Macedonian', and Plautus's *Poenulus*, containing mock 'Carthaginian'. Among the religious dramas we have bilingual situations in Rutebeuf's *Miracle de Théophile*, Bodel's *Jeu de St. Nicholas*, and a twelfth-century liturgical play presented at Montpellier.[4] In Vincente Espinel's romance, *Marcos de Obregon*, four men of four

---

[1] Edwards, xxxvii.

[2] P. W. Biesterfeldt, *Die dramatische technik Thomas Kyds* (Göttingen, 1935), p. 45; Edwards, xxxvii.

[3] The scene is echoed in many later works, including Rabelais, *Gargantua*, bk. I, Rotrou's *La Soeur*, and perhaps Molière's *Bourgeois Gentilhomme*: see Grace Frank, *The Medieval French Drama* (Oxford, 1954).

[4] Frank, p. 36.

nationalities in a boat cannot communicate even in Latin, because their pronunciation differs so greatly. And among earlier English plays two lost examples, *The Rock of Amity* (1518) and *Heretic Luther* (1527), seem to have been played in Latin or English and French at once; Kyd's audience may well have been familiar enough with the device to go along with a few incomprehensible lines. But for Hieronimo, perhaps, the most obvious precedent is the most familiar: like God and the builders of the Tower of Babel, he wreaks confusion with words, and with 'unknown languages' puts an end to the unchastised misbehaviour of his enemies.

Elizabethans like Thomas Nashe recognized the imitation of Seneca indulged in by their pre-Shakespearian dramatists. '*Seneca*, let bloud line by line and page by page, at length must needes die to our stage . . .': and by 1589, Nashe implies, the fashion was in the wane. But Kyd's play exhibits a number of Senecan characteristics, if in a lesser degree than the earlier and subsequent 'classical tragedies' like *Gorboduc*, *Jocasta*, *The Misfortunes of Arthur*, or Samuel Brandon's *Virtuous Octavia*.

Kyd's obligation to Seneca, direct and indirect, takes three forms: (1) the imitation of certain devices, particularly the ghost and the ghost's prologue, and the adoption of the general motif of revenge; (2) the use of actual phrases, in Latin or English, deriving from Seneca; and (3) a general stylistic debt to the Senecan rhetoric—a heritage common to all Europe. Now, the devices of ghost and prologue, as we have seen, go ultimately back to Euripides, and among sixteenth-century playwrights Kyd may have read, Robert Garnier and G. B. Giraldi Cintio employ both. Howard Baker has attempted to minimize the direct connexion between Kyd and Seneca, stressing the differences between Kyd's Andrea and Seneca's Thyestes (in *Agamemnon*) and Tantalus (in *Thyestes*), between Kyd's 'allegorical' Revenge and Seneca's Magaera, between the 'astonishing, almost gay' quality of Andrea's prologue and the overridingly horrific quality of Tantalus's, and, finally, between Kyd's thematic treatment of revenge, and Seneca's.

The real difference between the two authors lies in their dissimilar attitudes toward revenge. For Seneca revenge results from a family curse of long duration; betrayal, murder, and incest in preceding generations are sources of his tragedies . . . The ghost of Thyestes in *Agamemnon* is vengeful; but his machinations have caused the tragedy. The ghost of Tantalus is not vengeful; he is the unwilling victim of a Fury, and regrets what must take place. With Kyd, on the other hand, the Ghost of Andrea, unlike Thyestes, has no responsibility for the tragedy; nor is he in any ordinary sense the victim of Revenge. Andrea, moreover, has no vengeful tendencies until he is inspired to them by the events which he is witnessing . . . The revenge theme, which develops slowly in the mind of Hieronimo, develops with corresponding slowness in the mind of the Ghost. For a revenge movement to begin slowly and mount to a wild climax is foreign to Seneca, but it is the whole story of Kyd's play. . . .[1]

Now, this is perfectly fair, and it is indeed absurd to censure Kyd (as some critics have done) because his treatment of revenge is different from Seneca's—or because Andrea at the beginning of the play specifies no vengeable injury to himself—but the attempt to dissociate Kyd altogether from Senecanism is unconvincing. Obviously Kyd's characters differ from Seneca's; he is not simply a copyist; but knowing as we do that Kyd knew, and quoted, his Seneca, we would be foolish to dismiss all similarities in situation and choice of theme between the two writers as coincidental. Andrea and Revenge do evoke Tantalus and Magaera, Andrea's prologue does stem from a Senecan tradition at least as much as from the De Casibus 'Induction', and Seneca is certainly the principal progenitor of the revenge drama. As for the 'slowness' which Baker remarks, it may indeed be foreign to Seneca himself, but not to the earlier continental Senecans: we may note in particular the slowly evolved revenge dramatized by Giraldi Cintio in Orbecche, where action is preceded, as in Kyd, by long deliberation, dissimulation, and contrivance.[2]

Kyd's debt to Seneca in the matter of phraseology and style can scarcely be denied. Seneca is quoted in Latin in I. iii. 17 (Agamemnon) and thrice in III. xiii. (Agamemnon, Troades, Oedipus), while Hieronimo reads from a book (obviously Seneca) on the general topic of revenge. English echoes of Latin Seneca—and we have no indication that Kyd was familiar with the Heywood et al. translation of 1581—are less certain, but there remain a number of quite probable examples. And that Kyd's rhetoric employs figures favoured by Seneca—stichomythia above all—has been frequently demonstrated in the past. Whether Seneca, continental Senecans, or earlier English imitators of both supplied the primary stylistic influence need not be conjectured.

---

[1] Howard Baker, Induction to Tragedy (Baton Rouge, 1939), pp. 117–18.

[2] See also H. B. Charlton, The Senecan Tradition in Renaissance Tragedy (Manchester, 1946), esp. p. 163 on the italianate quality of Elizabethan Senecanism; and for the Senecan position stated in the extreme, J. W. Cunliffe, Early English Classical Tragedies, pp. xix–lviii.

Echoes of Robert Garnier, particularly in the General's narrative of the battle (I. ii) won by Spain, have been identified by Boas,[1] and pass unquestioned by Edwards. But the parallels are scarcely convincing, and A. M. Witherspoon, treating the influence of Garnier on Elizabethans, finds *The Spanish Tragedy* 'absolutely without any influence of Garnier'.[2] Seventy pages earlier, however, Witherspoon states that the General's narrative 'contains a good many details borrowed from the messenger's account of the battle of Thapsus in Garnier's *Cornélie*' which may redirect our attentions to Witherspoon's analytic technique. And, indeed, despite T. W. Baldwin's full endorsement,[3] Witherspoon's arguments against Garnier's influence are no more convincing than Boas's in favour of it. Garnier may or may not have been read by Kyd before *The Spanish Tragedy*; the evidence either way is minimal.

Similarly, no specific echoes remain to indicate whether Kyd knew Giraldi Cintio's tragedies, although a similarity of tone— more with Cintio than Garnier—might lead us to suspect he did. Hieronimo on two occasions has recourse to couplets in Italian: one is proverbial (see below), and the source of the other is unknown, but both might seem natural in the mouths of Acharisto (*Euphimia*) or Sulmone (*Orbecche*). Cintio, like Garnier, makes full use of the sententious aphorism, even when, as in Kyd, the burden of the aphorism is rather Machiavellian than pietistic. Compare Kyd's untraced couplet with two fragments from Giraldi Cintio:

> E quel che voglio io, nessun lo sa,
> Intendo io: quel mi basterà.
> > (*Sp. Tr.* III. v. 87–88)

> à me basta
> Ch'io sia, non men che Dio, da' miei temuto.
> > (*Euphimia*, II. i.)

> Chi volesse sempr'ir dietro à sospetti,
> Non si condurria à fin mai cosa alcuna.
> > (*Orbecche*, II. i.)

Minor echoes from a number of Latin writers give us some idea of Kyd's reading, although as a source only Virgil is important. Boas first showed how closely Andrea's description of the underworld was modelled upon Virgil's (*Aeneid* VI), and although a

[1] Boas, xxxii, 395; Edwards, pp. 10–11.
[2] A. M. Witherspoon, *The Influence of Robert Garnier on Elizabethan Drama* (New Haven, 1924), p. 160.
[3] Baldwin, p. 181.

number of later Virgilian expositions were available as well to Kyd, there is no reason to question his dependence on the original. Virgil is quoted approximately, in pastiche, in I. ii. 55, and II. v. 67 ff., and perhaps echoed in English in I. iv. 20 and III. xiii. 71. Statius, Claudian, and Lucan (III. xiii. 19) have been sought in a few lines, and one Latin phrase appears to originate in the unlikely text of Alanus de Insulis.[1] Ovid is paraphrased in II. v. 70.

In addition to the couplet quoted above, Kyd employs an enigmatic half-line of Italian (?), 'Che le Ieron', which seems to mean something on the lines of 'Come here, boy',[2] another half-line, 'Vien qui presto', and a proverbial couplet, 'Chi mi fa piu carezze che non suole,/Tradito mi ha, o tradir mi vuole' (III. xiv. 168). The proverb may be found in slightly varying forms in Sandford's *Garden of Pleasure* (1573), Florio's *Firste Fruites* (1578),[3] and in Puttenham's *Arte of English Poesie* (1589).[4] Pedringano calls Lorenzo 'Signior', and Serberine is murdered at 'Saint Luigi's Park' (III. ii. 83). Most of the characters bear Italian names, furthermore, and it is plausible that Kyd intended a play on the name Pedringano, with 'inganno' meaning 'deceive'.

The only truly Spanish touch, on the other hand, is the phrase 'Pocas palabras' ('in few words') in III. xiv. 118. Notwithstanding Carrère's impressionistic opinion that these two words manage to 'jeter sur la pièce des notes discrètes de couleur locale'—when linked, as he inexplicably states, with 'les noms de certains personnages, empreints de consonnances ibériques',[5] 'pocas palabras' in Elizabethan times testified no more authentic command of Spanish than 'bon voyage' testifies of French today. It was the commonest Spanish catch-phrase; even Christopher Sly mouthed it.[6]

The evidence *ab silentio* must be taken that Kyd did not know the Spanish language. 'Saint Luigi's Park' is especially telling, when we

---

[1] See W. P. Mustard, 'Notes on Thomas Kyd's Works', *PQ*, V (1926), 85–86; but the commonplace quality and the subsequent currency of this phrase (see Boas, p. 396) allow for the possibility that Kyd's immediate source was not Alanus.

[2] An attempt at paraphrase would be 'chi la', meaning 'some there' (as one might call for 'lights, there'), and 'Ieron', as Boas suggests, the name of the page Lorenzo is summoning. If 'Ieron' is, as is plausible, an abbreviation of Hieronimo, Lorenzo's line can be construed as an apprehensive reaction to hearing a noise.

[3] Sources pointed out by W. Keller, *Archiv* (CIII), 387.

[4] George Puttenham, *Arte of English Poesie*, ed. Edward Arber (London, 1869), p. 295.

[5] Carrère, pp. 97–98.

[6] See also Nares, *Glossary* (London, 1901), II, 628–9.

consider that the play is indisputably set in Spain. There is no trace of any Spanish reading either here or in the remainder of Kyd's extant writings, nor of any familiarity on his part with the Spanish Senecan playwrights of the same period or earlier.[1]

Among English writers of the period, Kyd's play exhibits the most definite traces of influence by John Lyly and Thomas Watson, by the first in what appear to be stylistic imitations, and by the second in one short passage of verse adapted from Watson's *Hekatompathia* (1582). Lyly's distinctive device of dramatic antithesis ('Ay but Euphues gave the onset; ay, but Lucilla gave the occasion; ay, but Euphues first brake his mind; ay but Lucilla bewrayed her meaning') is patently taken over by Kyd in II. i. 19 ff.:

> Yet might she love me for my valiancy,
> Ay, but that's slander'd by captivity.
> Yet might she love me to content her sire,
> Ay, but her reason masters his desire.
> Yet might she love me as her brother's friend,
> Ay, but her hopes aim at some other end.
> Yet might she love me to uprear her state,
> Ay, but perhaps she loves some nobler mate, &c.

Further instances of Kyd's Lylian rhetoric may be found in I. ii. 161–5, I. iv. 77–89, and possibly in the *palilogia* of II. i. 119–29.[2] Significantly, all these passages, including the first quoted, concern Balthazar; Kyd is not simply copying Lyly's mannerisms indiscriminately, but employing them to suggest character. Lorenzo, playing Hotspur to Balthazar's Owen Glendower, loses his patience three times after the latter's flowery and effete speeches:

> Tush, tush my lord, let go these ambages . . .
> (I. iv. 90)

---

[1] It is tempting to imagine a connexion between Kyd and the Spanish playwright Juan de la Cueva, whose work may have immediately preceded Kyd's, given the curious coincidence of four-act structure (for which Cueva provides elaborate justifications), a Spanish setting, a theme which can be stretched to involve 'pundonor', and Cueva's habit of writing plays in pairs, comedy before tragedy, compared with Kyd's putative fore-piece to *The Spanish Tragedy*, *The Spanish Comedy*. But beyond these piquant similarities I find no evidence of Kyd's knowing Cueva, or any other Spanish writer.

[2] Perhaps the prototype (but not the source) of these lines is in Watson: see F. G. Hubbard in *PMLA*, XX (1905), 366–7; Watson himself (*Hekatompathia*, XLI) characterizes his own use of the form as 'a somewhat tedious or too much affected continuation of that figure in Rhethorique, which of the Grekes is called *palilogia* . . .'

My lord, for my sake leave these ecstasies . . .
(II. i. 29)
Let's go my lord, your staying stays revenge . . .
(II. i. 134)[1]

Again, after the initial few scenes, when the action of the play picks up and develops, Kyd drops his euphuism and even Balthazar must speak directly. Kyd's use of Lyly's leisurely rhetoric depends no less on characterization than on dramatic tempo.

The only obvious use of Watson is less a dramatic adaptation than a plagiarism. II. i. 3–10 are a confident and close copy of Watson's *Hekatompathia*, XLVII; and it is beguiling to speculate whether Watson, Kyd's fellow playwright with the Queen's Company before 1585, supplied these unremarkable lines himself.

There are no reliable examples of factual borrowing from Lyly, although Schick points out an analogue in *Euphues* of Hieronimo's business of biting out his own tongue: 'Zeno, because he would not be enforced to reveal anything against his will by torments, bit off his tongue, and spit it in the face of the tyrant.' But the same story is frequently told of Anaxarchus of Abdera and Nicocreon, King of Cyprus,[2] and further instances may be found as close to home as in Whetstone's *Heptameron* (1582) or Hoby's Castiglione, and in Pliny.[3]

Considering Kyd's play as a whole in relation to its known sources, we cannot fail to be struck both by the originality and the ingenuity of the author. Few plays of the Elizabethan period exhibit so little dependence on narrative precedents, or so much imaginative variation upon what few are in use. And Kyd is never promiscuous in employing even those devices for which we can identify a source: euphuism, the play-within-play, contemporary history, a politic villain, all are woven skilfully into the main action, complementing each other and contributing singly to a cumulative theatrical effect.

III. *Date*

The date of *The Spanish Tragedy* is of peculiar importance to the study of Elizabethan drama. If the play precedes *The Jew of Malta* and *The Massacre at Paris* it contains the first Machiavellian villain;

[1] See Edwards, liii; Wolfgang Clemen, *Die Tragödie vor Shakespeare* (1955), pp. 91–102, 238–47, and M. E. Prior, *The Language of Tragedy* (1947), pp. 46–59 (Edwards).

[2] See Boethius, II, prose 6; Valerius Maximus, III, 3; Diogenes Laertius, IX, 59.

[3] See Thomas Izard, *George Whetstone* (New York, 1942), pp. 93–94.

if it precedes *John a Kent and John a Cumber*, it contains the earliest modern play-within-play; and if it precedes *Titus Andronicus* it may also be styled the first modern revenge tragedy. Given a date before 1587 and *Tamburlaine*, one might incontrovertibly call Kyd's play the first extant modern tragedy, without qualification.

But the date of the play is most difficult to pin down, and scholars have differed widely in their estimates. What we best can do in the following consideration is to discard a few of the more extreme dating arguments, evaluate the rest, add some new suggestions, and attempt to establish early and late limits narrower than those generally admitted.

The traditional *termini* for the play have been taken as 1582–92, the former because of Kyd's adaptation of *Hekatompathia* (entered 31 March 1582), and the latter because of performances recorded by Henslowe in February and March 1592, and the entry for publication on 6 October of the same year. Now, the early limit is not really firm, because, as we have pointed out, Watson and Kyd were co-playwrights for the Queen's Company shortly afterward, and if they were previously acquainted Kyd might easily have seen or received the lines in question in MS. But the Battle of Terceira took place in July–August of 1582, and Kyd might have had to wait until 1583 or even 1585 to have heard the name of the island (see p. 53 above). And the political scene-setting, as we have shown, reflects an actual situation in the Iberian peninsula after 1581; so the early limit of 1582 may with some safety be admitted.

The late limit of 1592 is quite solid, and we may note that the play as performed by Lord Strange's Men for Henslowe on 23 February was *not* designated 'ne'.[1] There is also an imitation of *The Spanish Tragedy* to be found in *Arden of Feversham*, which may be significant: Franklin's entering question, 'What dismal outcry calls me from my rest?' (III. i. 88) must be taken as a feeble echo of the most famous single line in *The Spanish Tragedy*. It requires considerable suspension of intelligence to argue this as evidence for Kyd's authorship of *Arden*. Now, *Arden* was entered on 3 April 1592, but is commonly dated 1591 or earlier. A more precise date for *Arden*, which hitherto has not been established, would bear on the date of Kyd's play as well.

---

[1] The standard discussion of Henslowe's 'ne' is in W. W. Greg, ed., *Henslowe's Diary*, II, 148, and in *Eliz. Stage*, II, 143–6; but see Foakes and Rickert, xxx–xxxi, and 'Two Notes on "A Knack to Know a Knave"', *NQ*, CCVII (1962), 326–7, for additional suggestions. Even if 'ne' does not always mean 'new', it seems very likely that any play *not* marked 'ne' was *not* new to Henslowe.

Evidence of questionable worth is provided by Jonson's *Bartho-lomew Fair* (1614). In the induction, a reactionary theatre-goer is said to 'sweare, *Jeronimo*, or *Andronicus* are the best playes' and he 'shall passe unexcepted at, heere, as one whose Judgement shewes it is constant, and hath stood still, these five and twentye, or thirtie yeeres'. This allusion, taken literally, sets limits of 1584-9, but beyond a general implication that *The Spanish Tragedy* is of the eighties, and so, in some form, is *Titus*, we would be rash to weight the humorous (and perhaps exaggerating) remarks of a competing playwright born in 1572. Perhaps the linking of *Jeronimo* with *Andronicus* is more significant than the dates mentioned, both as a guide to the antiquity of the latter and as a faint suggestion of common auspices.

Within the general limits, the often subjective estimates of scholars have ranged freely. T. W. Baldwin, as usual, offers the most surprising and specific date. Baldwin's argument is based primarily on the notion that the printed *Copie of a Leter* (1584) 'is a free and fictitious revision of the Manuscript form, *Letter of Estate*' 188 (i.e. P.R.O. MS. Dom. Eliz., Add. XXVIII, 113, ff. 369-88),[1] and that the changes made by the revisers may in part be explained by their dependence on *The Spanish Tragedy*. In other words, instead of Kyd's basing his Pedringano upon the Leicestrian Gates, as we have suggested, Baldwin supposes Kyd to have invented the episode independently, and the editors of the printed version of the Leicester book to have combined Kyd's fiction with a dissimilar 'source' (the *Letter of Estate*) to produce the anecdote as published in the *Copie*. Now, this theory demands that the *Letter of Estate* be the unique documentary source of *A Copie of a Leter*, rather than any one of the many manuscript versions which more closely approximate the wording of the printed version; and for such a contention there is simply insufficient evidence. Baldwin mentions no other manuscript versions of the book, but De Ricci's first census of manuscripts in America (to say nothing of Britain) records no less than eleven examples, and cursory examination of five of these had indicated that innumerable textual variations exist. Consider as well the passage in *A Copie* where Gates 'disclosed the same [i.e. his allegations against Leicester] to a Gentleman of

---

[1] The MS., which can be dated between 19 July 1584 and the end of the same year (Baldwin, p. 187) is discussed in *PCRS*, XXI, 58 ff., whence Baldwin draws many of his arguments. The printed version was ready by 18 September 1584 (Baldwin, p. 187).

worshippe, whom he trusted speciallie, whose name I may not utter for some causes (but it beginneth with H.)'. Baldwin concludes of this (p. 192) that 'it is the merest possibility that H. was suggested by Hieronimo', but the issue cannot be dropped so easily. Is it likely, if the printed version did indeed derive from the State Papers MS., that the revisers, anxious as they must have been to provide the utmost verisimilitude for their tales about the wicked Earl, would base such a tale on anything so familiar as a popular play—and effectively give themselves away with their enigmatic reference to an informant whose name 'beginneth with H.'? Is it likely that if they had even gone so far as to purloin Kyd's invention for their own political purposes, they would choose, of all fictitious letters, 'H'? Elizabethan Jesuits are not notable for their simplicity.

Given all this shakiness, do we not prefer to have Kyd's Pedringano based upon the 'historical' Gates, and the Catholic account, rather than the popular play to have been the earliest promulgation of the anecdote? Would Parsons or his agents be likely to glean their 'evidence' from so ignominous and available a source as the common stage? Is it not simply a more economical hypothesis to assume some intermediate manuscript source for the printed *Copie*, and to consider Kyd as the borrower, not the 'influence' wedged between MS. original and printed result? Without evidence beyond Baldwin's we shall have to discard a specific date of 1583–4 for *The Spanish Tragedy*. Of course, there is no reason to reject an early limit of 1584, if we agree that Pedringano is based on Gates, and that Kyd was more likely to have read the printed version of the Leicester slanders than the manuscript versions circulated primarily among Catholics.

At another extreme are the dating arguments of Philip Edwards and J. Dover Wilson. Edwards proposes *c.* 1590, denies the supposed allusion to the play in Nashe's *Menaphon* epistle (which we agreed to leave as problematic in Chapter I), and suggests some altogether unconvincing parallels between *The Spanish Tragedy* and Watson's *Meliboeus* (1590) as well as *Tamburlaine*, Part II (1588–90). In the first case, the similarities are both minimal and without any indication of precedence; in the second, there is simply nothing worth discussing. The same stringency of examination which discards the *Menaphon* evidence must discard, with even less hesitation, Edwards's 1590 parallels. If *Menaphon* is counted out, a date of 1590 remains possible, perhaps, although no more indicated than Baldwin's eccentric alternative. And Edwards's final argument that the 'modernity' of the play is closer in spirit to 1590 than the mid-eighties merely begs the question of Kyd's originality without offering reasons for doubting it.

Wilson's dating suggestion is made in a rather offhand manner during a discussion of *King John*.[1] He considers three lines in *The Spanish Tragedy*, I. ii. 170–3, as alluding to *King John*, II. i. 137–8. Since King John definitely alludes to *Soliman and Perseda*, Wilson must have *The Spanish Tragedy* following that play as well, and all three plays *c*. 1590–1. Sir Walter Greg[2] accepted Wilson's view, but few others will. It has been pointed out[3] that the 'allusion' in *The Spanish Tragedy* is no more than a proverb; and it will be shown how unlikely a proposition it would be to date *The Spanish Tragedy* later than *Soliman*.

F. S. Boas considers the evidence of *Menaphon* applicable, credits the Armada argument (see below), and suggests 1585–7, an estimate which most modern students, including the present writer, find plausible. E. K. Chambers disallows *Menaphon*, but apparently takes Jonson's 'five and twenty or thirtie yeeres' seriously, and for no obvious reason gives 1589.[4] W. Bang does the same, for similarly unclear reasons.[5]

It seems to me that the *Menaphon* epistle quite possibly does refer both to Kyd and *The Spanish Tragedy*, but given the understandable uncertainty on this point among scholars, it would be well to seek other bases for narrowing the limits of the play's dates. One point which deserves serious consideration is Kyd's failure to refer, directly or obliquely, to the defeat of the Spanish Armada by the English in 1588.

Now, at first glance the *ab silentio* argument seems extremely weak. Edwards (xxiv) points out 'it surely would have been foolish for Kyd to have introduced an allusion to it [the Armada] in the pageant before the King of Spain, for such an allusion would have placed the play squarely in a contemporary setting, inviting an identification of the King with Philip II, and corresponding identifications of his leading characters and the events of the story'. And this is not unreasonable, for, after all, Hieronimo is dwelling upon ancient

[1] *King John*, ed. J. Dover Wilson (Cambridge, 1936), liii, and pp. 115–16.
[2] *Shakespeare's First Folio*, pp. 254–5.
[3] See Edwards, pp. 15–16; 'Shakespeare and *Solyman and Perseda*', *MLR*, LVIII (1963), p. 485. Cf. also William Alexander, *A Paraenesis to the Prince* (London, 1604), sig. A3ᵛ, for another variation on the proverbial situation.
[4] *Eliz. Stage*, III, 395–6.
[5] *Englische Studien*, XXVIII (1900), 229 ff.

history. But let us examine the pageant more closely: Hieronimo's masque concerns three English 'conquerors' of Spain, popular heroes of the distant past. The King himself, with his guests the Portuguese Ambassador and Prince, interpret each tableau after Hieronimo explains it. Of Robert, Earl of Gloucester, who 'enforced the King, then but a Saracen/To bear the yoke of English monarchy', the Spanish monarch comments:

> by this you see
> That which may comfort both your king and you,
> And make your late discomfort seem the less.

Of Edmund, Earl of Kent's exploits, he adds:

> This is another special argument,
> That Portingale may deign to bear our yoke
> When it by little England hath been yok'd.

And of John of Gaunt's expedition, the Portuguese Ambassador takes occasion to say:

> This is an argument for our viceroy,
> That Spain may not insult for her success,
> Since English warriors likewise conquer'd Spain,
> And made them bow their knees to Albion.

The King is gracious enough to report that he is pleased by the masque.

Let us consider *why* the masque is presented in the first place: clearly, it is a concession to the feelings of an English audience watching a play about the military success of Spain, and expected to sympathize both with the vanquished and the victors. Particularly in a year when Spain and England were at odds, which might be practically at any time after 1580, but most probably between 1586 and the early nineties, something has to be said, in a popular production, about the Anglo-Spanish question—even if it is said in the most covert manner. What Kyd is doing is simply to clear up all his obligations along such lines with one quite patently super-added scene; there are no further references to England or the English in the play. The brief masque records the bravado and defiance of 'little England' toward a mighty power.

I suggest that the tone which Kyd takes, or his characters take, is a pre-Armada tone. Any reading of the literature about Spain published in England between 1582 and 1592 cannot fail to exhibit a marked change in the spirit of English writers, polemical or thoughtful, toward Spain precisely in 1588. Where before 1588 the defiance is a trifle shrill, the invective almost too violent—the violence of fear—and the prevailing mood one of drawing oneself up into a fighting pose, after the stunning defeat of the Spanish fleet a new kind of strength colours the language of very similar tracts, deliberate bravado is replaced by calm self-confidence, and the figure of the English nation suggests a triumphant warrior rather than a valiant underdog.[1] If we examine the way Kyd treats the Anglo-Spanish tension, we get the impression, I believe, of whistling in the dark, of deliberate afflatus: the Englishmen who 'likewise conquered Spain' are only popular trumperies, and long dead; their exploits, although chosen from popular tradition (see above), are overstated, as Kyd himself surely knew; and above all it is 'little England'. 'Spain may not insult for her success,' warns the Ambassador, and beyond the immediate dramatic relevance of the line it is obvious that Kyd intended a heart-warming thrill of historical immediacy to be shared by his audience—a co-operative gesture of warning from England, as well as 'Portugal', to the awesome power of Spain. After the Armada, I think, the point of the warning would not be the 'success' of Spain; the warning had by then been convincingly given in the open field, and the Spanish crest was drooping.

All in all, I think, the masque of Hieronimo and reactions of the

---

[1] As prewar examples, take Humphrey Mote, *The Primrose of London* (1585), recording 'the courageous attempt and valiant enterprise of the shippe called Primrose of London' in defeating, with twenty-eight Englishmen, a Spanish force of ninety-seven; Thomas Greepe, *The True and Perfect Newes of the woorthy and valiaunt Exploytes* [of] . . . *Syr Francis Drake* (1587), celebrating the audacity of 'a man of meane calling' who dares 'to deale with so mightie a Monarke [Philip II]'; Antony, Prior of Crato, *The Explanation of the true and lawfull Right and Tytle* (1585), G2ᵛ–G3ʳ: 'the King of Castile . . . through his excessive and unmeasurable ambition . . . would . . . invade not onely all christiandom, but also the rest of the worlde . . . This is the marke he shooteth at & wil easily hitte except thother christian Princes (before thevill creepe any further) have speciall regard to oppose themselves to his power.' As post-Armada tone, consider Robert Greene, *The Spanish Masquerado* (1589), 'a devise conteining the discoverie of the Spanish insolent pride alaied with a deepe disgrace, and their presumptuous braves pulled down with the resolution of English soldiers'; *The Copie of the Anti-Spaniard* (1590), A3ʳ: 'the Spaniard . . . at this present feeling his aged yeares to hasten in, winding up his latest days . . .'; and G. B., *A Fig for the Spaniard, or Spanish Spirits* (1591), A3ᵛ: 'though Philip of Spaine be olde and bed-redde, yet hee is not quite dead . . .' Relevant also are *STC* 6180 (1585), 12926 (1587), 847, 6558, 14257, 15412, 22999, 23011 (1588), and 842, 1038, 3056, 6790, 19537 (1589); but perhaps the examples quoted above will suffice.

stage audience reflect a pre-Armada attitude on the part of Kyd and his real audience; and if the play had followed 1588 and Kyd had chosen not to refer in any way to the English victory, I believe the tone of the writing would have suggested it. Edwards, after arguing against any politico-historical basis for the main action of the play, admits (xxiv–xxv), 'If Kyd's play was based on real events, then the absence of any reference to the Armada would be near to proof that the play was written before 1588.' Earlier in this chapter we have given our reasons for supposing that the play was indeed based on real events, and while perhaps in spite of Edwards's syllogism no rigorous proof can be adduced from the absence of any reference to the Armada, we have at least a modest excuse for dating the play before 1588.

There are a few perhaps tentative parallels between *The Spanish Tragedy* and *The Battle of Alcazar* (1589) which bear recording and suggest precedence on Kyd's part; and one possible echo of *The Spanish Tragedy* in the Gray's Inn play of 1587, *The Misfortunes of Arthur*, may give us a significant dating argument. Peele may be imitating the conclusion of Kyd's tragedy, where Andrea dooms the dead actors to all the traditional torments of Hell, by substitution:

> Let loose poor Tityus from the vulture's gripe,
> And let Don Cyprian supply his room:
> Place Don Lorenzo on Ixion's wheel . . .
> Hang Balthazar about Chimera's neck . . .
> Let Serberine go roll the fatal stone,
> And take from Sisyphus his endless moan . . .
> (IV. v. 31–40)

Compare Peele:

> Rackt let him be in proud Ixions wheele,
> Pinde let him be with Tantalus endlesse thirst,
> Praie let him be to Tityus greedie bird,
> Wearied with Sisyphus immortall toile . . .
> (IV. ii. 90–93)

Now, both Peele and Kyd may well be borrowing from the end of *Thyestes*, but Kyd is less prolix than Seneca, and Peele is the most concise of the three. Again, it is possible that Peele's description of a battle (V. i) derives in part from *Spanish Tragedy*, I. ii. 38 ff.:

> Meanwhile our ordnance play'd on either side,
> And captains strove to have their valour tried.

> Don Pedro, their chief horsemen's colonel
> Did with his cornet bravely make attempt
> To break the order of our battle ranks . . .
>
> Thick storms of bullets rain like winter's hail . . .

Peele describes the same sort of action:

> My Lord, when with our ordenance fierce we sent
> Our Mores with smaller shot as thicke as haile,
> Followes apace to charge the Portugall,
> The valiant Duke, the devill of Avero,
> The bane of Barbary, fraughted full of ire
> Breakes through the ranks, and with five hundred horsse
> . . . Assaults the middle wing.

Bullets in Peele are 'thicke as haile', and earlier (IV. i. 71) we have 'bullets as thicke as haile' again, while in IV. ii. 33, a company of men is 'as thicke as winters haile'. But the possibility of coincidence or commonplace is still admissible. Perhaps more to the point is II. i. 5 of *Alcazar*, 'Divine Architect of murthers and misdeeds', which well may be a reminiscence of Hieronimo's 'Confus'd and fill'd with murder and misdeeds', coming, as Kyd's line does, early in a quite notorious soliloquy ('O eyes, no eyes, &c.').

As for *The Misfortunes of Arthur*, we have in that play a curious non-Senecan detail in the alternate prologue, written by the future historian and legalist William Fulbeck, quite out of place in a description of Hell taken almost bodily from the Latin. Everything about Gorlois's experiences in the underworld is completely traditional, save that instead of receiving his instructions from the tribunal of infernal judges, it is Proserpina who issues the orders:

> My selfe by precept of *Proserpina*
> Commaunded was in presence to appeare,
> Before the Synode of the damned sprights . . .
>
> *Gorlois* quoth she thou thither must ascend, . . .
>
> She therewithall enjoynde the duskie cloudes, . . .[1]

Now, nowhere in Seneca or in any Senecan play I can discover does Proserpina figure as the 'supreme furie'. The only analogy seems to be in Andrea's prologue, where it is Proserpina who judges Andrea,

---

[1] Cunliffe, *Early English Classical Tragedies*, pp. 293–4.

commands him to return to earth, and makes appropriate arrangements with Revenge and the other infernal figures.

If there is no common source for this curious variation in the Senecan pattern, it is certainly more likely that Fulbeck, as a young law-student and belle-lettrist only to the extent of two passages of verse appended to one academic play, borrowed from Kyd, the professional of long standing (in 1587), rather than the reverse. Kyd, furthermore, combines classical sources with pure invention in about equal degrees in his prologue, whereas Fulbeck's only deviation from Senecan details is his treatment of Proserpina. While it is true that *Arthur* was in print by 1587, and *The Spanish Tragedy* was not, we have later evidence (see below) of the great notoriety of Andrea's prologue, and thus reason to suppose that it was commonplace in its own time as well. If we adduce, then, that Fulbeck extracted one detail of his literary Hell from Kyd's play, we have a late limit of 1587 for *The Spanish Tragedy*.

Boas's 1585-7 stands up well enough within the network of possible and just-possible factors of internal evidence summarized above. 1584-8, relying on *A Copie of a Leter* and the Armada idea, may be more conservative limits. And dates earlier than 1584 or later than 1588 remain, of course, possible, though in my opinion less likely.

CHAPTER IV

THE SPANISH TRAGEDY: STRUCTURE, STYLE, AND SUBSEQUENT HISTORY

I. *Structure and Style*

For all the gusto and sensationalism of the climax of Kyd's highly popular play, the manner of *The Spanish Tragedy* is essentially patient and graceful. For all that it has been called bombastic, crude, and rhetorical, Kyd's style is actually rather reserved, unimposing, and delicate. The leisurely beginning of the play establishes a beguiling, tale-telling atmosphere, and despite a quickening dramatic *tempo*, Kyd's plotting and language expose no remarkable awkwardness in the difficult transition from poetry to action. Perhaps by examining certain parts of the play in their natural order we can scotch the most extreme disparagements of Kyd as a tragedian and poet, and arrive at an estimate of his success in terms of his own intentions. Too much criticism of Kyd has verged on the patronizing; we shall suggest that there is in *The Spanish Tragedy* at least as much artistry to admire as weakness or crudity to condemn.

No prologue in Elizabethan drama has suffered so many parodies or travesties as Andrea's,[1] but we should not be led to believe that Kyd's contemporaries and successors found Andrea's lines altogether ridiculous in themselves. The parodies are scarcely more concerned with Kyd than the innumerable burlesques to our own day of 'To be or not to be' are with Shakespeare; both are essentially undirected spoofs on extremely familar passages, frequently used by other dramatic writers more to characterize the speaking parodist than the material parodied. In Beaumont, Heywood, Shirley, and Rawlins, it is playgoers who mouth these butcheries of the opening of Kyd's play, and playgoers who are thus characterized, not Kyd's rhetoric. For in point of fact, the prologue spoken by the Ghost of Andrea is as fine a piece of extended verse as the play contains.

---

[1] See Boas, pp. xciv–xcvii, 393–4; and below.

> When this eternal substance of my soul
> Did live imprison'd in my wanton flesh,
> Each in their function serving other's need,
> I was a courtier in the Spanish court.
> My name was Don Andrea . . .

There is a pleasing directness to Kyd's blank verse which marks it among the earliest truly dramatic applications of a form destined to predominate among the great playwrights of subsequent years. Along with Marlowe, Kyd is the first to do away with latinate noun-adjective order, with overwrought alliteration (where Kyd alliterates twice in a line upon occasion, Gascoigne frequently does three or four times),[1] and with the vocabulary of emphatic verbs and modifiers so favoured by earlier Senecan translators and imitative dramatists. Kyd strips his language to a modicum if not a minimum of passive constructions, and his employment of the plain verb 'to be' keys his speech consistently lower than Marlowe's. His epithets are less grand and less eccentric than Marlowe's, on the whole; his diction seems flatter, or perhaps less inflated. He seems deliberately to avoid three-syllable or longer words, where Marlowe seeks them out, and it is easy to imagine Kyd thinking Marlowe's style sensational and flashy, while Marlowe might find Kyd's simply dull.

Kyd is not unacquainted with the manipulation of imagery popular among Sidney's circle, but he does not allow himself to be carried away by it into extremes of classical accuracy. A seasonal cycle, from 'prime', through 'summer' and 'harvest', to 'winter' is lightly sketched in 7–13:

> For there in prime and pride of all my years,
> By duteous service and deserving love,
> In secret I possessed a worthy dame,
> Which hight sweet Bel-imperia by name.
> But in the harvest of my summer joys
> Death's winter nipped the blossoms of my bliss . . .[2]

Where Abraham Fraunce might have concluded this conceit with something along the agricultural-seasonal lines of blighting, blasting, or freezing, Kyd restrains himself and avoids overtaxing the metaphor by ending with simple statement:

> Forcing divorce betwixt my love and me.

[1] Kyd's alliterativeness is exhaustively tabulated in Karl Wiehl, *Thomas Kyd und sein Vers* (München inaug. diss., Kempten, 1911), pp. 29–37.

[2] There may be here a reminiscence of *Faerie Queene*, I. ii. 35 ('In prime of youthly yeares . . . it was my lot/to love this gentle Lady') although Kyd's work has been generally declared free of any influence of Spenser.

'Forcing' perhaps was less of a dead word among the Elizabethans than with us; and the phonetic device of 'forcing divorce' is one not overused by Kyd.

Characteristically, Kyd tempers his deliberately poetic lines with nearly prosaic follow-ups, but when the prosaic tends toward mere prose, he may counterbalance the effect again with rhyme:

> Ere Sol had slept three nights in Thetis' lap
> And slak'd his smoking chariot in her flood,
> By Don Horatio, our Knight Marshal's son,
> My funerals and obsequies were done.

In ensuing lines, we have 'slimy strond', 'fell Avernus', 'ugly waves', and 'honey'd speech' in the brief space of 28–30, but then more than four lines pass without a single qualifying epithet. The anadiplosis of 38–40, and a fair number of later modifiers ('dreadful shades', 'bloody furies', 'poor Ixion[1],' 'foul sins', etc.) may reflect in some measure a tradition of rhetoric both mechanical and effete which Kyd has not altogether managed to extirpate from his work. But we must bear in mind that his contemporaries found such a tradition as comfortable and natural as we may find the stripped language of journalism today, and, considered objectively, Kyd's most old-fashioned rhetoric is embarrassing only when it seems carelessly applied. Lines like 82–83, '. . . through the gates of horn,/Where dreams have passage in the silent night', cannot be faulted for classical allusion, or the simple adjective 'silent'; they deserve praise for their graceful phrasing and for their melodiousness alone.

After the prologue, Act I of *The Spanish Tragedy* falls into three preparatory scenes: the first, in conjunction with Andrea's soliloquy, establishes the situation and the events leading up to the main action; the second institutes the Portuguese sub-plot; and the third brings together Horatio and Lorenzo with Balthazar, and makes plausible Bel-imperia's actions and opinions which ensue. Edwards, for one, finds the first scene in the Spanish Court somewhat tedious, particularly with its sixty-two-line narrative of the battle by a Spanish General. Clemen[2] and Biesterfeldt[3] are less critical, but the modern reader does, as Edwards says, betray some impatience at the slow unfolding of what has passed in the wars immediately

---

[1] This rather pallid pair of lines (I. i. 65–66) maintained some neoclassical appeal: Hawkins comments, 'a smooth couplet not unworthy of Dryden'. *The Origin of the English Drama* (Oxford, 1773), I, ix).

[2] Wolfgang Clemen, *Die Tragödie vor Shakespeare* (1955), pp. 94–95.

[3] P. W. Biesterfeldt, *Die dramatische technik Thomas Kyds* (Göttingen, 1935), pp. 65–66.

before. Nevertheless, as a play for the state, in a time which endorsed the most discursive of Ovidian narrative poems, one must assume that *The Spanish Tragedy* pleased its audience no less with its long narrative reports than with its staccato on-stage action and dramatic exchanges. With the Spanish General's monologue we may compare the sixty-two-line factually reportorial speech of the Archbishop of Canterbury in the first Court scene of *Henry V*.

Another matter is the use of Latin. Castile offers a kind of prayer of three lines in Latin, and the General resorts to a line and a half in describing the battle; neither passage is a direct quotation, and later in the play it becomes clear that Kyd can compose with some freedom in the language. Here, perhaps, we have another relic of an academic tradition of composition, which some critics have seized upon to ridicule Kyd's pedantry and (particularly Nashe) the pretensions to learning which a college man would not find it necessary to put forward. Perhaps this is true, and perhaps the Latin intrusions represent a literary rather than a stage version of the play; but it is a mistake to suppose that even an unlettered audience would be altogether alienated by a few appropriate reflections in so familiar a second language. The artistic propriety of introducing these patches of Latin may remain in question, but Kyd's dramaturgy need not be judged too harshly on account of them.

The scene concludes by establishing reasons for resentment between Lorenzo and Horatio, and the protective pride of Hieronimo in his son. In some measure the social structure of the Spanish court is set out, and by placating and indulging Hieronimo the Spanish King suggests that attitude toward an almost senile man which will later become more pronounced. As the actions of Lorenzo and Balthazar toward Horatio will seem motivated primarily by injured pride, the social distinction between Horatio and Lorenzo is significant; and as Hieronimo will eventually succumb to a rational madness, the kid-glove politeness of his King at an early stage takes on a similar dramatic importance.

Scene ii of the act proper dispenses with unity of place, and initiates a subject which has disturbed some critics. 'It is very hard to justify the sub-plot. The Portuguese court could have been introduced more economically and the relevance of theme is very slight', comments Edwards (liii), which brings us to the question of what the 'theme' of *The Spanish Tragedy* is. Now, to a certain extent analysis of drama in terms of theme is artificial: themes are abstracted from plays by critics, in general, not installed in the text by the writers, and as the estimate of the moral point of a play may vary, so may the estimate of the theme. But if theme means preoccupation, the theme of Kyd's play may fairly be stated as revenge, or perhaps more generally as justice. Edwards characterizes the play rather neatly:

> The Spanish Tragedy is a play about the passion for retribution, and vengeance shapes the entire action . . . Marlowe never wrote a less Christian play than The Spanish Tragedy: the hate of a wronged man can speak out without check of mercy or reason; when a sin is committed, no-one talks of forgiveness; the word 'mercy' does not occur in the play.[1]

Elsewhere, however, Edwards calls attention to Hieronimo's extended attempt to gain legal redress, and the slow emergence of personal vengeance as the only remaining measure when due course of law fails. Revenge dramaturgically is the prime mover of the action, but in perspective it is more Hieronimo's creature than his creator; he is driven to revenge by injustice, not to injustice by revenge. Perhaps in the minds of Andrea and Bel-imperia desire for personal vengeance comes first in the sequence of motives, but Hieronimo is a judge and a man of feeling, and other avenues of conduct must first be explored by him. In so far as the play is about Hieronimo primarily, it is also about the development in Hieronimo of a lust for vengeance, by the deliberate thwarting of more 'Christian' measures of retribution. And to that extent the theme of The Spanish Tragedy is not revenge, but justice and injustice.

In fleshing out such a theme, Kyd has given us three subsidiary anecdotes, the punishment of Pedringano, which shows us the law not cheated of its victim; the supplication of Bazulto, which shows us injustice caused by a too tardy law; and the episode of Alexandro and Villuppo, which shows us the reverse, injustice nearly done because of haste in judging. If we are to understand the point of the Portuguese sub-plot, we must realize that Hieronimo is in much the same position as the Viceroy: both have lost sons, and both think they know the murderer. But the Viceroy is wrong; his son is alive, and Alexandro is innocent. Only the temporal power of the Viceroy enables him to coast so close to a monumental injustice—temporal power of which Hieronimo possesses less, and which Bazulto does not possess at all. With the Portuguese episode Kyd is explaining why Hieronimo cannot rush into the matter of punishing the villains

---

[1] Edwards, li–lii. We may note that the word 'merciless' does, however, occur (IV. iv. 106).

without true proof (we are apt to forget that although *we* know who are guilty, Hieronimo cannot be sure until Pedringano's note supports Bel-imperia's testimony; for Bel-imperia has made it clear early in the play that her aim is the ruin of Balthazar), and with the later episode of Bazulto he is recalling Hieronimo to the dangers of too long a preparation. Merely because Andrea, who single-mindedly represents the Senecan impulse to vengeance, calls again and again for blood, we should not infer that Hieronimo is only temporizing. 'There's not any advocate in Spain/ . . . will take half the pain/That he will, in pursuit of equity' (III. xiii. 52), and Hieronimo must work out his method of redressing injustice within the terms of his own character.

I think, then, that we may disagree with Edwards that in the Portuguese scenes 'the relevance of theme is very slight'. In addition to the emblem of too-hasty judgement which they provide, they serve the dramatic function of establishing some sympathy with Balthazar, if only as he is lamented. The Viceroy himself shares (as is natural) certain traits of speech with Balthazar, who has been introduced with Lylian conceits in the preceding scene. His long complaint against fate, something of a set piece in Elizabethan drama, proceeds with the slow stylized language we associate with his son. A couplet sums up the dramatic justification of this and un-numbered similar outcries:

> Why wail I then, where's hope of no redress?
> O yes, complaining makes my grief seem less.

And there is a genuine pathos in his concluding observation:

> O wherefore went I not to war myself?
> The cause was mine, I might have died for both:
> My years were mellow, his but young and green,
> My death were natural, but his was forc'd.

After the treacherous perjury of Villuppo, the stage is cleared and we are exposed to one of Kyd's summings-up, this by the villain, who states baldly what he has done and why. Like Bel-imperia and Andrea, Villuppo is an uncomplicated character with uncomplicated motives:

> Thus have I with an envious forged tale
> Deceiv'd the king, betray'd mine enemy,
> And hope for guerdon of my villainy.

The last scene of Act I brings Horatio and Bel-imperia together for the first time, and commences the main action of the play. Kyd is not at his happiest when representing either love or flirtation, and the exchanges of the pair are somewhat wooden. Horatio's suggestion that 'tears and sighs, I fear will hinder me' in his narrative of Andrea's death does not quite convince us, but Bel-imperia's reaction is refreshingly straightforward:

> Would thou hadst slain him that so slew my love.

There in a nutshell is Bel-imperia's motive for all her subsequent action. Horatio's keepsake of Andrea ('This scarf I pluck'd from off his liveless arm'), like Hieronimo's 'hankercher besmear'd with blood', proved a visually memorable part of the play: it is closely imitated in *The Atheist's Tragedy*, II. ii.

When Horatio has left her alone on the stage Bel-imperia reiterates her reactions and announces her intentions. Unlike the Viceroy and his foppish son, she is not one to complain for the sake of complaining:

> Yet what avails to wail Andrea's death,
> From whence Horatio proves my second love?
> . . .
> But how can love find harbour in my breast
> Till I revenge the death of my beloved?
> Yes, second love shall further my revenge.

In her own way, Bel-imperia is as Machiavellian as her brother, an appropriate trait:

> I'll love Horatio, my Andrea's friend,
> The more to spite the prince that wrought his end.

Her directness, like Villuppo's, signals an essentially simple character; she has some of the fire, courage, and wilfulness of Vittoria Accorombona, Ford's Annabella, and Middleton's Beatrice; there is much of the Italian heroine in her, and possibly a trace of Thomas Achelley's Violenta. Edwards appositely terms her 'a certain kind of woman', and her role in the plot is to provide spark on the 'good' side where her brother provides spark on the 'bad'.

The ineffectual exchanges between Bel-imperia and Balthazar bring us up to Hieronimo's pageant. The pageant serves perhaps primarily the function of clearing up Kyd's patriotic obligations (as suggested in Chapter III), but in terms of the play it provides a precedent for his more meaningful entertainment in Act IV. The fond and almost tender tact used by the Spanish King toward 'old

Hieronimo' maintains the suggestion of paternalistic indulgence begun in the first Court scene.

Act II belongs largely to Lorenzo. In the first scene he intimidates Pedringano into betraying Bel-imperia and Horatio, in the second he spies on the lovers, and in the fourth he murders Horatio. In between, a Court scene establishes the marriage contract between Spain and Portugal which will make legal redress nearly if not wholly impossible for Hieronimo.

In the exchanges between Lorenzo and Balthazar we are presented with an effective contrast between rhetorical inaction, and direct action linked to direct speech. While Balthazar pursues the courses of long complicated conceits, Lorenzo browbeats and threatens Pedringano into betrayal. Even when faced with the fact of Horatio's success in his suit, Balthazar returns to his verbiage, until Lorenzo, with an offhand allusion to a different sort of revenge, cuts him off:

> Let's go, my lord, your staying stays revenge.

The second of Bel-imperia's interviews with Horatio finds her well under way in confirming her 'second love'. Kyd pulls all stops from his rhetoric, employing long sequences of rhymed couplets and quatrains, *palilogia* or *reduplicatio* between Lorenzo and Balthazar, and one of his favourite and least effective devices, simple repetition:

> Hor. The less I speak, the more I meditate.
> Bel. But whereon dost thou chiefly meditate?
> Hor. On dangers past, and pleasures to ensue.
> Bal. [*Aside*] On pleasures past, and dangers to ensue.

Perhaps such repetition appears effective when used, as above, in dialogue as an echo, but in ordinary speeches (I. iv. 17–18, 44–45; II. i. 48–49, 57–58, etc.) it rarely seems to contribute any elegance. In I. ii. we observed some indication of the social distance between Castile's family and Hieronimo's, and the hauteur in Lorenzo which came of it. The aristocratic pride of both Lorenzo and Balthazar has been outraged by Bel-imperia's choice of a new lover (as she intended, in Balthazar's case, that it should), and the motive for Lorenzo's 'revenge' is expressed by the Portuguese Prince:

> Ambitious villain, how his boldness grows!
> (II. ii. 41)

Like Webster's Antonio, Horatio is violating caste in his affair with a powerful woman. After the hanging-up and murder (II. iv. 61) Lorenzo exults, humorously, 'Although his life were still ambitious proud,/Yet he is at the highest now he is dead.' It was family pride, rather than family honour, which Horatio had offended.

In the Court scene (II. iii.) Castile's character of Bel-imperia contains echoes of Lorenzo's, two scenes earlier, in the hawking image: 'Although she coy it as becomes her kind . . ./I doubt not, I, but she will stoop in time' (II. iii. 3–5). Lorenzo has explained, 'My lord, though Bel-imperia seem thus coy . . ./In time all haggard hawks will stoop to lure' (II. i. 1–4). The marriage arrangements are entered upon, will or nill Bel-imperia, who is expected to come around; and Castile shows one of his less sympathetic sides as he proposes nearly to compel her acceptance of Balthazar: 'Yet herein shall she follow my advice,/Which is to love him or forgo my love.' By his extraordinary settlement of the whole kingdom upon the male offspring of Balthazar and Bel-imperia, the childless King creates a situation where Hieronimo's suit for justice will have little hope of success: Balthazar will be the presumptive father to the heir apparent to Spain, and Lorenzo the heir's uncle—both villains above all law but the personal, or at least so in Hieronimo's consideration. The King's inappropriate allusion to Bel-imperia ('Young *virgins* must be ruled by their friends'), in addition to its perhaps unintentional irony, exposes his ignorance of the girl's volatile character.

The murder of Horatio in II. iv. is handled with dramatic dispatch and some fine touches: when Balthazar attempts to help, Lorenzo excuses him with a delicate irony acting might heighten:

> O sir, forbear, your valour is already tried.

We have heard earlier of Balthazar's 'valour' in assassinating Andrea (I. iv. 23–26). Bel-imperia shows her courage and Balthazar his oiliness in a well-written sequence:

> Bel.   O save his life and let me die for him!
>   O save him brother, save him Balthazar:
>   I lov'd Horatio but he lov'd not me.
> Bal.   But Balthazar loves Bel-imperia.

It is typical of Balthazar to be making a declaration while Lorenzo's agents are busy stabbing the trussed-up body of his rival.

Hieronimo's entrance, along with his later lament ('O eyes, no eyes, etc.') and Andrea's prologue, provided perhaps the most notorious moments of the play for parodists and imitators to seize upon; some of the echoes of 'What outcries pluck me from my naked bed' will be noted below. But the speech itself is not unaccomplished, with Hieronimo's dawning realization that 'A man hang'd up and all the murderers gone,/And in my bower, to lay the guilt on me' is indeed 'Horatio my sweet son'. Perhaps the ensuing rhetoric is overcharged, but Isabella's subsequent appearance contains an affecting couplet:

> And I'll close up the glasses of his sight,
> For once these eyes were only my delight.

As Kyd's rhetorical power lies in milder description, his weakness may emerge in moments of emotional stress. The long Latin dirge that concludes Hieronimo's lament is something of an admission of inadequacy on Kyd's part, but it does serve to bring back the *tempo* to that calm level where the dramatist's strength and skill may best assert themselves once more. A slowly rising *tempo* is Kyd's forte; climaxes, for ever difficult to convey literally, lie somewhat beyond his best scope.

As at the end of Act I, Andrea chafes at the direction of the action. Revenge reassures him, with a conceit later to figure in *England's Parnassus*:

> Thou talk'st of harvest when the corn is green.

We are to rein in our impatience and follow the slow but thorough process of the several retributions now called for.

Act III is one of the longest acts in English drama, and it belongs mainly to Hieronimo: substantially it concerns the slow evolution in Hieronimo's mind of the idea of revenge. Beginning with him baffled and helpless, it concludes with him resolved past any influence; and as personal vengeance consolidates its hold on Hieronimo's thoughts, so the madness which has been prepared in Acts I and II flourishes alongside.

The point of the Portuguese sub-plot has already been registered upon the observer, and Kyd winds it up early, in scene i. Following it we turn to Hieronimo, for the first time since Horatio's murder and his discovery of the corpse, and the long lament ('O eyes, no eyes') leads into his reception of Bel-imperia's 'bloody writ', and his attempt to speak with her. The lament has often been parodied, and perhaps it is the most overwritten speech in the play; but Kyd's rhetoric is never as excessive as the academic Senecans'. Hieronimo's struggle for the *mot juste* to describe the murder of his son ('un-hallow'd . . . inhuman . . . barbarous . . . incomparable') can,

of course, be interpreted as Kyd's personal struggle with an emotion-
ally impoverished vocabulary, or, more generously, as the difficulties in expression a confounded and stunned father might
encounter. Hieronimo's first appeal is to the heavens:

> If this incomparable murder thus
> Of mine, but now no more my son,
> Shall unreveal'd and unrevenged pass,
> How should we term your dealings to be just,
> If you unjustly deal with those that in your justice trust?

And it is a cast of 'direful visions', 'ugly fiends', and 'dreams'
which 'drive me forth to seek the murderer'. Hieronimo is flounder-
ing for a direction when Bel-imperia's letter 'falleth', presumably
from the balcony which represents Bel-imperia's 'window' (see III.
ix.), but his reaction to her note is characteristic of the judicial turn
of mind:

> Hieronimo beware, thou art betray'd,
> And to entrap thy life this train is laid.
> Advise thee therefore, be not credulous:
> This is devised to endanger thee . . .
> Dear was the life of my beloved son,
> And of his death behoves me be reveng'd:
> Then hazard not thine own, Hieronimo,
> But live t'effect thy resolution.

He is naturally a little suspicious of Bel-imperia's motives:

> What might move thee, Bel-imperia,
> To accuse thy brother, had he been the mean?

And when Lorenzo fobs him off with Bel-imperia's 'some disgrace'
which has 'awhile remov'd her hence', the chary father does not
evidently pursue the matter. When we next meet him he is back to
lamenting. Perhaps at this moment, in the staged play, Revenge (who
is sound asleep at the end of the act) may begin to nod.

   The little device by which Lorenzo rids himself of both accomplices, his page and Balthazar's, has been commented upon above;
it, too, is closely imitated in *The Atheist's Tragedy*, IV. ii. Poor
Pedringano, like Kyd himself after him, pins his hope on his patron:

> As for the fear of apprehension,
> I know, if need should be, my noble lord
> Will stand between me and ensuing harms.

But the trap closes, and Lorenzo celebrates his success with a state-

ment of the Machiavellian code. Appropriately, even his cohort
Balthazar is kept partially in the dark about Lorenzo's devices, and
unwittingly 'prosecutes the point' designed by the plotter; secrecy
is Lorenzo's watchword, and he prefers an underhanded but private
way of effecting his ends to a simple agreement between the Portuguese Prince and himself, which undoubtedly he could arrive at.

> Why so, this fits our former policy,
> And thus experience bids the wise to deal.
> I lay the plot, he prosecutes the point,
> I set the trap, he breaks the worthless twigs,
> And sees not that wherewith the bird was lim'd.
> Thus hopeful men, that mean to hold their own,
> Must look like fowlers to their dearest friends.
> He runs to kill whom I have holp to catch,
> And no man knows it was my reaching fatch.
> 'Tis hard to trust unto a multitude,
> Or anyone, in mine opinion,
> When men themselves their secrets will reveal.

Later, alone again, he reiterates:

> I list not trust the air
> With utterance of our pretence therein,
> For fear the privy whisp'ring of the wind
> Convey our words among unfriendly ears,
> That lie too open to advantages.

By this point in the play Lorenzo's initial motive, which appeared to
be partly injured pride, partly family ambition, and partly pure
cruelty, has become almost buried in complications, and he has
begun to delight, like subsequent stage villains of his stamp, in the
intricacies of plot for their own sake. In future scenes he will remind
himself of the material advantages to be derived from an alliance of
Balthazar with Bel-imperia, and redirect his activities to that end.

Kyd is sometimes described as humourless, but scenes v–vi, the
execution of Pedringano, are grimly amusing. We may note that the
comic relief, as in *Soliman and Perseda*, is presented in prose.
Perhaps Kyd intended to foreshadow the catastrophic conclusion of
Hieronimo's play-within-play, for the boy who holds 'no pardon,
but an empty box' speaks of the irony of Pedringano's 'jesting' in
the face of Lorenzo's ultimate jest: 'Is't not a scurvy jest, that a man
should jest himself to death?' Now, in the sense that a stage play is
also a 'jest' (compare Ralegh's 'Only we die in earnest, that's no

jest') the same end will come to Lorenzo and his co-conspirator. Hieronimo delivers himself of judicial reflections in an orderly fashion:

> For blood with blood shall, while I sit as judge,
> Be satisfied, and the law discharg'd.

But the parallel the situation offers to his own does not escape him:

> Despatch, and see this execution done:
> This makes me to remember thee, my son. *Exit* Hieronimo.

By scene vii Hieronimo's inertia has reached its heaviest, and he is once again ineffectually soliloquizing; now, however, there is a kind of hopeless fatalism to his complaints, and Revenge in the observer's box must have dropped off. Hieronimo's elegiac tone accommodates his grief admirably:

> The blust'ring winds, conspiring with my words,
> At my lament have mov'd the leaveless trees,
> Disrob'd the meadows of their flower'd green,
> Made mountains marsh with spring-tide of my tears . . .
> Yet still tormented is my tortur'd soul
> With broken sighs and restless passions,
> That winged mount, and, hovering in the air,
> Beat at the windows of the brightest heavens,
> Soliciting for justice and revenge:
> But they are plac'd in those empyreal heights
> Where, countermur'd with walls of diamond,
> I find the place impregnable, and they
> Resist my woes, and give my words no way.

The particularly fine last couplet is also a rare example of enjambment in Kyd. The passage is echoed at one point in *Titus Andronicus* (IV. iii. 49–51) and parodied at a few others by Marston (*Antonio and Mellida*, V. i.).

But at the nadir of Hieronimo's inaction, half-way through the long act, as before, a letter jolts him into resolution. Pedringano's letter to Lorenzo falls into the wrong hands, and at last luck begins to turn against the villain. Hieronimo realizes 'That Bel-imperia's letter was not feign'd', and his *furor parentis* is revived. Still, however, he will seek the legal method of dealing with the malefactors; only when that avenue is closed to him does personal action become inevitable:

> I will go plain me to my lord the king,
> And cry aloud for justice through the court,
> Wearing the flints with these my wither'd feet,
> And either purchase justice by entreats
> Or tire them all with my revenging threats.

Scenes viii and ix continue to compare inaction with action, now in the persons of the two bereaved women. Horatio's somewhat ineffectual mother 'runs lunatic', in circumstances reminiscent of Ophelia's madness, while Bel-imperia, 'at a window', fulminates against 'this outrage that is offer'd me' in sequestering her from the Court. When in scene x Lorenzo confronts his furious sister, he meets his own match in deviousness. Bel-imperia feigns belief in Lorenzo's tale of spiriting away Horatio, and cloaks her anger in irony:

> You, gentle brother, forged this for my sake,
> And you, my lord, were made his instrument:
> A work of worth, worthy the noting too!

But Lorenzo and Balthazar are deaf, here as in the future with Hieronimo, to all irony, and Bel-imperia lays the groundwork for revenge by seeming to fall in with their plans to marry her off. Elegant and self-pitying to the end, Balthazar sums up his conduct during the whole play, which he has plodded through for ever 'incertain':

> Led by the lodestar of her heavenly looks,
> Wends poor oppressed Balthazar,
> As o'er the mountains walks the wanderer,
> Incertain to effect his pilgrimage.

The sanctimoniousness of his image of himself is particularly telling.

In scenes xi and xii revenge and madness come together in Hieronimo. Where before he was grief-stricken and circumspect, now he is outspoken and resentful, approaching vindictiveness. To the two Portuguese who inquire for Castile's house, Hieronimo gives a succinct and apocalyptic description of Lorenzo, 'bathing him/In boiling lead and blood of innocents'. When one laughs Hieronimo laughs back, and the second concludes, 'Doubtless this man is passing lunatic.' Perhaps it is grief which has unhinged Hieronimo, but it may also be observed that for a judge the notion of personal vengeance can hardly be squared with respect for the law; perhaps in order to revenge himself Hieronimo *must* become mad. And, like Hamlet's madness, Hieronimo's serves his turn of making him appear harmless, and rendering his victims heedless.

Hieronimo's attempt to speak with the King and Lorenzo's interference constitute the last attempt of the wronged man for legal redress; after scene xii there is no turning back. Resolution has made the old man audacious (III. xii. 29, 68 ff.), but also crafty (81–82), and a little truculent ('go by, go by', another familiar quotation from the play). For Lorenzo, things have stopped running smoothly and he fails in his attempt to have Hieronimo's marshalship discontinued.

Scene xiii gives us a Hieronimo completely committed to the revenge Andrea has been crying for since the prologue. And here we may emphasize again the difference between Hieronimo's revenge, arrived at after painful prevarication and pursuit of alternatives, and Andrea's, or Bel-imperia's—on the one hand, a stock Senecan family-directed, unpitying blood-lust, and on the other, a lover's passion provoked by loss. Hieronimo is a father and a judge, Andrea a soldier, and Bel-imperia a lover, and their several desires for retribution take dissimilar forms. Most critics lump everybody's revenge into one dramatically driving force; and Fredson Bowers goes so far as to suggest, implausibly, that Kyd and his audience joined in their disapproval of the action Hieronimo finally takes, in so far as it is 'un-Christian'. Edwards (lix–lx) more sensibly reflects,

What an Elizabethan might think of Hieronimo's actions in real life may be irrelevant to the meaning of *The Spanish Tragedy*. Hieronimo may still be a sympathetic hero in spite of Elizabethan indignation against private revenge . . . [the play] is not written to advocate a system of ethics, or to oppose one. If its moral attitudes are mistaken for the 'real life' attitudes of the dramatist, then the play has an appalling message. But if the play is seen as a thing of great—and skillful—artificiality, with standards of values which we accept while we are in the theatre, there is no problem at all about sympathizing with the hero. . . .

The question of whether the final disposition of retaliation meted out by Hieronimo is quite justifiable, however, we can reserve for a moment. The point here is not that Hieronimo has lost his humanity by falling in with the demands of Andrea and his supernatural ally, but that he has come to a human decision based on his own human problems. That he becomes as well the agent of Andrea's revenge (revenge for Balthazar's unfair tactics in battle: see I. iv. 23 ff.) is the fatalism of the play, fatalism eked out by dramatic ironies in abundance, as Edwards (lii) has indicated. Within the framework of destiny, however, Hieronimo sets his own pace and shapes at least the particulars of his conduct.

Kyd takes pains, in scene xiv, to make Castile a sympathetic character, and we well may wonder why. Lorenzo's and Bel-imperia's father has heretofore seemed rather neutral, but after his interview with Lorenzo we cannot fail to be convinced of his good-heartedness:

> Myself have seen thee busy to keep back
> Him and his supplications from the king.

Now, inasmuch as Castile will figure among Hieronimo's victims in the concluding catastrophe, some readers may be led by this scene to believe, with Bowers, that Kyd intends us to disapprove of Hieronimo's revenge, or at least of the extreme form it takes. And it is true that Castile is essentially an innocent victim, and that this scene ensures our appreciation of the fact. On the other hand, there is one other essentially innocent victim of the final tragedy, as we shall point out, namely Hieronimo himself, and Castile's death redresses an imbalance of Mosaic justice: Balthazar for Bel-imperia, Lorenzo for Horatio, Castile for Hieronimo. Whether Kyd does well to include Castile among the victims may be debated; but what this scene almost certainly indicates is that Kyd purposely desires Castile to appear sympathetic, and that, assuming that he intended all along to kill off the father with his children, Kyd had something more in mind than one last outrageous atrocity. For if Kyd merely wished to bathe the stage in blood, would he have taken the trouble to humanize Castile? By doing so he ensured either (*a*) that we should temper our enthusiasm for the punishment of the villains with pity for the loss of the likeable, and/or (*b*) that we should appreciate the enormity of Lorenzo's crime in the extreme retribution it eventually calls down. Which of these alternatives he intended will remain in question (see below), but meanwhile we can keep in mind the fact that the scene which humanizes Castile is deliberately introduced into the action; it is not a by-product of another episode; and thus we may assume that if Kyd knew what he was doing, the death of Castile finally is not, as some have suggested, either an accident or a gross dramatic error in the interest of pure sensationalism.

Furthermore, in the exchanges between Lorenzo, Castile, and Hieronimo, after Lorenzo has pulled the wool over his father's eyes, we come for the first time to see a Hieronimo who is beyond conciliation. If there is any possibility of legal redress still held out, now that Castile has taken an interest in the matter and is so manifestly willing to be fair, it is already too late: Hieronimo is all guile and disbelief. The die has been cast.

Hieronimo's guile goes deep enough to take in Andrea, who complains at once that 'Hieronimo with Lorenzo is join'd in league/And intercepts our passage to revenge'. During the long act Revenge has fallen asleep in his seat—an amusing touch, and one which lends body to the overall play-within-play structure already commented upon—but to Andrea's supplicating he awakes and explains that 'in unquiet, quietness is feign'd,/And slumb'ring is a common worldly wile'. Despite the first scene of Act IV, where Bel-imperia upbraids Hieronimo for giving up his plan of revenge, there is no reason to suppose, as Andrea does, that Hieronimo has really let the project slide. Revenge himself is clear enough on that score, and Hieronimo's protestations to Castile and Lorenzo are obviously dissembling. In my view, Hieronimo's revenge takes shape as early as III. vii., but more definitely in III. x-xii., and never significantly wavers from then on: acting would bring out more continuity than an unemphasized text can. And when in IV. i, Bel-imperia accuses the father 'Of such ingratitude unto thy son', Hieronimo can reply, 'Nor think I thoughtless think upon a mean/To let his death be unreveng'd at full.' Now that he is sure of Bel-imperia's honesty and support—for, after all, he has had reason to suspect aid offered by the immediate family of the chief villain, and by the fiancée of the accomplice—he can reveal that 'the plot's already in my head'.[1]

The passage which follows (IV. i. 53 ff.) contains some of the best dramatic writing in Kyd. Hieronimo's irony is at its deftest, his 'madness' most deliberate, and the future victims cavort before him sublimely unsuspecting. From the first request for 'a show . . . or any such like pleasing motion', the audience, if it is, as certainly it came to be, acquainted with what is eventually to take place, can

---

[1] The ballad of the play makes this point clear: 'Whereto I straightway gave consent,/Although in heart I never meant . . . Sweete *Bellimperia* comes to me,/Thinking my sonne I had forgot,/To see me with his foes agree/The which I never meant, Got wot:/But when wee knew each others mind,/To worke revenge a meanes I find' (Boas, pp. 345–6). Evidently, then, contemporaries took it for granted that Hieronimo was always only shamming lack of enthusiasm for accomplishing the revenge; but cf. T. S. Eliot, 'Hamlet and his Problems', *Selected Essays* (New York, 1950), p. 122, where, after a number of unwarranted logical leaps and errors, it is asserted that the delay in Hieronimo's vengeance, 'is caused . . . solely by the difficulty of assassinating a monarch surrounded by guards'.

savour a succession of fine ironies and hints from Hieronimo falling on deaf ears:

> Hier. Is this all?
> Bal. Ay, this is all.
> Hier. Why then I'll fit you, say no more.

After Lorenzo interrupts Hieronimo's rumination on the profitlessness of 'fruitless poetry', with a curt 'and how for that', Hieronimo continues to play his part of a somewhat ruffled, garrulous, harmless old pedant:

> Marry, my good lord, thus—
> And yet methinks you are too quick with us—

More intimations follow:

> I mean each one of you to play a part—
> Assure you it will prove most passing strange
> And wondrous plausible to that assembly.

The supreme touch, however, administered with a cloak of indignation to the supercilious Balthazar, is Hieronimo's allusion to Nero:

> Bal. What, would you have us play a tragedy?
> Hier. Why, Nero thought it no disparagement . . .

The importance of this line in relation to the authorship of the play has been noted already; but, as Heywood knew, what Hieronimo is actually talking about is the on-stage carnage which Nero sponsored for his own amusement, and which Hieronimo is about to duplicate.

But Lorenzo and Balthazar are no scholars, and this most deliberately piquant allusion passes them by. The slightly patronizing facetiousness of the intended victims continues (IV. i. 104–7, 127, 171), with Hieronimo apparently too Polonian to appreciate their gibes. Bel-imperia, however, perceives his drift, and when the plot of the playlet has been sketched she who 'must needs be employed in your play' asks curiously about the fate of the architect:

> But say, Hieronimo,
> What then became of him that was the Bashaw?

> Hier. Marry, thus, moved with remorse of his misdeeds
> Ran to a mountain top and hung himself.

The trap is laid, and Hieronimo's irony becomes almost flamboyant:

> I'll play the murderer, I warrant you.

But the coltish victims pay no heed. Hieronimo instructs the cast about 'unknown languages', and cryptically promises 'a strange and wondrous show besides,/That I will have there behind a curtain'. And in soliloquy he predicts, by the muddling of languages, 'the fall of Babylon/Wrought by the heavens in this confusion'.

As if to demonstrate what Hieronimo's end might have been, had he allowed grief and irresolution to dominate him entirely, Isabella, mad, is brought on to the stage to wrench pity from the viewers with her suicide. Little can be said to defend this superfluous episode, save that the extirpation of Hieronimo's whole family makes his assassination of Castile somewhat more plausible.

Scenes iii and iv bring *The Spanish Tragedy* to its violent conclusion, although the acting out of the catastrophe, by the fine touch of its primary device, seems as moderate and stylized as any of the delicate conversational scenes earlier; prior to the disruption of decorum by Hieronimo's stabbing Castile, we have observed a very minuet of death, with the characters falling singly and silently, as if in jest. The Court is no wiser after all but one of the deeds have been done, and Hieronimo's extremely long speech of explanation is so constructed as not to give away the true meaning of the stage play until close on the end. His literally captive audience tolerates a long and quite formal peroration, which swells into invective, and concludes with plain speaking, by the end of which no doubt of the effected revenge can remain; they break in and interrupt Hieronimo's intended suicide.

Now, the conclusion of the play has been called more into question, dramatically, morally, and aesthetically, than any other part. To begin with, Hieronimo makes much of his refusal to 'speak', or 'tell'. What exactly he is concealing remains obscure, as his long narrative (IV. iv. 73–152) has made plain everything about the plot and counterplot which we ourselves know. Nevertheless, the King woodenly demands, 'Why hast thou done this undeserving deed?' and the Viceroy and Castile echo his question. Such can be perhaps explained by shock, disbelief, or inattention during the dawning realization of Hieronimo's import (IV. iv. 135 ff.), but what are we to think of Castile's question:

> But who were thy confederates in this?

The Viceroy himself answers Castile, but from his own observation, and without reference to Hieronimo's plain statement (IV. iv. 138–45) that Bel-imperia conspired with him; beyond Bel-imperia, we know of no accomplices, and it is puzzling to hear Hieronimo defending his silence in the face of 'the tortures':

> What lesser liberty can kings afford
> Than harmless silence? then afford it me:
> Sufficeth I may not, nor I will not tell thee.
> . . .
> . . . never shalt thou force me to reveal
> The thing which I have vow'd inviolate.

To effect his intention, Hieronimo 'bites out his tongue', and we are left bewildered by what the King wants to be told, and what Hieronimo insists on concealing. Edwards's conjecture (xxxiv–xxxv) that the text is corrupt, and that in the original version containing Hieronimo's 'vow' no long explanation to the courtiers was included, is not borne out by the independent plot summary provided by an undated ballad:

> Then for to specifie my wronges,
> With weeping eyes and mournefull hart,
> I shew'd my sonne with bloody wounds,
> And eke the murtherers did impart . . .
>
> But when they did behold this thing,
> How I had slain their onely sonnes,
> The Duke, the Viceroy, and the King
> Uppon me all they straight did run.
> To torture me they doé prepare,
> Unlesse I shuld it straight declare.
>
> But that I would not tell it then . . .[1]

What exactly is it that Hieronimo must 'straight declare', but 'would not tell'? Whether or not the ballad is based on a printed text, which is possible, but from what we know of the relations between ballads and plays of the period unlikely, the balladeer (a) did not find the contradiction impenetrable, and (b) did not bother rectifying it or investigating the corruption which brought it about. Evidence of a sort that Kyd's contemporaries might have found Hieronimo's adamant secrecy excusable in itself is offered by a parallel incident in *Othello* (V. ii. 301–4). Iago has been named and captured, and the agonized Othello asks Lodovico:

> Will you demand that demi-devil
> Why he hath thus ensnared my soul and body?

[1] Boas, p. 346.

And Iago, in the face of 'torments', replies coolly:

> Demand me nothing. What you know, you know.
> From this time forth I never will speak word.

J. D. Wilson finds Iago's silence 'a mystery into which criticism cannot penetrate',[1] given that practically all of Iago's misdoing has been disclosed, and no confederates remain concealed. But the natural explanation might be that Iago is simply getting in one last stab at Othello, deliberately piquing Othello's doubt (so easy to arouse) that some major conspiracy has made him its victim, that there is more to Iago's pointless vindictiveness than meets the eye. Iago might find a final satisfaction in fuelling such a maddening suspicion in the mind of an already paranoid victim. Can it be thus with Hieronimo? The scene is undoubtedly corrupt, as Edwards declares, but if the balladeer and eight reprinters did nothing to alter it, the possibility remains that readers, publishers, and theatre-goers put the apparent inconsistency down to Hieronimo's devilish irony—countering the physical tortures threatened by the King with psychological tortures of his own.

The death of Castile raises a question mentioned before. Had Hieronimo not been taken in the midst of his suicide, Castile would have lived, and the crux of the conclusion would not exist. Kyd has often been accused of sacrificing Castile to nothing more than the popular appeal for blood, but some justification may be proposed for the death of that essentially harmless bystander. I referred earlier to the proportionate justice involved in demanding the life of one innocent father (Castile) for another (Hieronimo), for, except in so far as he takes the law into his own hands while implementing justice, Hieronimo has not offended. Another explanation, offered by Bowers, would make Castile's death a reminder of the godlessness of private revenge, and how easily out of hand it can grow; or perhaps it merely attempts to temper with pity, by a pathetic death, a climactic revenge which has been conceived in intransigent hatred. For Kyd has taken pains to make of Castile a sympathetic figure.

Edwards (lx) observes, 'It may be that Kyd was trying to give a Senecan touch of the curse upon the house . . . Castile's death appears to make Andrea's peace perfect. Revenge is satisfied, and we had best try not to worry about the bloodthirstiness of it all.' This is indeed an apposite notion if with Edwards we regard Andrea and Revenge as the figures of destiny who manipulate the action of

---

[1] J. D. Wilson, ed., *Othello* (Cambridge, 1957), xxvi.

the whole play; but if we regard Andrea and Revenge as characters, superhuman where the others are all too human, their feelings deserve only the consideration which we give any character on a crowded stage. It is true, however, that Andrea and Revenge have the last word: after a most solemn and humanly sad speech of the Viceroy (209 ff.), we have a particularly brutal interchange between the infernal observers, self-congratulatory and nearly gleeful. The pity of the final tragedy, which Castile's death has gone into implementing, is dashed by the 'piling-on' Kyd indulges in with his Andrea. Castile, indeed, is sentenced by Andrea to replace Ixion on the wheel.

Need we gather, then, that Kyd, beginning with Seneca (prologue and theme of revenge) determined to end with Seneca (house-curse and stern judgement), and to this purpose either altered his conclusion or stretched it out of natural proportion? Respect for the dramatic skills he shows throughout the play should prevent us from theorizing that the end comes mainly out of carelessness. The alternative possibility that during the catastrophe Kyd means us to feel pity while we exult, to modify our self-righteous blood-lust with horror at wanton punishment, and furthermore to recognize the superhuman characters for the cold fish they are, may be oversubtle; but at least it offers us an explanation of the denouement consistent both with Christianity and with dramatic artistry, and we have no *a priori* reason to suspect that Kyd lacked either.

II. *The Play on the Stage*

While the artistic excellence of *The Spanish Tragedy* is perhaps inevitably open to debate, there is no questioning the theatricality of the piece, the 'stage force' which made it the most popular dramatic entertainment of its era, and might still move an audience in ours. The play has come down to us now chiefly as a book to be read, a literary or historical text, but its success in its own time and indeed its ultimate importance in history are more results of its impact as once staged than as a surviving construct for study. Although more difficult to isolate than the stylistic and thematic—literary—considerations dwelt on above, it may be desirable to examine certain strictly theatrical characteristics of the tragedy, from the viewpoint, as far as possible, of a spectator rather than listener or reader, and evaluate its achievement as a contemporary play-goer—Jonson's thirty-year reactionary, for example—might understand it. What specifically are the component qualities of this theatrical striking power, we may inquire, and to what extent traditional or original with Kyd? And how far has the author succeeded, by his dramaturgy large and small, in converting practical innovation into theoretical advance—or, conversely, theory into practice?

Beginning with theory, it is arguable that Kyd's major achievement in *The Spanish Tragedy* is the creation of a certain compromise in dramatic form, and that a great deal of the force of the play as staged derives from the compromise itself, or the tension thus established between antithetical traditions. On the one hand as precedent lay a group of English and Anglo-Latin 'classical' tragedies (*Gorboduc, Absolon, Jocasta, Antigone*), plays cast in the mould of Seneca, Terence, the continental Senecans, and the antiquarian academicians, with many of their rhetorical and characterizational habits carried over unaltered from 'authority': long fact-filled narratives, like Kyd's Lord General's report, stichomythic dialogue, formal declamatory monologue, codas of summing-up in speech or symbolic dumb show; and characterization founded upon decorum and convention—the flawed hero, the personification of revenge, the implicated innocent—all nearly indistinguishable from play to play within the *oeuvre* of one writer, or indeed a whole school. On the other lay a body of now largely perished popular drama of the seventies and eighties, broadly dissimilar to the classical in many significant ways. Plays like *The Cruelty of a Stepmother* or *Murderous Michael* (1577, both lost) must have inclined, as do the extant *Cambyses, Common Conditions*, and *Promos and Cassandra*, toward more naturalistic, unvarnished dialogue, quicker, more direct movement from action to reaction; must have employed more sensational subject-matter, and exhibited physical conflict and violence even to the point of irrelevance; must have mingled genres and distorted history with cheerful inattention to the rules of art—for Sidney to deplore as 'mungrell tragi-comedies', or the captious Stephen Gosson to characterize with the contempt, simultaneously, of Puritan and collegian:

. . . If a true Historie be taken in hand, it is made like our shadows, longest at the rising and falling of the Sunne, shortest of all at hie noone. For the Poets drive it most commonly unto such pointes as may best showe the majestie of their pen in Tragicall speaches; or set the hearers a gogge with discourses of love; or paint a fewe antickes to fitt theire owne humors with scoffes & tauntes; or wring in a shewe to furnish the Stage when it is bare . . .[1]

[1] *Eliz. Stage*, IV, 216, quoting Stephen Gosson, *Playes Confuted in five Actions* (1582).

Kyd's way lay between these two contemporary traditions, opening him, perhaps, to a double scorn in his own day. In speech, for example, he can be said to have hewn a line between the choral rhetoric of *Gorboduc* and the alternating conversation and bombast of *Cambyses*, *The Famous Victories of Henry V*, and Robert Wilson's flimsy comedies; in characterization between type-cast decorum and largely rootless originality, between the classical figure-heads enriched but limited by their precedents, and those popular 'personalities' (historical figures, 'humours' characters, newsmakers like Arden of Feversham or Cesare Borgia) liberated but dislocated from an associative past by their individuality. Kyd's characters balance, at their best, the weight of their lineage against the immediate appeal of their eccentricity, their traditions against their traits.

We recognize now that aesthetic conflict, even to the yoking of opposites, may generate healthy artistic cross-breeds of style, form, preoccupation—and surely theatrical viability as well. A tension central to the whole Elizabethan drama comes about from the juxtaposition of a deliberately artificial speaking medium, verse, on a realistic *materia*, a plot or action 'to be believed'; can an analogous tension made physical by its stage embodiment yield gains in physical theatricality? It is specifically a theatrical force, a stage power we seek to explain, and the link between that and the playwright's essentially literary choice or compromise will bear establishing.

A primary effect of rhetorical compromise, to begin with, is upon the *tempo*[1] or pace of action—an element of drama far more clearly to be appreciated by an audience in the playhouse than by the reader of a book. Within an individual scene or sequence of scenes we can observe the antithesis of styles at work on *tempo*: Andrea's slow, stately monologue, and the unhurried response of Revenge—ninety-one lines of traditional induction—break off sharply with the entry of the Spanish Court, and the King's abrupt one-line inquiry:

> Now say Lord General, how fares our camp?
>
> (I. ii. 1)

The pace thus stepped up rolls smartly forward for a matter of ten lines, and then subsides into the Lord General's lengthy declamatory narrative of battle (22–84). We have been given a taste of conversation and a full course of declamation; hereafter the styles and speeds will at times seem to alternate and at times seem to progress.

[1] See the interesting analysis by Wolfgang Clemen, *English Tragedy before Shakespeare* (London, 1961), pp. 110–12.

Progression, for example, from declamation to action occurs in I. iii., the long formal complaint of the Viceroy (5–42) giving way to short outcries:

> Alex. O wicked forgery: O traitorous miscreant!
> Vice. Hold thou thy peace!
>
> (72–73)

and culminating in rough hands being laid on the innocent victim (89). Likewise III. i. builds from the Viceroy's by now characteristic rumination (1–14), past a quickening exchange between Villuppo, the Viceroy, and a Nobleman (15–30), past conversational half-lines:

> 2 Nob. Yet hope the best.
> Alex.   'Tis heaven is my hope.
>
> (35)

to peremptory, sharp imprecations ('Why linger ye? . . . No more, I say! To the tortures! Injurious traitor, monstrous homicide!') and, finally, to the breaking-point of a cathartic interruption:

> Amb. Stay, hold a while . . . Lay hands upon Villuppo.

III. ii. similarly begins with declamation ('O eyes, no eyes, etc.', 1–24), accumulates formally and operatically toward a maximum of

> Eyes, life, world, heavens, hell, night, and day,
> See, search, shew, send, some man, some mean, that may—

and with the fall of the 'bloody writ' snaps suddenly into a completely antithetical rhetoric:

> What's here? a letter? tush, it is not so!

By the force of this abrupt drop in tone Kyd achieves a formidable gain in playing pace; the next lines accelerate toward the brief and chaffing colloquial exchanges of Hieronimo and Pedringano (53–54), and the considerably quickened action of 54–99. Again progressing from traditionally extended speech to naturalistically choppy dialogue, IV. i. makes use of an interruption (52) to mark the division of styles.

Kyd also alternates, when occasion arises, between the declamatory and conversational modes, thus (as in III, viii., where a block of plain prose sets off the two long soliloquies around it) preventing the pace from settling too firmly into one low speed, while sustaining the mood and matter of complaint as long as the plot or characterization demand it. Or conversely, a scene like IV. iv. can profitably be braked as it travels from violence to violence by slow, explanatory monologue (73–152), the harangue here serving to keep excitement from snowballing into incoherence, and to allow the horror of the final action time to crystallize in the understanding of both the stage and actual audiences.

Another pace-setting technique pits a deliberately inappropriate rhetoric against an implied action, as when in II, iv. 14–46 the lovers' wholly formal, choral rhyming dialogue fills the ear while the perfidy of Pedringano and the imminence of Lorenzo's intervention fill the mind: by slowing and stylizing his dialogue here Kyd is creating a suspense all the more devastating for the 'prettiness' of the talk. The violent action and curt speech of 50–63 come almost as relief.

Over the period of the whole play the final effect of such alternations of style, of activity and declamation, violence and oratory, is the creation of a series of peaks, plateaus, and valleys of movement, or more simply a varying pace of action; and the effect of such variation must be ultimately to broaden the playwright's opportunity to move his audience. The higher the drop, the steeper the rise, the sharper the contrast, the more the potential for releasing or provoking emotion—short, one expects, of the crude exploitation melodrama attempts. The starts and stops, the pauses, relaxations, and occasional shocks serve also to undermine the spectator's natural will to resist, to disbelieve: he is lulled into sympathy by slow poetry and brought up sharply to immediate involvement with an action by violence. Thus it is tactically understandable that the pace of the early action would advance slowly, in the successive small waves a pattern of declamation-to-action produces. The peaks of the play begin, for our purposes, with II. iv., the murder of Horatio, and recur henceforth with increasing frequency. III. i., the near escape of Alexandro, may be the next; III. iii–vi., from Pedringano's assassination of Serberine to the hanging of the assassin, provides a high plateau of excitement and pace; III. xiii. 133, Hieronimo's symbolic tearing of the suppliants' bonds, peaks again, and, of course, the catastrophe, rising swiftly from IV. i. to IV. iii., builds to the most intense moment, visually as well as rhetorically, Kyd is capable of providing—at which time the speed of speech and surely its vehemence or volume in a staged production must be at their maximum.

Between these peaks and plateaus lie deep valleys like III. vii. and II. v. 67–80, Hieronimo's Latin dirge, long, solemn soliloquies following short and sharp action. The epilogue, IV. v., likewise fulfils the function, perhaps superfluous to our taste, of relaxation after violence, or soothes to the level of the prologue the involvement of the audience with the play—much as recorded music after a cinema is calculated to palliate the shock of the house-lights.

I think that if we recognize Kyd's technique of pace-setting or manipulation of *tempo*, and compare it with the achievements of earlier, more 'consistent' playwrights, or even contemporaries like the Marlowe of *Tamburlaine*, we will be struck above all with the sophistication in this respect of *The Spanish Tragedy*, and its importance once again as a precedent for later dramatists. Kyd's judgement is not always unflawed, of course, and there are slack or static passages (III. x–xi., for example) and perhaps one scene (IV. ii., the suicide of Isabella) where the choice of rhetoric and the effect thereby achieved on the precession of Act IV seem unfortunate, but generally, as the evident theatricality of the piece we began by conceding must testify, his success has been extraordinary. As a technical development by one man in one play, Kyd's rhetorical compromise and, through it, control of playing pace, are not the least of his legacies to the Elizabethan stage.

Some lesser aspects of Kyd's rhetoric have their theatrical importance as well. Half-lines and outcries we have already noted as speeding up or breaking off accelerating action: no consciously classical tragedy contains either a line like Bel-imperia's

> Murder! Murder! Help, Hieronimo, help!

or the on-stage physical conflict which accompanies it. Traditional abstract *exclamatio*, on the other hand, to be distinguished from person-to-person outcry—Thomas Wilson gives as example 'O Lord, O God, O worlde, O life, O maners of men? O Death, where is thy sting? O Hell, where is thy victorie?'[1]—traces its origins to the earlier formal drama, and survives in Kyd rather more abundantly than later fashions would favour; indeed, this aspect of his rhetoric is the one most often chosen for parody. Hieronimo's recognition of his son dead in the arbour (II. v.) leads him from conversational self-interrogation (1–12) to his first deliberately exclamatory complaint (14–33); and it is grief and frustration—the Viceroy's, Isabella's, Hieronimo's—which continue to be associated rhetorically with this most unmanageable of speaking styles. The question must remain here, as elsewhere in a theatrical analysis of

[1] B. L. Joseph, *Elizabethan Acting* (Oxford, 1951), p. 77.

The Spanish Tragedy, whether we are genuinely in possession of a script 'as acted' or of a literary amplification: and the stage viability of long exclamatory passages like III. vii. will depend in our day as in Kyd's on the patience of the audience as well. But an operatic rendition, *stilo recitativo*, enhanced by the formal gesturing and posturing which accompanied traditional declamation, would perhaps solve the immediate problem of tediousness. Half-way playing measures would be disastrous: 'O eyes, no eyes' is a *cri du coeur* to be dwelt on syllable by syllable, wrung dry of its emotional content, not slipped past in an embarrassed undertone.

Noting the high rate of survival in *The Spanish Tragedy* of *exclamatio* (I would specify such passages as II. v. 15 ff., II. v. 42–45, III. i. 1–11, III. ii. 1–23, III. vii. 1–18, 45–48, 57–60, 60–66, III. viii. 23–25, III. ix. 1–11, and IV. ii.), it may seem curious to discover a comparatively low proportion of straightforward sententious generalization. The use of *sententia*, or sentence, often rhymed for emphasis and isolation, 'to hint at a motif underlying a scene, or to sum up and stress the theme of a play' (Joseph, p. 63), is widely identifiable in later Elizabethan drama; one might expect so essentially unwieldy and preacherly a device—and one viewing of *The White Devil* fully freighted with *all* its sententious couplets will show how heavy-handed the device can be—to form more a part of Kyd's technique than, for example, Shakespeare's. But Kyd's resort to such emphatics is a matter only of some three or four unobtrusive English examples. Homiletic Isabella counsels patience to Hieronimo:

> The heavens are just, murder cannot be hid,
> Time is the author both of truth and right,
> And time will bring this treachery to light.
>
> (II. v. 57–59)

But Hieronimo's own aphorisms in IV. i. 93, 189 ('For what's a play without a woman in it?' 'For there's no pleasure ta'en in tediousness') are clearly ironic in context. The majority of the play's obvious *sententiae* are, in fact, in Latin (I. iii. 15, III. xiii. 6, 12–13, 31) or Italian (III. xiv. 168–9) or in rhetorical questions geared to a particular rather than common condition—as if their author blushed a little at the presumptuousness of generalization; and the failure either to rhyme or to 'sum up' epigrammatically in the last lines of IV. iv. is further evidence of a certain shyness on Kyd's part with respect to this device.

The implicit directions for acting and staging the play which we can extract from the printed text of *The Spanish Tragedy* lead us further toward defining its theatrical appeal. Like his rhetoric, Kyd's instructions for gesture and arrangement of groups on the stage range from stylized and traditional to naturalistic and even startling. A stylized form of gesture, itself fixed by long-standing convention, as B. L. Joseph has shown, is called for in representations of pleading (III. i. 101: '*Alexandro seems to entreat*'), recoiling (III. xii. 28–31, Hieronimo's sullen 'go by, go by'), and defiance (III. xiv. 141: '*Hier. . . . Grant me the combat of them, if they dare./Draws out his sword*'); the last being a particularly significant brave, considering its seriousness in the presence of royalty (in England the penalty was still death). Spoken grief likewise has its repertory of accompanying movements: Hieronimo touches his heart at III. vi. 16, presumably where the bloody handkerchief is cached; and Isabella and her husband take their last leave of Horatio in ceremonial sequence:

> Hier. I'll kiss thee now, for words with tears are stay'd.
> Isab. And I'll close up the glasses of his sight . . .
>   (II. v. 48–49)

The bereaved Viceroy '*Falls to the ground*' (I. iii. 9) to dramatize his collapsed fortunes, a decorous action much affected by Elizabethan playwrights early and late; and Hieronimo twice considers and rejects suicide in equally stylized manner (II. v. 66, 80: '*Hieronimo sets his breast unto his sword . . . Here he throws it from him and bears the body away*'; III. xi. 1, 19, 20: '*Enter Hieronimo with a poniard in one hand, and a rope in the other . . . He flings away the dagger and halter . . . He takes them up again*').

While we cannot be sure, it is at least possible that the action prescribed in III. viii. 5, '[Isabella] runs lunatic', was traditional, or at least that traditional hand gestures accompanied the running; and it is also conceivable that when Hieronimo 'diggeth with his dagger' (III. xii. 71) he is reproducing a conventional mannerism of the mad. But other actions in the play (stabbing and hanging up Horatio (II. iv), cutting him down (II. v. 12), firing a pistol (III. iii. 32), struggling with constables (III. iii. 36), executing Pedringano (III. vi. 104), tearing the supplications (III. xii. 123), cutting down the arbour (IV. ii. 5), and all the final violence of IV. iv.) are necessarily naturalistic. Something of an odd compromise occurs in the staging of Hieronimo's play and in the bower scene between Bel-imperia and Horatio: in the first the action is almost certainly stylized and masque-like, but the slaughter of each 'actor' may verge on naturalism—or create a conflict between two forms of gesture which mirrors the predicament each victim suddenly finds himself in: naturalism, and actual death, struggling to free themselves of the gauzy net stylization and Hieronimo's ingenuity have drawn over them. Skilful acting might bring out the dawning horror of the design, by allowing some breach in the formality of movement as this *danse macabre* nears its end. In the love-making scene (II. iv. 36 ff.) an extremely stylized sequence of gestures serves to depict the seduction, by nature an event more suited to naturalism. Bel-imperia sets the tone of it:

> Speak thou fair words, I'll cross them with fair words,
> Send thou sweet looks, I'll meet them with sweet looks,
> Write loving lines, I'll answer loving lines,
> Give me a kiss, I'll countercheck thy kiss:
> Be this our warring peace, or peaceful war.
>
> (II. ii. 34–38)

And indeed the encounter itself is as elaborate and formal as Bel-imperia's rhetoric. The 'wars' allow Horatio to put forth his hand; Bel-imperia meets it with hers, offers a foot, takes 'a look' instead, counter-checks with a kiss, and so forth. While indeed the intent of the action is extremely sensual, and the interruption presumably avoids an unstageable consummation, each step toward it has been dramatized as if in ballet. Here, as we observed of the rhetorical arrangement of the scene—formal, patient speech set against the nervous imminence of disaster—the conflict of traditions of gesture creates extreme tenseness; which in turn renders an eruption into informal violence no less than relief.

Certain positionings of individuals and groups directed by the text may seem to offer emblematic significance as well as theatrical advice; much as props, costumes, and even sound effects—devices we usually credit Strindberg and his contemporaries with exploiting fully for the first time—may possess symbolic connotations beyond their immediate utility. Balthazar enters the Spanish Court as the object of contention between Horatio and Lorenzo, and physically between them as well (I. ii. 151). The serial seating prescribed in I. iv. 127–31, like the sequence of departure from Macbeth's banquet, suggests a social ordering of great importance to our understanding of the Spanish Court. And the mutual support offered by

Hieronimo and the Old Man ('Lean on my arm; I thee, thou me shall stay', III. xiii. 171) as they pass from the stage represents pictorially the need for reassurance in his proceedings which Hieronimo has come by now to admit. The most obviously suggestive properties employed in *The Spanish Tragedy* are probably the blood-drenched scarves—Andrea's presented to Bel-imperia by Horatio, and the handkerchief Hieronimo dips in the blood of his son—the letter with specifically red ink (III. ii. 23), the poniard and rope (III. xii.) and the empty box of III. v., like the fair and hollow shell of worldly expectation itself. Some slight extra-material significance may attach to a few other physical objects: the chain of office in I. ii. 87, the Viceroy's hateful crown (I. iii. 87), the bower—which the woodcut of 1615 implies is a middle-sized, latticed arch, not a Spenserian garden—the stake Alexandro is bound to, herbs for Isabella (III. viii.), the suppliants' bonds (III. xii.: remember Kyd's paternity), and the key to the stage gallery (IV. iii. 13) which Hieronimo insists upon having back. Beyond these, as the uncurtained Elizabethan stage necessitated, Kyd employed few large or small objects: swords, halberds, a pistol, gold, a cup, papers and letters, escutcheons for the masque, lit torches, a ring, a book, a playbook, title-board, chairs, tables, and a cushion for the King. About costuming we know little, save what the 1615 woodcut shows us: modern dress, Horatio booted and spurred as he hangs, Hieronimo untrussed but with pantaloons, Bel-imperia in a vast farthingale, and Lorenzo evidently masked in black. And, of course, Balthazar wears a beard in the play-within-play, as Hieronimo does in the woodcut. The young men are all clean shaven.

A last aspect of Kyd's stage-craft to be explored is his use of stage areas, in so far as the text and our somewhat hypothetical understanding of the Elizabethan theatrical structure makes this clear. First, vertical spacing of the actors is prescribed in at least two places and possibly four. In II. ii. 17 Balthazar's line is delivered from 'above', which indicates that the stage direction following II. ii. 6, '*Pedringano showeth all to the Prince and Lorenzo, placing them in secret*', intends the conspirators to overhear Horatio and Bel-imperia from some partially concealed elevation—presumably a gallery running along the back of the stage. In III. ix. Bel-imperia delivers her soliloquy '*at a window*', and the space she occupies is sufficiently large and unobstructed that Christophil can be seen entering to her (14) and leading her away. It is presumably this window from which '*A letter falleth*' in III. ii. 23. Hieronimo in IV. iii. 12 specifies 'the gallery' as the area the King and his train will occupy during his presentation, and requests Castile 'to throw me down the key' when all are arrived; but this matter of staging requires further exploration (below).

The stage, we are aware, is wide enough to accommodate 'the army' at I. ii. 109 and 127, and in IV. iv. the King, Viceroy, Castile, retainers, Hieronimo, Bel-imperia, Balthazar, Lorenzo, and the corpse of Horatio; and at III. vi. 65 the boy with Lorenzo's empty box is sufficiently far away from Pedringano to be descried as 'yonder boy'. Andrea and Revenge, furthermore, must have a niche to sit in visible to the audience and with a sight-line to the action: this may be an extreme corner of the main stage or apron, or alternatively, a scaffold at one side or a portion of the gallery.

Can we reconstruct from these hints something of the setting Kyd intended, or was obliged to employ? In III. xi. 6 Hieronimo points out 'yon house' as the Duke of Castile's, and double doors (both presumably to the same 'house') are required by the ensuing stage direction: '*He* [the First Portingale] *goeth in at one door and comes out at another.*' It would be logical to presume that Bel-imperia's 'window' occupies the area over this pair of doors, assuming again that certain locations are kept by convention constant. Hieronimo's house, or the space from which he enters 'in his shirt' at night (II. v. 1), must then be across from Castile's, and the arbour or bower, whether portable, raised by a trap, or permanent, should lie alongside it, probably toward stage centre.

There is a good likelihood that these areas are indeed meant to be kept constant throughout the play, even though action, of course, takes place as far away as Portugal, in Court, at a place of execution, and elsewhere. But the two uses of Bel-imperia's window, coupled with mention of Castile's house and doors, and the reappearance (or survival) of the bower in IV. ii., suggest strongly that these locations were conventionalized, and may call to mind examples of the Italian 'street' or perspective settings as shown in Serlio's woodcuts of 1551 (*Elizabethan Stage*, IV, 359, 361). On the other hand, there is no evidence at all for an 'inner stage'; indeed, as Edwards points out, Hieronimo's being obliged to hang up a curtain himself in order to conceal his son's body (IV. iii. 1) provides impressive negative testimony. May we posit, then, a pair of 'houses' facing each other obliquely, with a gallery running above them—perhaps with wide windows on Castile's side—double doors,

an arbour, tree, or complex of trees[1] on the other, and a section of
the gallery or a corner of the main stage reserved for Andrea and
Revenge? Possibly a post of the arbour served as the stake to which
Alexandro is bound in III. i., while torch-bearers (III. i. 48) prepare
an *auto-da-fé*. The gallows of III. vi. may require additional explanation, involving perhaps a trap and mechanical aids.

Postulating such a basic arrangement, how would the staging of
three difficult sequences be managed? II. iv.–v., from the encounter
of Horatio and Bel-imperia to Hieronimo's discovery of his son's
body, takes place while 'the night begins with sable wings/To over-
cloud the brightness of the sun', a state probably conveyed dramatically by Pedringano's bearing a torch. Horatio urges, 'Come
Bel-imperia, let us to the bower' (4), apparently then crossing the stage
from Castile's side to Hieronimo's. Bel-imperia posts Pedringano
'without the gate' (10), while the pair go on to sit 'within these
leafy bowers' (24)—a space wide enough, evidently, to be still in
full view of the audience. The narrow trellised arch shown in the
1615 woodcut is, after all, limited by the dimensions of the quarto
page, but here again is some evidence of a fairly large structure not
easily moved about during the course of the play. At line 50 the
assassins enter 'disguised'—Lorenzo masked as in the woodcut, and
the two servants (57) hang Horatio by what appears as a noose in
1615 from the top of the bower, a few inches off the ground, and
stab him to death. The woodcut conflates some action here, showing
Lorenzo leading off his sister while Hieronimo makes his delayed
discovery; the lines reproduced in 'balloons' are II. iv. 62, 63, and
II. v. 14, but the picture is obviously attempting to capture two
high-points of excitement simultaneously. Hieronimo enters then
hard on the assassins' departure, dragging off Bel-imperia. He is 'in
his shirt, &c.', possibly carrying a torch (woodcut) and certainly a
sword (II. v. 68, 80) with which '*He cuts him down*' (12).

If he indeed has a torch, perhaps Isabella takes it from him before
line 67, as the action of setting one's breast to the sword cannot very
effectively be done one-handed. If so, again, the discrepancy between
Hieronimo's 'Come Isabel, now let *us* take him up' (64, my italics),
and the final direction '*Here he throws it* [the sword] *from him and
bears the body away*' (80) may be explicable: Isabella is simply
lighting him in. We need not, at any rate, postulate a hybrid of stage
and literary versions to rationalize the inconsistency.

----

[1] It is variously described by Horatio, Bel-imperia, Isabella, and Hieronimo:
see Edwards's note to II. iv. 4.

III. vi., the hanging of Pedringano, requires a gallows for the victim to mount ('So then, must I up?' (50)) and be turned off (104). The actors are grouped severally: Hieronimo with his deputy together, the officers, boy, Pedringano—bound—and hangman entering together at line 16. The boy is near enough to Pedringano to be spoken to in an undertone (18–22), but far enough from the gallows by line 65 that the prisoner can address the hangman:

> Sirrah, dost see yonder boy with the box in his
> hand?
> Hangm. What, he that points to it with his finger?

Some 'business' is implied by Pedringano's 'Grammercy, boy' (18); presumably the emissary has been reassuring him of Lorenzo's good faith. Hieronimo calls the prisoner 'forth' (24), condemns him (39–40), and departs (98) before the sentence is executed, leaving his deputy to oversee it. Pedringano is soon aloft (50–51), but the hangman is even higher—probably on a ladder fixing the noose about his neck (63). Now some sort of securing of the rope, comparable to that done for Horatio in II. iv., must be effected here: probably it is looped about hooks in his clothing so that the fall will not actually strangle him. For apparently he is turned off in full view of the audience, as the deputy orders his visible body borne off (105) by the officers. Thus the machine serving as gallows need not be more elaborate than a portable wood framework, perhaps to be raised from a trap in the stage floor; no curtain or concealment, such as covers the Jew of Malta's cauldron of hot oil, is required here. The arbour may even double as the gallows, as Edwards (p. 41) suggests, thus adding a little emblematic justice to Pedringano's fate. We may note that the hangman's contemptuous reply to the prisoner's hope of pardon ('Stand you on that?') implies that at this point the boy has finally thrown open the box and revealed it quite empty.

The sequence which offers the most provocative problems in staging is certainly IV. iii.–iv., from the preparation of the little theatre to the final catastrophe. The main question is one of levels: do the King and his retinue watch the playlet from an elevated gallery, as Hieronimo implies (IV. iii. 12–13), or from a 'hall', presumably beneath the gallery, and certainly segregated enough from the main stage to be 'pass'd into' (12), locked (13), and broken out of (IV. iv. 156), as Edwards, following suggestions of Richard Hosley, maintains?[1] Hieronimo does say 'throw me *down* the key'

[1] See IV. iii. 1 n.

(my italics), does specify 'gallery', and we know from earlier scenes that a gallery was indeed available and rather commodious. Hosley, however, points to the action of Balthazar bringing 'a chair and a cushion for the king' as evidence that the royal party are placed on the main stage with all the others, and Edwards glosses 'down' as 'down [on the floor]'. I think this unnecessarily bleak. Why does Hieronimo give Castile the play-book to present to the King (IV. iii. 5–7), who turns up with it upon entry (IV. iv. 9–10), when the presentation could be made merely by walking across the floor? If the king's party are indeed locked in, as Edwards agrees (IV. iv. 156 n.), in what or with what are they locked? Cannot Balthazar's entrance with the chair and play-title (IV. iii. 17) be aloft, into the gallery where the King will come, while Hieronimo addresses him from below? Balthazar's exit at IV. iii. 20 gives him twenty lines and a stately entrance to get downstairs and ready to come on at main-stage level, beard completely in place; and Castile's exit at IV. iii. 14 provides him as well sixteen lines to reappear aloft. The problem of such a reconstruction, however, is still to be faced: between IV. iv. 156, when the Viceroy cries 'Break ope the doors, run, save Hieronimo', and 201, when Hieronimo stabs Castile—a passage of unabated pace and constant excitement—the royal party has got to get from wherever it is confined to the main stage. It may indeed be that the initial breaking in and holding of Hieronimo is done by attendants or guards, entering from off-stage (Edwards, IV. iv. 156.1 n.), but the rest must arrive there, too, and the quicker the better. May one conjecture a struggle long enough to allow the others time to descend? Or additional steps, possibly for this occasion only, leading from the gallery directly to the stage? I would myself prefer to imagine a rather long piece of physical action following 156, involving attendants from off-stage, the unlocking or breaking of a door between gallery and a short curved staircase— like an Elizabethan pulpit's—to the stage, with the pell-mell descent of the observers following; but if this seems unnecessarily uneconomical, we shall have to return to a wholly main-stage arrangement, and leave the elevation and locking to the imagination—as Hieronimo's apparent inability to give the King his play-book personally may well be designed to reinforce.

Granted the gallery, however, we would expect Hieronimo's curtain (IV. iii. 1) to cover a door, behind which the raised body of his son lies: when the arras is 'knocked up'—hung upon prepared supports—the doors can be opened from off-stage without giving away Hieronimo's 'wondrous show'. The actors assemble and perform and ultimately lie dead in that area of the main stage, in front of the curtain, and in full view of both audiences. Having revealed all, Hieronimo '*runs to hang himself*'—action difficult to suggest, but with the arbour hewn down (IV. ii.) perhaps its frame is meant to represent the 'mountain top' he has specified as his place of suicide (IV. i. 129–30); at any rate, the action is long enough and complex enough to allow the others, clamouring all the while, time to break in—from any part of the theatre—and save him. Tongue-biting, pen-mending, and the last stabbings occur with the Court close about the hero; and the dead march concluding clears the stage for the ghostly epilogue.

When one considers the approximate contemporaneity of *The Spanish Tragedy* with *Tamburlaine*, or even *The Jew of Malta* and the earliest chronicle histories, what we can reconstruct of Kyd's use of the stage seems, as other aspects of *The Spanish Tragedy* have seemed, remarkably in advance of its time. The inevitable castles and cliffs, towers and pits, caves, ascensions, and trap disappearances, by comparison with Kyd's subtler and more varied stage-imagination with an apparently fairly bare repertory of mechanical aids, show up the limitations of the medium in the hands of rival practitioners. Kyd makes the most of his elevations and spaces, drains a single large property, an arbour, a gallows, of significance both practical and symbolic, and among the early empiricists whose technical innovation made available, to an artistically more accomplished succession, the full theatrical potential of a fundamentally elementary stage, he must stand for us as a formidable primogenitor.

III. *Printing History*

The Spanish Tragedy was entered for publication in the Stationers' Register on 6 October 1592, by Abel Jeffes:

> Abell Ieffes   Entered for his copie vnder thandes
> of mr Hartwell and mr Stirrop, a
> booke wche is called the Spanishe
> tragedie of Don Horatio and Bellimpera &c.
> vjd debt hoc[1]

But no copy of Jeffes's edition survives; instead, we have an undated octavo in fours printed by Edward Allde for Edward White, 'newly corrected and amended of such grosse faults as passed in the

---

[1] Arber, II, 293.

first impression'. From the unique copy of this edition, commonly assigned to 1592, every responsible text of the play (excluding the additions) must derive.

White had evidently no title to the play he printed, but then Abel Jeffes, who was in and out of trouble throughout his career, had had no right to publish an edition of *Arden of Feversham*—either before or after this piracy—which belonged to White, and so both were fined ten shillings and reprimanded. The actions and sentences preserved in the records of the court of the Stationers' Company have been printed by Greg and Boswell in full,[1] while the relevant passages may be found collected in the introduction to the Malone Society Reprint of *1592* (1948), and abstracted as well in Edwards; it seems unnecessary to reprint them here. Far from nursing an inveterate enmity because of their conflict, Jeffes and White collaborated in future printings of both disputed plays.

Edwards (xl) has given us a full and convincing evaluation both of the copy for *1592*, and of what Jeffes's lost edition might have been like, based on the text of *1592* itself.

1592 is a good text, deriving from a manuscript of the dramatist which had probably not been worked over for the stage. There is some corruption, irregularity, and inconsistency in the last act and the last scene of the third act, though the 'affected area' is small . . . If Jeffes' edition, which preceded White's, did indeed contain an 'unauthorized' text, the inconsistencies and corruptions could be explained on the ground that the printer of *1592* used Jeffes' text as copy to supply defective parts of his manuscript copy.

Such an arrangement would enable us to conjecture the following sequence of events: (1) Jeffes prints the play, from either a stage copy with prompter's notes, or from a reporter's (faulty) reconstruction; (2) White procures, perhaps from Kyd himself (who might already have left off play-writing, and been properly annoyed at seeing a butchered text of his tragedy), an authorial manuscript, perhaps the 'foul papers', and perhaps salted with 'literary' amplifications, such as Hieronimo's Latin dirge; (3) to eke out lacunae in the manuscript, White has recourse to Jeffes's text: hence the 'inconsistencies and corruptions' of the last scenes. It may further be noted that while the Latin passages are on the whole printed with reasonable accuracy, the Italian couplets suffer horrible mutilation.

[1] *Records of the Court of the Stationers' Company* (Register B) (London, 1930 pp. 42 ff.

Given the clarity of Kyd's handwriting and the fact that errors seem based on mispronunciation, rather than on misreading, we can guess that the Italian tags derive from a reportorial text, presumably Jeffes's. It may be conjectured that Kyd himself had stricken them from his own manuscript, but that White's compositor replaced them from Jeffes's version.

Between 1592 and 1633 nine separate editions of *The Spanish Tragedy* remain to us, testimony to the enormous popularity of the play in its own day.[1] With the exception, however, of *1602*, with its important non-Kydian 'additions', none of the later editions possesses any independent bibliographical importance: the changes in *1594*, for example, are all in the nature of compositor's 'corrections', and give no evidence of manuscript authority. *1599* is a direct reprint of *1594*, and with two exceptions[2] each seventeenth-century edition is based on its immediate predecessor.

On 13 August 1599 Jeffes transferred his rights in *The Spanish Tragedy* to William White. White brought out an edition dated 1599, and on 14 August 1600 he in turn sold, along with a number of other properties, his own title in the play to Thomas Pavier. Perhaps a commercial understanding was reached at the same time, for White was subsequently engaged as the printer for Pavier's new edition.

Now, Pavier was a busy publisher, and he took some time to make use of his new material; White's books trickled out of Pavier's shop severally during the next three or four years. And unless an interim edition of *The Spanish Tragedy* has wholly perished, Pavier's first edition of Kyd's play emerged in 1602, 'newly corrected, amended, and enlarged with new additions of the Painters part, and others, as it hath of late been divers times acted'. The nature and importance of these interpolations are touched on below, although they are not strictly relevant to a study of Kyd; but we can say something here about the new copy which *1602* required.

Presumably Pavier himself acquired the supplementary material, which consists of 340 lines in five passages, and presumably after

---

[1] Title-page transcriptions and locations of copies are given by W. W. Greg, *A Bibliography of the English Printed Drama to the Restoration*, vol. 1 (London, 1962), pp. 187–91, and cf. J. Schick, ed., *Thomas Kyd's Spanish Tragedy* (Berlin, 1901), pp. xxii–xxxxii.

[2] *1602*, of course; and Edwards (xliii) asserts that *1610–11* goes back primarily to *1602*, by-passing *1603*. The provenance of copy for *1603* is somewhat confusing: cf. Schick, xxx–xxxi, and Edwards, xliii (n.). But after *1602* all subsequent quartos do include the additions first published by Pavier.

1599, for if White had possessed the new matter before that date no doubt he would have printed it. The basis of *1602*, except for the additions, is simply *1599*.

A clue to the nature of the additions copy is provided by the curiously inconsistent 'joining' that occurs between some of the additions and the main text. The first, second, and fifth passages are neatly enough inserted, but, as Levin Shücking pointed out,[1] the third and fourth present difficulties. The fourth addition is almost certainly intended to *replace* a lengthy passage in the text—i.e. the scene of bereaved Bazardo is intended to be substituted for the scene of bereaved Bazulto—but in the text of *1602* as it stands both scenes are retained, and Bazulto follows Bazardo. Schücking argues, and Boas and Edwards agree, that the play as printed in 1602 is too long for acting, and that the Bazulto scene should be, as it probably was, dropped from a stage production. Schücking also points out the awkwardness of the 'joins' cementing the third addition to its context.

Given these irregularities, regardless of whether (with Schücking) we consider *1602* a 'reading' and not an 'acting' text, we must account for White's and Pavier's uncertainty about placing the additional material. The simplest explanation is that White used as copy his own text of *1599* plus a transcript of 340 lines of new material, upon which there was no infallible indication of placing or replacement, and did his best to make everything come out logically. Where did the transcript come from? W. W. Greg and Nichol Smith suggested,[2] on account of the metrical roughness of the additions, that 'a reporter relying on his memory' provided it. Now, this is unlikely, if only because the second addition consists of no more than ten lines, which replaces two lines of the original text; and no one, even an actor, could plausibly be expected to remember both the original lines and the new lines, as well as the join (which is perfect)—and then turn around and blunder grossly on the third and fourth additions while generally damaging the metre of all.[3] We must agree with Edwards that the 'shortcomings in the text' of the

---

[1] L. L. Schücking, *Die Zusätze zur 'Spanish Tragedy'* (Leipzig, 1938).

[2] Malone Society Reprints, *The Spanish Tragedy (1592)* (1948), xv.

[3] The possibility remains that in the fourth addition, as well as the first, where corruption is especially evident reportorial copy was supplied. But if one insists upon the integrity of the additions' copy, the reporter hypothesis must be scrapped. Given the existence of two different kinds of copy (reportorial and transcribed) we have yet more evidence (see below) for subsequent revision and variety of auspices.

additions, which Schücking, Greg, and Smith all point to, are more likely due to 'a careless and hurried transcript'.[1]

But a transcript of what? Clearly of passages from an acting text or prompt-book. An important consideration is that whoever made the transcript knew enough to copy the additions and not the main text; which indicates that there was something physically different about the appearance of these additions, enabling the copyist, whether actor, proprietor, publisher, or spy, to pick them out. Now, there is only one surviving Elizabethan manuscript prompt-book, and its appearance sheds light on this problem: the manuscript of *The Book of Sir Thomas More*, in the British Museum, consists of a basic text, apparently by Anthony Munday, but extensively revised by a number of hands. It is significant that the revisions in the manuscript occur as (1) slips of paper inserted over existing lines and (2) slips inserted over actual excisions. There are six inserted passages, and two segments of the original text cut out and now missing. And, what is important for comparison to our case, one of the inserted passages 'appears to have been misplaced'.[2]

If the play-book of *The Spanish Tragedy* resembled the play-book of *Sir Thomas More*, which is plausible, we can explain our copyist's procedure simply as transcribing whatever was written on inserted slips, taking note, where it was obvious, of where the new matter was to be placed. Possibly he did not notice that the Bazulto scene had been eliminated, or possibly he was instructed to provide only additions, not cuts—which may have been extensive.[3] Surreptitious haste, or insufficient indication in the prompt copy, might explain the mislocation of the third addition.

Leaving further implications of the analogy with *Sir Thomas More* for a little later, we can offer this reconstruction of procurement of copy for *1602*. Later editions, tabulated by Schick and by Greg, need not detain us; editions after 1700 will be mentioned below (part V).

We have no record of any English printing of Kyd's play between 1633 and Dodsley (1744), but the booksellers continued to hawk it. Copies[4] of an early quarto existed in John Harington's collection (no 84, as 'Spanish Tragedy. Ronimo.'), and in the extensive Oxinden

---

[1] Edwards, lxiii.

[2] *Eliz. Stage*, IV, 32.

[3] The two lines which are *replaced* by the ten-line second addition might have been crossed out or excised with a razor in the prompt book. *More* exhibits both such methods of cutting.

[4] Greg, *Bibliography*, III, 1311, 1315, 1324, 1333, 1336, 1345; IV, 1657.

collection (two copies, one, no. 38, dated 1615, the other, no. 67, apparently undated). In the Rogers and Ley catalogue of 1656 we find 'Hieronimo, both parts', and in Kirkman's lists (1661, 1671) there is 'Hieronimo 2. part/T[ragedy]'. Archer's catalogue of 1656 lists the play twice: 'Hieronimo, both parts/H[istory]/Will. Shakespeare', and 'Spanish Tragedye/T[ragedy]/Tho. Kyte'. Archer's latter attribution, although perhaps offset by his flyer on Shakespeare, is the sole seventeenth-century corroboration of Heywood on the authorship, and has gone curiously unremarked. In Marsh's play-list of 1662, again, we have 'Hieronymo/t/two parts'. Presumably at least ten quarto editions had made the play sufficiently available to forestall further printings in the seventeenth century, but by Dodsley's time only a copy of the unreliable *1633* could be located by that editor.

IV. *Stage History*

The earliest recorded performance of *The Spanish Tragedy* falls on 14 March 1592, by Lord Strange's Men at the Rose Theatre, under the management of Philip Henslowe. 'Jeronymo' is not designated 'ne' by Henslowe, and the lost companion piece 'spanes comedye donne oracioe', which, as we will argue below, may have been composed after *The Spanish Tragedy*, played as early as 23 February 1592; doubtless Kyd's play had a stage history earlier than this, but no record survives.

There is no evidence whatever for assigning *The Spanish Tragedy*, with Baldwin, to the Queen's Company,[1] merely because Kyd is known to have written for that group. Lord Strange's Men seem to have been in continuous existence since at least 1576[2] and in collaboration with the Admiral's Men had captured the services of such a celebrated leading actor as Edward Alleyn and so promising a talent as Richard Burbage. The length of Alleyn's involvement with the Company is problematic, however, and we cannot theorize with much safety that he played the original Hieronimo. Presumably Alleyn would take the part when *The Spanish Tragedy* was revived by the Admiral's Men under Henslowe's auspices early in 1597.

Between 14 March and 20 June 1592 Lord Strange's Men presented 'Jeronymo' about thirteen times for Henslowe at the Rose; the exact number is in question because of confusions between the tragedy and the lost comedy, but the total of performances of both

[1] *Genetics*, p. 200.
[2] *Eliz. Stage*, II, 118; see also Chambers, *William Shakespeare*, I, 39–41.

was twenty. From 23 June to 28 December playing in London was inhibited by plague, and Lord Strange's Men took to the road; but they were back with Henslowe and still featuring 'Jeronymo' between 29 December 1592 and 1 February 1593, giving *The Spanish Tragedy* on three occasions, but apparently not the comedy. Plague again interrupted the London season, and the Company returned to the provinces for the duration of 1593, one of the leanest years in Elizabethan dramatic history.[1] On 25 September 1593 Lord Strange's father died, and with their patron's accession to the earldom the Company became known as Derby's Men; but although the inhibition was lifted on 27 December, they remained in the country and made no further appearances at Court. On 16 April 1594 the new Earl of Derby died.

Now, as far as we can reconstruct the history, Derby's company disintegrated into three groups: in May, at Winchester, some played under the patronage of the Countess, and there are further provincial appearances of 'Derby's Men' throughout 1594–9. Chambers has demonstrated that 'Alleyn took the leadership of a new body of Admiral's Men, that several other members of the old combination including Pope, Heminges, Kempe, and Phillips, joined with Burbage, Shakespeare, and Sly, under the patronage of the Lord Chamberlain, Henry Lord Hunsdon, and that, after a short period of co-operation with each other and Henslowe, the two companies definitely parted'.[2] The period of co-operation under Henslowe's management, 'at newington my Lord Admeralle men & my Lorde chamberlen men', began on 3 June 1594 (the Admiral's Men had gotten in three earlier performances in May) and concluded, in all probability, only ten days later. During their short and rather unprofitable co-operation the two companies played seven different plays, but not *The Spanish Tragedy*.

What happened to Kyd's play as a property after the break-up of Lord Strange's Men? We know that the Admiral's Men took over a number of play-books including *Tamar Cham* and *The Battle of Alcazar*, and that others fell to the Chamberlain's Company (*Henry VI*, *Titus Andronicus*).[3] *Hamlet* was played once by the

---

[1] Some index of the effect of this plague year may be seen in the number of extant plays entered for publication during 1594 (at least 23: see *Eliz. Stage*, IV, 383–4), as opposed to 1593 (5 entries) and 1595 (8).

[2] *Eliz. Stage*, II, 126; further evidence is presented in *Shakespeare*, I, 47 ff.

[3] *Eliz. Stage*, II, 126; but here Chambers, as habitually, assumes that *Titus and Vespasian* is an early version of *Titus Andronicus*, a supposition which the popularity of the quite discrete story of the destruction of Jerusalem from

combined companies in 1594, but never by the Admiral's Men thereafter; the old version existed before 1589, of course, and it is reasonable to suppose that its book was among the spoils of Lord Strange's Company which accrued to the Chamberlain's. A third category of material, however (*Orlando Furioso, Friar Bacon and Friar Bungay, The Jew of Malta*), seems to have fallen, perhaps through publication, into public domain, or at least into joint or multiple proprietorship by agreement. *The Spanish Tragedy* may have been such a play, for there is evidence at least of dual auspices after 1594.

Henslowe or the Admiral's Men maintained an interest, if not the sole one, in the play, and we find it revived as 'ne' thirteen times in 1597;[1] something, according to Henslowe, was new, either about the production or the book itself. And in 1601 and 1602 Henslowe records payments made (or intended) for Ben Jonson's 'adicians in geronymo', viz:.

Lent unto m^r alleyn the 25 of septemz 1601 to lend vnto Bengemen Johnson vpon hn writtinge of his adicians in geronymo the some of . . . . xxxx^s

and:

Lent vnto bengemy Johnsone at the A poyntment of EAlleyn & w^m birde the 22 of June 1602 in earneste of A Boocke called Richard crockbacke & for new adicyons for Jeronymo the some of . . . . x^{li}

But there is evidence also that the Chamberlain's Men (later the King's Men) staged *The Spanish Tragedy* as well, possibly before 1600, and almost certainly before 1604. There are two references to Richard Burbage in the part of Hieronimo, to begin with, and Burbage in his maturity was always a member of the Chamberlain's: an elegy on Burbage's death enumerates among the actor's parts 'young Hamlett, ould Hieronymoe/Kind Leer, the Greved Moore, and more beside';[2] and in *II Return from Parnassus* (1600), Burbage is represented instructing young Studioso in acting:

> I thinke your voice would serve for Hieromino,
> observe how I act it and then imitate mee:
> Who calls *Jeronimo* from his naked bedd?[3]

---

medieval times onward belies. Derby's Men are cited, among others, as having played *Titus Andronicus*, by the quarto of 1594.

[1] Foakes, *Henslowe*, p. 55. The performance of 7 January is designated 'ne'.
[2] John Munro, ed., *The Shakespeare Allusion Book* (London, 1909), I, 272–3.
[3] *Three Parnassus Plays*, ed. J. B. Leishman (London, 1949), p. 341.

Perhaps Edwards is right in minimizing this second allusion, 'considering the authors' scorn for the public theatre and its ways', but the elegy cannot so easily be discounted. It is strictly unlikely, as Edwards says, that Burbage would have played such a part as Hieronimo before 1594, and noteworthy that all the other parts enumerated are *circa* or post-1600.

We have also a statement in John Webster's induction to Marston's *The Malcontent* which provides further evidence. One of the actors is explaining how the Chamberlain's-King's Men come to be staging a play (*The Malcontent*) which belongs not to them but to the Children of the Chapel (*alias* of the Queen's Revels), and he offers:

Why not Malevole in folio with us, as Jeronimo in Decimo sexto with them. They taught us a name for our play, wee call it *One for another*.[1]

Clearly he means that the Children had 'borrowed' a play, 'Jeronimo', from his Company, which in turn is retaliating by presenting a play belonging to the Children.[2] 'Folio' and 'Decimo sexto' are, of course, allusions to the stature of the actors. Now, a common interpretation of this passage takes 'Jeronimo' to mean *The First Part of Jeronimo*, a short comedy published in 1605, but there is little justification for doing so. First, 'Jeronimo' has always been taken, in Henslowe's accounts and in the numerous contemporary allusions, to denote *The Spanish Tragedy*, not the perished fore-piece. Second, if *The First Part* is what the Children pilfered, and what Webster is alluding to, the play that has come down to us is curiously altered (see Chapter VI). *The First Part* contains numerous literary echoes from *c.* 1600, at least one contemporary allusion, and evidence of being acted by the Children throughout; and it is also too short to play alone. Edwards surmises that the Children adapted (or burlesqued) the original *First Part*, owned by Burbage's Company, which might account for both the accusation in *The Malcontent* and the traces of Children's use in the extant *First Part*; but there are a number of improbabilities: (1) that so extensive a revision would have been wasted on such a worthless property, and a theft at that, (2) that the Chamberlain's Men would own the fore-piece of Kyd's play and not the play itself, (3) that the fore-piece would have been played

---

[1] John Marston, *Plays*, ed. H. H. Wood (Edinburgh, 1934), I, 143.
[2] The standard gloss is provided by F. L. Lucas, ed., *Webster's Works* (London, 1927), III, 307; see also W. J. Lawrence, *Elizabethan Playhouse*, First Series (Stratford, 1912), p. 79; Chambers, *Shakespeare*, I, 148, discusses 'shared' properties, including *Jeronimo*.

alone,[1] and (4) that the Burbage elegist's reference to Hieronimo, clearly a tragic part, as are all the others he cites, can be squared with the comic figure the perished *First Part* must have contained, and the extant text indicates. And it is no more than arbitrary to propose in solution that 'the references to Burbage as acting the *great* Hieronimo are mistakes' (Edwards, p. 147).

I take it, then, that Henslowe and the Admiral's Men revived the play in 1597 and attempted another revival about 1602, but that simultaneously the Chamberlain's Company were apt to stage it; that the Children of the Chapel appropriated it some time before 1604 and that the King's Men retaliated by producing Marston's *Malcontent*; and that at some time between 1600 and 1605, perhaps in conjunction with their theft of the main tragedy, the Children borrowed and burlesqued, or perhaps reconstructed, the original 'spanes comedye', and subsequently allowed their version to reach the press.

The implication of dual ownership by both the Admiral's and the Chamberlain's can be supported by the following considerations: (1) Webster's and the Chamberlain's Men's accusation is directed against the Children for 'taking' *Jeronimo*, but not against any other company; nor is there any record of animosity or litigation by the Admiral's Men toward the Chamberlain's–King's on this score. (2) An understanding about when each company might play the tragedy is suggested by the fact that Henslowe records no performances whatever between 1593 and 1597. Why was it not staged, if that company owned it? It had been among the most consistent of Henslowe's money-makers, and it was scarcely more old-fashioned and laughable than *The Jew of Malta* or the other chestnuts Henslowe continued throughout those years to sponsor. All contemporary references suggest the popular appeal, even in the teeth of the new elegance, which the play maintained; and Henslowe was not one to eliminate a crowd-pleaser from the repertory for aesthetic considerations. (3) The run of performances for Henslowe in 1597 ends after thirteen, and coincides with Alleyn's retirement;[2] again, Henslowe's

---

[1] We may recall that our only records of performances of the comedy link it with the tragedy always, even in Germany (see below); and that in the booksellers' catalogues cited above, comedy and tragedy were treated as one entity— 'Hieronimo, 2 parts'.

[2] Alleyn had 'leafte [p]laying', according to Henslowe, by 29 December 1597, but in all probability was not an active player after 11 October (see *Eliz. Stage*, II, 156–7). The Admiral's Men played *Jeronimo* twelve times between 7 January and 19 July, and when the perhaps reconstituted Company began its winter season, playing with Pembroke's Men, *Jeronimo* was the first play given (October 11: *Henslowe*, p. 60). However, since Henslowe's records stop naming

commissioning of 'adicians' follows Alleyn's return to the stage. Between 1597 and 1601 there is no more mention in Henslowe of 'Jeronimo', but in the meantime (see below) Marston was burlesquing for Paul's Boys the Painter's scene of the 'additions', and quite possibly the theft and counter-theft referred to above was enacted.[1] Perhaps Burbage and Alleyn had a personal understanding about taking turns with the vehicle. (4) Whether or not the common proprietorship of the Admiral's and Chamberlain's was set up sequentially, with each company taking its turn, or involved actual transfer of the property each time, there are precedents for multiple auspices of plays, particularly the older ones, in the same period: *Orlando Furioso*, *Titus Andronicus*, *The Jew of Malta*, and *Friar Bacon* all exhibit a plurality of indicated auspices, arrived at either by double dealing (as in Greene's case)[2] or possibly by agreement between companies. It must also be remembered that *The Spanish Tragedy* was in print, and the City companies would have little power to inhibit provincial players from using the book: even Ben Jonson is supposed to have acted Hieronimo, possibly in 1597, with a company of strolling actors.[3]

Thus we have evidence of productions of Kyd's play by no less than four companies between 1592 and 1604. From one or a number of these productions, presumably, came the 'additions' which Pavier published in 1602.

It is unlikely, however, that the additions we now possess were those which Henslowe paid Ben Jonson for writing, or promising to write, in 1601–2. To begin with, there is a stylistic incompatability which seemed insurmountable even to Jonson's recent editors,

---

the plays shown after 5 November 1597 we have no evidence that Henslowe's tenants did *not* enact *Jeronimo* after Alleyn's retirement. Alleyn returned to the stage early in 1600 (see *Eliz. Stage*, II, 173).

[1] Chambers, *Shakespeare*, I, 148, suggests that the *Malcontent-Jeronimo* allegations are in the way of a jest, and assumes that *The Spanish Tragedy*, which he takes to be the referent of 'Jeronimo', was shared by at least three companies (I am offering reasons in support of such a theory). Whether *Jeronimo* was 'stolen', or merely revived independently, the evidence suggests that the Children played it.

[2] Greene sold the book of *Orlando* twice, the second time to the Admiral's Men while the Queen's were 'in the country'. See *Eliz. Stage*, II, 112, and III, 329.

[3] He is represented doing so in *Satiromastix* (1602), IV, i. 130–2: 'Thou hast forgot how thou amblest (in leather pilch) by a play-wagon, in the high way, and took'st mad Jeronimoes part, to get service among the Mimickes.' Cf. also I. ii. 354–8; and see Herford and Simpson, eds., *Works*, I, 12.

Herford and Simpson.[1] Further, there is considerable variation in both style and skill between the additions themselves and plain external indication (see below) that *some* additions had been made before 1600, or even 1597. Thirdly, Jonson's payments indicate that his work on the play, if it was done at all, was done after September of 1601, and there is an undeniable parody of the Painter's scene (the fourth addition) in a play which precedes that date.

The third point is sufficient alone. Levin Schücking[2] and Harry Levin[3] showed independently (although the point was originally made by Fleay)[4] that V. i. of Marston's *Antonio and Mellida* contains an elaborate parody of the fourth addition, namely the 'painter's part'. Quoting Levin:

Here it is Balurdo the clown, at the beginning of the fifth act, who confronts a painter and commissions him to paint a device, 'a good fat leg of ewe mutton, swimming in a stewed broth of plums.' *Inter alia*, he asks (1, 2, 29, 30):

And are you a painter? sir, can you draw, can you draw? . . . can you paint me a driveling reeling song and let the word be, Uh.

And the Painter, protesting that he cannot make canvas sing, replies (33–44):

It cannot be done, sir, but by a seeming kind of drunkenness.

This courts comparison with Jeronimo's questions (108, 109, 120):

Art a Painter? canst paint me a teare or a wound, a groan or a sigh? canst paint me such a tree as this? . . . Canst paint a dolefull cry?

And Bazardo's answer, that he can by a kind of optical illusion (121):

Seemingly, sir.

Levin goes on to record some less obvious echoes from the preceding scene. The lines following those quoted from *Antonio and Mellida* continue and extend the parody, with Balurdo's 'instructions' to the Painter paralleling Hieronimo's; and even Marston's Painter's exasperated reply, 'O Lord, sir, I can not make a picture sing', recalls his counterpart's 'O Lord, yes sir', in the additions. Although

[1] Herford and Simpson, eds., *Works*, II, 245.
[2] Schücking, *Zusätze*, pp. 33–35.
[3] Harry Levin, 'An Echo from *The Spanish Tragedy*', MLN, LXIV (1949), 297–302.
[4] F. G. Fleay, *A Biographical Chronicle of the English Drama* (London, 1891), II, 75.

there is really no question of the order of the parody (i.e. of whether the 'additions' passage could be an echo or parody of Marston's scene) Levin, and Schücking before him, consider this possibility and reject it. It would help to realize that the remainder of the Marston scene contains a number of other overt parodies upon earlier sections of *The Spanish Tragedy*, Kyd's own lines, which, of course, would be recognizable as stock matter for ridicule by Marston's audience. The stichomythic exchange between Feliche and Alberto quoted below is a play on the famous speech of Balthazar (later again parodied by Nathan Field in *A Woman is a Weathercock*):

> Fel. Hast writ good moving unaffected rimes to her?
> Alb. O Yes, *Feliche*, but she scornes my writ.
> Fel. Hast thou presented her with sumptuous gifts?
> Alb. Alas, my fortunes are too weake to offer them.

Balthazar feels he is unattractive to Bel-imperia because:

> The lines I send her are but harsh and ill,
> Such as do drop from Pan and Marsyas' quill.
> My presents are not of sufficient cost,
> And being worthless all my labour's lost.
>   (II. i. 14–17)

Alberto, in the parody, concedes the hopelessness of his suit and concludes:

> Ile goe and breath my woes unto the rocks,
> And spend my griefe upon the deafest seas.
> Ile weepe my passion to the senseless trees,
> And loade most solitarie ayre with plaints . . .
> Farewell, deare friend, expect no more of mee,
> Here ends my part in this loves Comedy.

The first four lines are a travesty of Hieronimo's soliloquy (III. vii. 1 ff.):

> Where shall I run to breathe abroad my woes,
> My woes whose weight hath wearied the earth?
> Or mine exclaims, that have surcharg'd the air
> With ceaseless plaints for my deceased son?
> The blust'ring winds, conspiring with my words,
> At my lament have mov'd the leaveless trees . . .

while the last couplet is generally reminiscent of Hieronimo's epilogue to his own tragedy as 'author and actor' (IV. iv. 146 ff.), concluding his part as executioner. Marston's burlesque of *The Spanish Tragedy* continues into *Antonio's Revenge*, where Balurdo's 'beard half-off, half-on' plays on Balthazar's stage-beard (IV. iii. 19).[1]

Proceeding to the question of date, we may observe that Henslowe's first payment to Jonson, 'vpon hn writtinge of his adicians in geronymo', implies strongly that Jonson had not yet supplied the additions in question. Henslowe, whatever his spelling may lead one to believe, preserved meticulous distinctions in his accounts between loans and payments, and between work done and work promised: 'vpon' in the above phrase specifically means that the loan is an advance, not a payment in purchase, and that the work being advanced against is not yet done. Compare folio 43[v]: 'lent vnto Bengemen Johnson the 3 of desembz 1597 *vpon* a boocke w[ch] he showed the plotte vnto the company w[ch] he promysed to dd vnto the company at cryssmas next the some of . . . xx[s]' (my italics). Like all of Jonson's purported work for Henslowe, no trace of this 1597 enterprise seems to have survived,[2] and no further payments for it are recorded. At any rate, Henslowe seems to have trusted him enough in 1601 to lend him two pounds toward writing new scenes for *The Spanish Tragedy*. If we have construed 'vpon' correctly, these scenes were not written at the time of payment.

Whether Jonson ever did fulfil his part of the bargain with Henslowe, the Painter's scene cannot have been part of it; for *Antonio and Mellida* can be dated, by internal evidence, 1599. There is little reason to question Chambers's and Small's establishment of the date,[3] but if external limits are required, we have the date of entry for both *Antonio and Mellida* and its sequel, *Antonio's Revenge* (between the compositions of which some time must have passed)[4] as early as 24 October 1601, although the pair were not published until 1602. It is scarcely likely that Jonson could have written the scene, Henslowe staged it, Marston seen it, parodied it, written two plays, seen them produced, and the books of them given the press, all within less than a month. This is proof enough that the Painter's

[1] See Edwards, p. 111.

[2] See *Eliz. Stage*, III, 374.

[3] Ibid., III, 429; R. A. Small, *The Stage-Quarrel between Ben Jonson and the So-called Poetasters* (Breslau, 1899), p. 92.

[4] Wood, p. xxii: 'It is necessary to postulate a considerable interval between their composition.'

scene was composed and acted before Jonson began working on the additions Henslowe commissioned.

If such were not sufficient, there is also the problem of style, which has troubled equally the admirers of Jonson's poetry, and of the additions: there is simply no trace in Jonson's writings of either the manner or the particular skills of the author of the Painter's scene. Another objection, less cogent but in any case unnecessary, has been that Henslowe's payment is disproportionately large for the mere 340 lines of additions which have come down to us.[1]

It can also be observed of the additions that there is considerable unevenness in both their quality and their style. A discussion of the possible authorship, which seems to be multiple, falls outside our province; but here we may recall the example of *Sir Thomas More* cited in the previous section: it will be remembered that *More* was revised or added to by more than one writer on more than one occasion, and that the play-book preserves as a working text these subsequent accretions and revisions. In *The Spanish Tragedy* we have some indication of a similar process of subsequent revision. Ben Jonson, again, in *Cynthia's Revels* (pub. 1601, composed 1600), characterizes an old and reactionary play-goer as one who will 'swear that the old Hieronymo (as it was first acted) was the onely best, and judiciously pend play of Europe'.[2] The phrase 'as it was first acted' can and has been taken to mean that *The Spanish Tragedy* in 1600 had already been tampered with.[3] We have also Henslowe's 'ne' in 1597, which implies revision or refurbishment, and the parody in Marston, which suggests the existence of the Painter's scene before 1599, or certainly before 1601. And if we follow the passage quoted from Webster's induction to *The Malcontent* for a line longer, we have Sly inquiring of Condell, who has explained

---

[1] This objection is less convincing because (1) it is not clear how much of the latter ten pounds were intended for the additions, (2) Henslowe habitually overpaid Jonson, or underpaid his other writers, (3) despite frequent mention of Henslowe's lower payments to other writers for additions (ten and twenty shillings for *Oldcastle*, *Cutting Dick*, and *The Black Dog of Newgate*, part II) it is rarely pointed out that Henslowe paid a full four pounds to Bird and Rowley on 22 November 1602 for the longer but quite wretched additions to *Doctor Faustus* (Henslowe, p. 206), and it is peremptory to suppose that quality played no part in the cash value of Elizabethan theatrical property.

[2] Jonson, *Works*, IV, 42.

[3] Herford and Simpson comment on this possibility, with bewildering circular logic, that Jonson cannot have intended a reference to any additions, because the additions were not commissioned until 1602 (*Works*, II, 239), while elsewhere they agree that the extant additions are probably *not* those commissioned by Henslowe.

about 'one for another', 'What are your additions?' If 'your' is
emphasized, the suggestion might be that the Children had again
altered *Jeronimo* when they appropriated it; whereas the King's
Men's additions to Marston are 'not greatly needefull, only as your
sallet to your greate feast, to entertaine a little time'. In the travesty
published as *The First Part of Jeronimo*, Jeronimo may be attempting
a similar allusion, when he offers his wife 'wondrous newes':

> Go, tell it Abrod now;
> But see you put no new aditions to it.
>
> (I. iii. 94–95)

And, of course, Jonson's additions for Henslowe, if ever they were
accomplished, represent yet another stage of revision of the play
which seems not to have survived.

The question of the order and possible origin of the various additions will be passed over here, as it does not have to do strictly with
Kyd, and more consideration of *The First Part of Jeronimo* will be
undertaken in Chapter VI. Recapitulating, then, I propose that the
inconsistencies in the later stage history of *The Spanish Tragedy*
can be resolved by supposing joint or sequent auspices for the play,
with title at one time pertaining both to the Admiral's Men and the
Chamberlain's-King's; that the 'Jeronimo' borrowed by the Children
of the Chapel from the King's Men was the same play, and not the
comedy; and that the additions surviving through Pavier's printing
of 1602 represent revisions at different times and possibly by
different companies of the acting text, but are not those commissioned by Henslowe from Ben Jonson in 1601–2.

After the flurry of activity, licensed and piratical, which we have
described in the nineties, there is little to record in the way of
professional performance. The continuous printing of the play, and
the familiar allusions to it and echoes of its lines which extend to the
closing of the theatres, imply that it was at least occasionally to be
seen on the stage;[1] but in a period of growing sophistication and
refinement one can hardly expect Kyd's pioneering tragedy to hold
its own with an audience. Edwards is not quite right in declaring
that 11 October 1597 was 'the last datable professional performance
in England', however, as Pepys saw a performance at the Nursery

---

[1] The allusion in Rawlins's *Rebellion* (1640) to 'wide mouth'd Fowler' appar-
ently in the past of Hieronimo suggests that Kyd's play was to be seen at the
Fortune in those days. See Edwards, lxviii, and Bentley, *Jacobean and Caroline
Stage*, V, 996; but the allusion may only be half serious.

on 24 February 1667/1668: 'Their play was a bad one, called "Jeronimo is Mad Again", a tragedy. Here was some good company by us who did make mighty sport at the folly of their acting, which I could not neither refrain from sometimes, though I was sorry for it.'[1] Of course, Pepys had similar reservations about *The Duchess of Malfi* and *The White Devil*, but no doubt Kyd's play would find few enthusiasts among Restoration audiences. Nor are there any records by Genest or in *The London Stage* of eighteenth-century productions, and in our own day performances have been, it seems, reserved to those of amateur, festival, and academic companies.

V. *Echoes, Parodies, and Imitations*

Kyd's influence, in a general sense, can be traced or posited in practically all the succeeding Elizabethan revenge tragedies, and not least in the greatest of them, Shakespeare's *Hamlet*. In so far as *The Spanish Tragedy* seems, among extant examples, to be the earliest play combining fundamental characteristics of the later drama —elaborate plot, sub-plot, and comic relief, evolving characters, blank verse, intrigue, and on-stage violence—perhaps the whole of dramatic literature after Kyd owes him a debt; and it may be observed that Kyd's intertwined, alternating plot structure, with trains of dramatic development interrupting each other, rather than Marlowe's more orderly, static, and medieval precession of events, came altogether to dominate the stage in Shakespeare's era. But here we can only treat briefly of specific indications of the notoriety and influence of *The Spanish Tragedy*, as they emerge from contemporary literature in echo, parody, and in conscious and unintentional imitation.

Among the earliest traces of Kyd's influence I have already cited what seem to be unintended echoes in *The Misfortunes of Arthur* (1587), *The Battle of Alcazar* (c. 1589), and *Arden of Feversham* (before 1592), as well as what may be a direct scoffing allusion in Nashe's preface to *Menaphon* (1589). Allusions or echoes or sources of echoes in Marlowe's plays have been suggested,[2] but are inconclusive.

Reflections of *The Spanish Tragedy* in Shakespeare's plays fall

[1] Samuel Pepys, *Diary*, ed. H. B. Wheatley (London and Cambridge, 1923), VII, 339.
[2] Parallels with *Tamburlaine* and *The Jew of Malta* are suggested by a number of scholars: see Edwards, 141–2, Boas, p. 407, and Bakeless, *The Tragicall History of Christopher Marlowe* (Cambridge, Mass., 1942), I, 262–5; but there is almost nothing to go on in the way of precedence, and most of the parallels cited are quite weak.

more toward imitation than parody. The 'handkercher' which Hieronimo dips in the blood of Horatio, a bit of business popular enough to be illustrated in the woodcut of 1615,[1] possibly inspired the action in *3 Henry VI*, I. iv., where Margaret presents the Duke of York with a handkerchief dipped in the blood of York's son, Rutland.[2] *Titus Andronicus* and *Hamlet* present special problems in assessing the supposed influence of *The Spanish Tragedy*, because in each case there is some likelihood that pre-Shakespearian versions of the plays were composed by Kyd himself; and the distinguishable echoes of *The Spanish Tragedy* which crop up especially in the bad quarto of *Hamlet* may be explained[3] as memorial intrusions in a reporter's reconstruction of the latter play. But in both *Titus* and *Hamlet* Shakespeare is cultivating ground cleared off by Kyd, and some traces of Kyd's prototypical revenge tragedy are inevitable.

Boas stretches a point considerably to find echoes of *The Spanish Tragedy* in *Venus and Adonis*, *Romeo and Juliet*, and *The Merchant of Venice*, but Don Pedro is certainly quoting Lorenzo in *Much Ado*, I. i. 262: ' "In time the savage bull doth bear the yoke." ' 'Go by, S. Jeronimie', a quippish misquotation of Hieronimo's 'Go by, go by', is found in *The Taming of the Shrew*, induction, line 9, and possibly Edgar (*King Lear*, III. iv. 47) intends an echo of Hieronimo's night-shirt scene with his 'go to thy cold bed and warm thee' (Boas).

Jonson's use of *The Spanish Tragedy*, on the other hand, is almost exclusively by way of ridicule; if indeed he ever came to write additions to Kyd's play, his obsession with deriding Kyd's rhetoric might take on interesting psychological implications. *Every Man in his Humour* (1598-9), I. iv., makes sport of Hieronimo's 'O eyes, no eyes' at some length, but quotes it precisely. The slighting allusion to '*Hieronimo*, as it was first acted' in *Cynthia's Revels* (1600) has been above remarked on, as has the passage in the induction to *Bartholomew Fair* characterizing '*Jeronimo* or *Andronicus*' as hopelessly out of date. Several examples of Kyd's rhetoric are parodied in *The Poetaster* (1601), and Doll in *The Alchemist* mockingly quotes a lesser-known line from I. ii., 'Say, Lord Generall, how fares our Campe?' (III. ii.; the stock 'Go by, Hieronimo' recurs in *A Tale of a Tub*, III. iv).

[1] The woodcut on the title-page is the only early illustration of the play, and presumably inspired by a stage performance; see pp. 110, 112.

[2] See Boas, lxxxii. Cf. also *Richard III*, IV. iv. 275-6.

[3] See G. I. Duthie, *The Bad Quarto of Hamlet* (Cambridge, 1941), *passim*, and below.

Thomas Dekker is another late contemporary of Kyd's upon whom *The Spanish Tragedy* made a powerful impression. In *Satiromastix* (1602) he gives a satirical description of Ben Jonson in the part of Hieronimo, has Tucca characterize the widow Miniver as 'my smug Bel-imperia', and has recourse to a 'Go by, Jeronimo'. In *Westward Hoe!* (1604) a woman is likened to a play—'If stale, like old Jeronimo, go by, go by.' Among allusions contained in Dekker's prose pamphlets we have already mentioned the biographical passage of *A Knights Conjuring*, and we may also notice 'the ghost in Jeronimo crying "Revenge"' and 'What Outcries . . .' (*Seven Deadly Sinnes*, 1606), and '*Baltazar's* part in *Hieronimo*' (*Wonderful Yeare*, 1603).[1]

Miscellaneous parodies of the notorious passages in *The Spanish Tragedy* abound: the favorite butts were (1) Andrea's prologue, (2) Balthazar's Euphuism, and Lorenzo's speech in the beginning of II. i., (3) the murder of Horatio and Hieronimo's discovery of the body, and (4) Hieronimo's 'O eyes, no eyes' speech in III. ii.[2] Marston's parodies in *Antonio and Mellida* and *Antonio's Revenge* (1599–1601) have been cited; Beaumont travestied Andrea's prologue in *The Knight of the Burning Pestle* (1600), V. iii., as did Thomas Heywood, in *The Fair Maid of the West*, part I (1610), I. v., Nathan Field's *A Woman is a Weathercock* (I. ii. and I. i) contains parodies of 'In time the savage bull' and Hieronimo's first receipt of a letter from Bel-imperia, and Thomas Tomkis's academic *Albumazar* (1615) battens on both Andrea's induction and 'O eyes, no eyes'. Another academic effort, *Narcissus* (1602), line 301, chooses the same speech for ridicule; while Barry's *Ram Alley* (1611), V. i., parodies the murder of Horatio. There seem to be a few digs at Kyd and *The Spanish Tragedy* intended in the *Parnassus* trilogy, beyond Studioso's acting lesson from Burbage, but specific points of reference are somewhat tenuous.[3]

Parody sometimes carries over into imitation, as in *Wily Beguiled* (1606) which plagiarizes in one breath what is mocked in another.[4]

---

[1] Dekker, *Non-Dramatic Works*, ed. Grosart (1884), I, 133; II, 46.

[2] A number of analogues, but not echoes, of speeches in *The Spanish Tragedy*, are listed by R. S. Forsyte, 'Notes on "The Spanish Tragedy",' *PQ*, V (1926), 78–84.

[3] The parallels suggested by Boas (xcii–xciii) are not especially convincing; but others were noted by Sarrazin, pp. 89–91, and two lines in the first part of *The Return from Parnassus* are quoted directly from Kyd: see J. B. Leishman, ed., *Three Parnassus Plays* (London, 1949), p. 184.

[4] Boas, xciv–xcv. See also W. P. Mustard, 'Notes on Thomas Kyd's Works', *PQ*, V (1926), and Sarrazin, pp. 75–77.

Poems like Thomas Andrew's *The Unmasking of a Feminine Machiavell*
(1604) and *Diaphantus* (1604) simultaneously jest at and echo the
play, while in the latter poem we may note with some interest that
the lines spoken by Diaphantus, 'much like mad *Hamlet*', are actually patent travesties of Hieronimo:

> Who calls me forth from my distracted thought?
> . . .
> I'll fallow up the wrinkles of the earth,
> Go down to hell, and knock at Pluto's gate!
> I'll turn the hills to valleys, &c.[1]

(Cf. *Sp. Tr.* III. vi. 9–10, III. xiii. 109.) *Diaphantus* also contains an
imitation, perhaps half-humorous, of 'O eyes, no eyes'.[2] Individual
studies of Wentworth Smith's *The Hector of Germany*, Tourneur's
The Atheist's Tragedy, and Chettle's *Hoffman*[3] reveal the extensive
influence, both in general terms and in details, of *The Spanish
Tragedy*.

Mere echoes, particularly of 'go by, go by', are extremely common, and may be found in Middleton's *Blurt, Master Constable*
(1602), IV. i., Fletcher's *The Captain* (1612), III. v., John Taylor's
Superbiae Flagellum (1630), *A New Dittie in Praise of Money* (1607),
in *The Blind Beggar of Bethnal Green* (1600) and Prynne's *Histriomastix*; 'What outcry' is quoted or travestied in Prynne again, in
Fletcher's *The Chances*, Randolph's *Conceited Pedlar* (1630), in the
anonymous *The Fatal Marriage* (after 1610); and 'Ifs and Ands'
comes up in parallel context in *The True Tragedy of Richard III*.[4]
More general use of *The Spanish Tragedy* can be found in Shirley's
The Bird in a Cage (where Bonamico quotes Andrea's prologue to
signify that he has returned from the dead),[5] in Rawlins's *The
Rebellion* (1640), where four tailors rehearse for a production of
Kyd's play—an echo as well of *Midsummer Night's Dream*—and in
Braithwaite's *English Gentlewoman* (1631), recounting an anecdote:
a lady of 'good rank' on her death-bed was so outrageous as to
decline the ministrations of a priest, calling instead for a play:

> Hieronimo, Hieronimo, O let me see Hieronimo acted!

---

[1] An. Sc., Gent., *Diaphantus, or the Passions of Love* (London, 1604), in E.
Arber, ed., *An English Garner* (London, 1883), VII, 409.

[2] Ibid., VII, 400.

[3] See Boas, xcii, and above; also cf. Bowers, *Elizabethan Revenge Tragedy*,
pp. 125 ff.

[4] *True Tragedy*, ed. B. Field (London: Shakespeare Society, 1844), p. 33:
'If, villain, feedest thou me with ifs and ands . . .'

[5] III. i (Boas, p. 394). See also Shirley's *The Constant Maid* (1640), I. i. (ed.
Gifford and Dyce, IV, 451); and Fletcher's *Rule a Wife*, IV. i. 48–49.

Prynne retails this story in *Histriomastix*, that we may be properly appalled; but there is a kind of pathos to the tale which far transcends Braithwaite's irony and Prynne's indignation. And perhaps the noblest testimony (if unintentional) to the true power of Kyd's dramatic creation is rendered by Thomas May, in *The Heir* (1620):

> Roscio: Has not your lordship seen
> A player personate *Hieronimo*?
>
> Polymetes: By th' mass 'tis true. I have seen the
> knave paint grief
> In such a lively color that for false
> And acted passion he has drawn true tears
> From the spectators. Ladies in the boxes
> Kept time with sighs and tears to his sad accents
> As he had truly been the man he seemed.

There is extant a ballad titled *The Spanish Tragedy, containing the lamentable murders of Horatio and Bellimperia with the pittiful death of old Hieronimo*, 'Printed at London for H. Gosson', without date, which has been of some use in confirming that the ballad audience and balladeer were used to the same occasionally inconsistent plot which has come down to us in print. But the ballad may, of course, have been based on the play as printed, rather than as acted. In general, Elizabethan ballads on the same themes as extant plays seem to be more in the way of puffs for or capitalizations upon the dramatic version than either sources or independent tellings of the same story,[1] and we might expect this ballad to have originated with the play's first popularity, perhaps even before the printing of 1592. But the two copies that have survived of the ballad, both in the Roxburgh collection and evidently not duplicates, but different editions,[2] are not early printings: *STC* dates one *c.* 1620, without mentioning the other; and it is even possible that the ballad was composed after 1624, as it does not appear by name in the list of 124 ballads with Henry Gosson and his colleagues in the Ballad Partnership entered and re-entered—presumably the entire holdings of all the partners—on 14 December 1624.[3] Boas, citing Sir Sidney

---

[1] See C. J. Sisson, *Lost Plays of Shakespeare's Age* (Cambridge, 1936), pp. 120–1.

[2] I am indebted to the notes made by the late Prof. W. A. Jackson and F. S. Ferguson toward the as yet incomplete revision of Pollard and Redgrave's *Short-Title Catalogue*.

[3] See W. A. Jackson, *Records of the Court of the Stationers' Company, 1602 to 1640* (London, 1957), pp. xiii–xiv.

Lee in *DNB*, says that seven editions of the ballad were printed between 1599 and 1638, but Lee is merely misunderstanding a rather ambiguous note in the *Roxburgh Ballads* (II, 454), which meant to say (inaccurately) that seven editions of the *play* were printed in that period.[1]

Given the uncertainty about the date and composition of the ballad, it is perhaps unwise to weigh it heavily as evidence of the integrity of the plot of the dramatic version, but it at least demonstrates (see above) that the inconsistencies which puzzle us did not greatly distress a contemporary; for the balladeer might as easily have cut out Hieronimo's refusal to 'tell it then' as he eliminated the superstructure of Andrea and Revenge, and the episode of Pedringano's entrapment and betrayal.

The career of Kyd's play in Germany and the Netherlands has been amply described by Boas, and by Rudolph Schoenwerth, *Die Niederländischen und Deutschen Bearbeitungen von Thomas Kyd's Spanish Tragedy* (Berlin, 1903). A troupe of English actors presented the play, presumably in English, at Frankfurt-am-Main in 1601;[2] and an English company presented a *Comoedia von Konig in Spanien und dem Viceroy in Portugal* (surely some version of the lost forepiece, as Boas suggests) at Dresden on 6 and 19 June, 1626, while *Tragoedia von Hieronymo Marschall in Spanien* was staged on 28 June following. Further productions, perhaps of the German version, are recorded at Prague in 1651 and at Lüneberg in 1660.[3]

In Germany, Jacob Ayrer of Nurnberg (d. 1605) composed a free translation of Kyd's play which has been highly praised by German scholars.[4] Its date is uncertain,[5] but it seems to be based on a quarto earlier than 1602; like the balladeer, Ayrer dispenses with Kyd's Senecan framework of ghostly observers, and there is considerable inventiveness shown in modifying the plot line. In Holland *The Spanish Tragedy* in translation and adaptation maintained a popularity, as Boas remarks, 'even greater than in Germany, and more enduring than in the very land of its birth': a curious adaptive translation into Dutch of *Orlando Furioso* by Everaert Syceram (1615) contains imbedded in it a narrative version of the

[1] There is actually no indication of registration of this ballad, and Rollins's *Analytical Index* does not include it. The melody was 'Queen Dido': see Chappell, p. 372, and *Roxburgh Ballads*, VI, 547–51.
[2] *Anglia*, II (1883), 15; Boas, xcix.
[3] Boas, xcix–c.
[4] C. H. Kaulfuss-Diesch, *Die Inszenierung* (Leipzig, 1905), pp. 169–74.
[5] It was published posthumously in a collected edition of 1618.

main plot of Kyd's play, and by 1621 Adriaen van den Bergh had contributed a Dutch translation of the play, based upon one of the post-1602 English quartos. In 1638, moreover, a second Dutch translation, anonymous, appeared at Amsterdam, and became popular enough to undergo ten editions by 1729; like all the continental adaptations before it, the anonymous version omits the induction and framework of Andrea and Revenge. Another German dramatization, Kaspar Stieler's *Bellimperie* (printed at Jena, 1680), is based in turn on the Dutch anonymous adaptation rather than the English original; there is furthermore included in a list of early eighteenth-century plays what may be yet a different adaptation, *Der Tolle Marschalk aus Spanien*, presumably lost. The variations in plot and considerations of textual transmission raised by these Dutch and German versions are dealt with in some depth by Schoenwerth, who has also edited the three Dutch texts; Boas reprints Ayrer's version with Kyd's *Works*.

VI. *Criticism*

Before 1773 and Hawkins, criticism of *The Spanish Tragedy*, save that inherent in the early seventeenth-century parodies and imitations, consisted almost entirely of catalogue descriptions. An occasional half-line of opinion colours the Restoration listings of Edward Phillips, William Winstanley, and Gerard Langbaine, but in these compilations Kyd is considered only as the author of *Cornelia*—about which none of the above offers an estimate—and *The Spanish Tragedy* either anonymous or (Phillips) the work of 'William' (alias Wentworth) Smith, author of *The Hector of Germany*. In 1744 Dodsley produced the first edited edition of *The Spanish Tragedy*, and the first printing of any sort in English since 1633, but evidently generated little critical sympathy for the play among his contemporaries: Boas quotes aptly from Peter Whalley, *An Enquiry into the Learning of Shakespeare* (1748), dismissing the still anonymous tragedy as 'little else but a continued String of Quibbles and Conceits even in the most passionate and affecting parts', although he allows there are 'about six good Lines [II. ii. 45–51], describing the time of an Assignation appointed by two Lovers, which are tender and natural enough'.

Hawkins, however, provided in *The Origin of the English Drama* (1773) not only a respectable text of the play, roughly collating four editions (where Dodsley had employed only *1633*), choosing primarily readings from the best quarto (*1592*), and identifying and separating the additions, but also disclosed Kyd's authorship for the first time since 1656, gave a surprisingly accurate estimate of the date of the play ('about 1589'), conjectured for the first time Kyd's authorship of *Soliman and Perseda*, and in some measure made possible the slow growth of critical appreciation for Kyd and *The Spanish Tragedy* during the ensuing century.

But appreciation came slowly indeed. Beyond his exposition of the 'Kidde in *Aesop*' passage from Nashe, Malone scarcely deals with Kyd or his plays, and for D. E. Baker *The Spanish Tragedy* was no more than 'the constant object of ridicule among [Kyd's] contemporaries and immediate successors'.[1] Only the additions interested Coleridge,[2] while Lamb characterized the text as Kyd wrote it as 'a *caput mortuum*, such another piece of flatness as *Locrine*',[3] reserving admiration for the additions as 'the salt of the old play'. Schlegel comments only on the crudeness of the play; Taine does not even mention it by name.

Perhaps it was John Payne Collier, the many-faceted scholar of no mean taste, who first entered a plea for the serious consideration of Kyd and *The Spanish Tragedy*. In 1831 he speaks of Kyd as 'a poet of considerable mind', who 'deserves, in some respects, to be ranked above more notorious contemporaries'.[4] Perhaps by 'more notorious contemporaries' Collier means to suggest Lyly or Greene, an evaluation which might well find support among present-day readers. In 1874 Hazlitt's edition of Dodsley's *Old Plays* collected for the first time plays definitely by Kyd along with conjectural attributions like *Soliman and Perseda* and *The First Part of Jeronimo*, and collated, for the first time since Hawkins, the undated quarto which forms the basis of his text. Subsequent editions showed the ameliorating influence of new bibliographical methods, beginning with Manly's old-spelling edition of 1897 (of which Schick quotes, '*Enfin Malherbe vint!*'), continuing with Schick's editions of 1898 and 1901, and Boas's *Works* of 1901; since Boas, the most important contributions have been Malone Society Reprints of *1592* and *1602*, and a fresh and generally valuable edition by Philip Edwards in the Revels series.

Criticism and scholarship since Hazlitt have been voluminous, and one can only refer the reader to the brief abstracts provided by

[1] *Biographica Dramatica* (rev. ed., London, 1812), I, 442.
[2] *Table Talk* (London, 1888), p. 203.
[3] *Specimens of the English Dramatic Writers*, ed. I. Gollancz (London, 1893), I, 73.
[4] *History of English Dramatic Poetry* (London, 1831), III, 207.

Boas, both in the original edition of Kyd's *Works* and in the 'Corrections and Additions' provided with his reprint of 1955, and to the *Concise Bibliography* assembled by Samuel Tannenbaum in 1941. The publications of Félix Carrère, T. W. Baldwin, Fredson Bowers, and Charles Crawford (a Kyd *Concordance*) have been frequently cited in my notes; and the work of German scholars, among whom Koeppel, Sarrazin, and Schücking may be named, has made a mark on the field. In general, among critics of the drama or the Elizabethan period, Kyd has been treated as a literary figure of considerable historical importance, and almost negligible poetical worth—a traditional view which may easily result in a corresponding overestimation of Kyd's aesthetic and poetic capabilities now and in the immediate future, if only to redress a bad balance. And indeed one might lean far to counterweigh such a description of Kyd and his work as is given by J. A. Symonds,[1] a composite of superciliousness, inaccuracy, and smug ignorance thinly disguised as offhandedness. But the text of the tragedy itself has already outlived its disparagements from Nashe and Jonson onward, as presumably it will outlive our own latter-day lip-service.

[1] *Shakespeare's Predecessors in the English Drama*, 1884.

CHAPTER V

SOLIMAN AND PERSEDA

I. *Authorship*

The evidence for Kyd's authorship of *Soliman and Perseda* is entirely internal; prior to Hawkins's suggested attribution to Kyd in 1773 all publishers and critics had treated the play as anonymous, and to the present some scholars, notably E. K. Chambers, prefer to exclude *Soliman* from Kyd's canon.[1] But the case for Kyd is quite strong, perhaps as strong as the attribution of *Tamburlaine* to Marlowe, and it would unnecessarily curtail any study of Kyd's works not to consider *Soliman* as at least tentatively his. I will summarize the main arguments for Kyd's authorship below.

Hawkins's original reason for attributing *Soliman* to Kyd, and the starting-point of most discussions, is its coincidence of plot with *The Spanish Tragedy*; for the main source of *Soliman* is the same as Hieronimo's play-within-play, the tale of Solyman and Persida as told by Henry Wotton, in *A Courtlie Controversie* (1578). No other playwright of the era shows any familiarity with Wotton's compilation, nor with the tale in its earlier continental forms.[2]

F. S. Boas (lvi–lix) pointed furthermore to a number of similarities in dramatic technique between *Soliman* and *The Spanish Tragedy* which strongly suggest common authorship: (1) the shift of locale for the purpose of introducing early another constellation of characters, in *Soliman* from Rhodes to Constantinople, in *The Spanish Tragedy* from Spain to Portugal; (2) the early exchanges between Ferdinand and Lucina, compared with Horatio's second and third interviews with Bel-imperia—passages extremely close both in spirit and in actual language; (3) the repartee between Perseda and Erastus (II. i. 153–66) akin to that between Balthazar

---

[1] See *Eliz. Stage*, IV, 46–47. Baldwin takes both positions: compare 'On the Chronology of Thomas Kyd's plays', *MLN*, XL (1925), 346, with *Genetics*, p. 198. A summary of the positions assumed by various authorities is given by John J. Murray, 'The Tragedye of Solyman and Perseda', unpubl. doctoral diss., New York University 1959 (available xeroxed from University Microfilms), pp. xliii–xlvii.

[2] Sarrazin, pp. 40–41 [123].

and Bel-imperia (I. iv. 77–89); (4) Alexandro's arraignment on false charges, and the similar trial on similar charges of Erastus; (5) the timely reprieves, at the point of death, of both Alexandro (III. i) and Perseda (IV. i. 110–37). Now, of all these coincidental episodes, only the trial of Erastus is provided by Wotton, and there it is no more than hinted at; Boas let his authorship argument rest almost entirely upon these parallelisms in dramatic construction, and his reasoning has seemed sufficient to most scholars.

We can add to this compilation some characteristics of melodrama and dramatic irony in both plays which are pointed out in detail by Carrère, as 'éléments charactéristiques du drame Kydien'. Furthermore, we have a superstructure of allegorical figures in both plays, who comment in a similar manner on the proceedings throughout; and as it is specifically indicated in *The Spanish Tragedy* that Andrea's prologue is *not* an induction but a part of Act I proper—in other words, that Andrea is to be considered more a part of the action than, for example, Tantalus in *Thyestes*—so in *Soliman* the trio of gods who oversee the main action are not set off in prologue and epilogue, but included in the regular act-scene structure.[1] In both cases the placing of 'supernatural' scenes is unusual, and if the author and not the compositor determined it, another coincidence of peculiar technique is to be identified.

Beyond the general compositional parallels we may specify some coincidences in language, style, versification, and terminology, which flesh out the authorship argument substantially. Sarrazin isolated a number of lines and phrases which, quoted in parallel with others from *The Spanish Tragedy*, are far more revealing of common authorship than usual with this technique. Selecting from his perhaps overburdened list, we can quote the following: 'What boots complaint, where there's no remedy?' (*Sp. Tr.*, I. iv. 92); 'What boots complaining where's no remedy?' (*Soliman*, V. ii. 87); the allegorical Revenge in *The Spanish Tragedy* urges Andrea to sit down 'And serve for Chorus in this Tragedy' (I. i. 91), while the allegorical Love in *Soliman* thinks herself fittest 'To serve for Chorus to this Tragedie' (I. i. 17). Hieronimo characterizes his dead son as 'Sweet lovely rose, ill pluckt before thy time' (II. v. 47), while Erastus styles dead Perseda 'Faire springing rose, ill pluckt before

---

[1] There is no act-division in *1592* after the initial 'Actus Primus', which, however, *precedes* the first scene of Love, Death, and Fortune: Murray (p. 108) is probably right in assuming that Kyd intended no separated 'Induction', as Boas, p. 164, arranges it.

thy time' (V. iv. 81). Told of Balthazar's death, the Viceroy in
Sp. Tr. laments, 'Aye, Aye, my nightly dreams have told me this'
(I. iii. 76), while Perseda, hearing of Erastus's death, puts aside the
discussion of Lucina with 'Ah no; my nightly dreames fortould me
this' (V. ii. 25). Boas quoted, in connexion with Ferdinand's invita-
tion to Lucina 'As fits the time, so now well fits the place/To coole
affection with our words and lookes' (II. i. 1–2), the quite similar
suggestion from Horatio to Bel-imperia (II. ii. 3) that the two lovers
repair somewhere 'And that with looks and words we feed our
thoughts'. In the ensuing scene between Lucina and Ferdinand
both lovers employ military imagery for their 'blissful war', or love
combat; while Horatio and Bel-imperia in the bower scene (II. iv)
do likewise. Certain other scraps of similar diction were picked
out by Sarrazin ('second self', 'translucent breast', 'eternal night',
etc.) and by Murray ('sable weed', 'with all convenient speed'), but
these are less impressive data. The point of the verbal coincidences
is that they occur in essentially cliché forms, but not merely in
proverbial or commonplace phrases: they are the sort of coincidence
which is far more likely to appear within the corpus of one author's
work than, by virtue of imitation, in another's. Thus while it is
possible, if strained, to imagine the similarities in dramatic technique between *The Spanish Tragedy* and *Soliman* coming about
through clever, or at least faithful, imitation of Kyd by some contemporary, it is more difficult to imagine anyone so struck with Kyd's
exact wording as to plagiarize such phrases as those quoted above.
None is memorable enough to suggest notoriety, and hence conscious or unconscious reminiscence; nor is any so common a phrase
or line for us to assume that someone else arrived at the same words
by accident. This kind of verbal parallelism, it seems to me, is (if
it goes deep enough) a fair sign of one writer's hand in two places;
but it is, of course, dangerous to build an entire case for attribution
upon such evidence.

Hence it is reassuring to turn more broadly to the question of
style and versification in the two plays. Sarrazin (pp. 3–4) points
out parallel use of comparatively uncommon rhetorical figures like
anaphora, stichomythia, antithesis, and *palilogia* in both plays.
Euphuism colours the verse of *Soliman* about as distinctly as the
verse of *The Spanish Tragedy*; and Sarrazin has attempted (p. 6) to
find echoes of Watson's *Hekatompathia* in *Soliman* as well as in the
earlier tragedy. But the test of stylistic similarity between the plays
must rest on extended passages; a reading of any long speech in

Soliman leaves one with an impression, difficult to account for in detail, of Kyd's compositional technique, and enumerating or tabulating the stylistic characteristics which can be isolated—proportions of masuline to feminine line-endings, proportion of similes, alliteration, long words, *sententiae*, generalizations, vocabulary, etc. —seems not to convey to the full the qualitative similarity which exists, nor sufficiently to take account of the possibility of poetic growth or versatility in the author.[1] For it is the quality of the verse, taken as a whole, which we would like to appraise, and the quality of the author's mind which the verse seems to represent. To this end we might observe that the language of *Soliman* is essentially subdued, as is the language of *The Spanish Tragedy*, that eccentric or violent epithets are rare in both plays, and that most sentences and phrases in both are delivered in a balanced syntax, and in periods of about the same duration. Perhaps it is mere impressionism to record that the levels of dramatic and poetic skill exhibited in the plays are quite comparable, and that no flight or descent in either play seems beyond the capability of the author of the other; but despite the fact that *Soliman* is both slighter and less finished than *The Spanish Tragedy*, one cannot but sense behind its text an author of approximately Kyd's level of intelligence and artistry. Nor are there in *Soliman* the lapses of patience nor the flashes of brilliance that illumine or disfigure the work of Marlowe; there is little of Greene's patent cheerfulness, Munday's crudeness, or Peele's more luxuriant poetic manner. Instead, as in *The Spanish Tragedy*, *Soliman* maintains a fairly even and moderately high level of craftsmanship and carefulness, tinged with the moderately stoical melancholy characteristic of Kyd, neither soaring nor sinking, but at all times at least competent.

But presumably there were other men of Kyd's time with similar temperament and quality of mind, and we may go on to record more specific stylistic coincidences. Both plays contain a considerable number of laments, long and short, most frequently in soliloquy. With any of Hieronimo's, Isabella's, or the Viceroy's lamenting speeches in *The Spanish Tragedy* we may compare such monodies as Soliman's for the death of his two brothers:

---

[1] See K. Wiehl, 'Thomas Kyd und die autorschaft von *Soliman and Perseda*', *Englische Studien*, XLIV (1912), 343–60; and, by the same writer, *Thomas Kyd und sein Vers* (Kempten, 1911), *passim*. Another attempt to demonstrate Kyd's authorship on stylistic grounds is S. J. Mitchell, 'Rhetoric as a Dramatic Element in the Plays of Thomas Kyd', unpubl. diss. (Texas, 1951).

O *Haleb*, how shall I begin to mourne,
Or how shall I begin to shed salt teares,
For whom no wordes nor teares can well suffice?
. . .
Come, Janisaries, and helpe me to lament,
And beare my joyes on either side of me—
I, late my joyes, but now my lasting sorrow.
Thus, thus, let *Soliman* passe on his way,
Bearing in either hand his hearts decay.
(I. v. 83 ff.)

'Help me to lament' recalls Hieronimo's request to Isabella (II. v.
36), 'Here, Isabella, help me to lament', and, like the constant harp-
ing on the *efficacy* of lament as palliating sorrow (*Soliman*, V. iv.
10–11; *Sp. Tr.*, I. iii. 31–32, among other instances) co-operation
in misery is a familiar theme of Kyd's. Similarly close to the spirit of
The Spanish Tragedy is the connexion Soliman expresses between
grief and revenge (III. i. vi): 'Then farewell sorrow; and now,
revenge, draw neere.' The irony Kyd exploits to the full in the
preparation for Hieronimo's playlet is paralleled in the oaths taken
by Erastus's false accusers, suborned by Soliman:

1 Wit.: Foule death betide me, if I sweare not true.
2 Wit.: And mischiefe light on me, if I sweare false.
(V. ii. 73–74)

Of course, they are both lying, and promptly after the execution of
Erastus, Soliman will do away with his accomplices summarily, by
tumbling them from a tower—an act in itself somewhat comparable
to Lorenzo's methods with his agents.

Pedringano is compelled by Lorenzo to swear allegiance on the
hilt of his sword, as Basilisco is similarly forced by Piston to 'swear
upon my Dudgin dagger'. No other articles are sworn on in either
play. In *Soliman*, as in *The Spanish Tragedy*, there is a short and
gratuitous incidental glorification of England (*Soliman*, I. iii. 181–4),
and a masque-like procession of warrior knights before a monarch
(I. iii. 1–115).[1] As *The Spanish Tragedy* ends with carnage strewn all
over the stage, we have multiple deaths twice in *Soliman*, at the
conclusion, and after the execution of Erastus.

Kyd is much given to lamenting soliloquies, and rhetorical

---

[1] Boas, lvii, notes the similarity of the enumeration of national types in this
sequence with *Cornelia*, I. 59–63, and IV. ii. 44–51.

questions are a familiar part of such speeches in *The Spanish Tragedy*. Compare, from *Soliman*, IV. i. 10 ff.:

> But what helps gay garments, when the minds oprest?
> What pleaseth the eye, when the sence is altered?
> . . . For what is misery but want of God?

Or I. v. 95:

> Ah, what is dearer bond than brotherhood?

Or III. i. 249 ff., with *Sp. Tr.*, III. v. 16–17, III. xiv. 86–87, IV. l. 97, etc. Another rhetorical trick which we have pointed out before in *The Spanish Tragedy* is the 'Yet might . . . Ah, but . . . 'construction so favoured by Balthazar. Compare from *Soliman*, I. iv. 126 ff.:

> Come therefore, gentle death, and ease my griefe;
> Cut short what malice *Fortune* misintends.
> But stay a while, good *Death*, and let me live;
> Time may restore what *Fortune* tooke from me:
> Ah no, great losses sildome are restord.
> What, if my chaine shall never be restord?
> My innocence shall cleare my negligence.
> Ah, but my love is cerimonious . . . &c.

One may observe that the rhetorical pattern is less slavishly followed by Erastus than by Balthazar, but a subsequent scene of *Soliman* (III. ii.) contains seventeen lines of perfectly overelaborated conventional echoing, viz.:

> Perseda: Accursed Chaine, unfortunate *Perseda*.
> Lucina: Accursed Chaine, unfortunate *Lucina*.
> My friend is gone, and I am desolate.
> Perseda: My friend is gone, and I am desolate.
> Returne him back, faire starres, or let me die.
> Lucina: Returne him backe, fair heavens, or let me die. &c.

The vocabulary of both plays is similar, as we have said, but scarcely identical. Several of Kyd's favourites ('butcher', 'solicit', e.g.) recur; and the few Latin tags in *Soliman* sort well with those in *The Spanish Tragedy*.

J. J. Murray (lii–liv) has attempted to connect the few legal scraps quoted in Latin in *Soliman* with the scrivener's training Kyd may or may not have been exposed to; and his discussion is not unconvincing. Whatever aspects of metre and style can be submitted to statistical analysis have been so treated by K. Wiehl, as a part of his study of the mechanics of Kyd's language; and Wiehl's results led him as well to endorse the attribution. Of perhaps more significance is J. E. Routh's interesting analysis of the rhyme scenes found in *Cornelia*, *Soliman*, and *The Spanish Tragedy*, but altogether non-existent in the spurious *First Part of Jeronimo*;[1] an extension of Routh's tabulation to include other playwrights of the late eighties and early nineties might render almost unimpeachable the case for Kyd.

The weight of the evidence is definitely for Kyd's authorship of *Soliman*, and further subjection of the play to metrical and stylistic tests, comparison of techniques of characterization and thematic preoccupations (as, for example, the quality of modified fatalism inherent in the play) can only, I believe, reconfirm what may be nearly a maximal probability. By the most conservative standards of cataloguing, of course, the play must remain 'anonymous', but for the special purposes of scholars and readers in the period I think it safe to assign *Soliman and Perseda* to Kyd.

II. *Sources*

The main source of *Soliman* is Wotton's first story of Solyman and Persida from *A Courtlie Controversie of Cupids Cautels* (1578), which we have already discussed in connexion with *The Spanish Tragedy*. Sarrazin has reprinted the source-story, studied the use made of it by Kyd, and traced earlier versions of the same story (with which Kyd appears to have had no acquaintance) to 1540 and Fontaine's *De Bello Rhodio*.

While the main action of the play is for the most part modelled closely upon Wotton, even to an occasional verbal echo, the following are some aspects of the plot not found in Wotton, or changed in transmission: (1) the comic scenes, and the vaudevillian sub-plot of Piston and Basilisco, are not in Wotton; (2) neither are the deaths of Soliman's two brothers, Haleb and Amurath; (3) Brusor in Wotton is an unmitigated villain, while in *Soliman* he emerges somewhat of a tragic figure, beset on one occasion by an envious spitefulness which he is ever after regretful of; and Brusor in Wotton is Soliman's cousin; (4) Soliman in Wotton is not remorseful about Erastus's death, nor are the false witnesses and judge done away with; (5) Lucina disappears from Wotton's story after relinquishing her

---

[1] J. E. Routh, 'Thomas Kyd's Rime Schemes and the Authorship of *Soliman and Perseda* and of *The First Part of Jeronimo*,' *MLN*, XX (1905), 49–51.

chain—there is no marriage with Brusor—but there is a basis for Perseda's suspicion of double dealing in Erastus which Kyd does not reproduce: for Lucina gambled away her chain because she 'knew his [i.e. Erastus's] chapman, otherwise she would hardly have departed from the Jewell she esteemed past all earthlye treasure'. In Kyd (II. i. 229 ff.) Lucina thinks the masker is actually Ferdinando, but Wotton makes it clear that she has an interest in the young hero as well. (6) In Wotton, Perseda dies by 'two bullets sent from a Musket' of a rank-and-file soldier, while in Kyd she induces Soliman himself to do the deed; and subsequently in Wotton, Soliman survives to erect a pyramid to the memory of the lovers, from the pinnacle of which the villainous Brusor is hanged. In Kyd, Soliman turns maliciously on a repentant Brusor, and has him beheaded, but dies himself from the poison Perseda has 'sawst' her lips with. (7) The framing scenes of Fortune, Love, and Death are, of course, not in Wotton, but perhaps suggested by a line in the concluding verses.

Beyond these changes, Kyd has also brought Brusor to the tournament of foreign knights, converted Soliman from a simple and passionate tyrant to a complex character in whom rage and remorse alternate with heroic rapidity, likewise deepened the characters of Brusor and Lucina, introduced a few minor characters, and above all added the comic action which remains the most attractive aspect of the whole play. Kyd's control of dramatic *tempo* is considerably greater than Wotton's, but both versions coincide in their leisurely and somewhat long-winded beginnings—a characteristic of Kyd's plotting which we have already remarked in *The Spanish Tragedy*.

Subsidiary sources may be noted. J. J. Murray (xxvi–xxxiii) has drawn attention to the analogues of Basilisco in Italian *commedia dell' arte* and *commedia erudita*, where various 'Basiliscos' of similar nature take comic parts ranging from clever servant to *miles gloriosus*. Murray goes on to suggest a direct source for Kyd's Basilisco in the comedy *La Furiosa* of G. B. Della Porta; *La Furiosa* is, however, much too late to be a source. But there is some possibility that a source of close anterior analogue of the character and the comic sub-plot may be identified in Pasqualigo's *Il Fedele*, Englished before 1584 by Munday as *Two Italian Gentlemen*, and made Latin by Abraham Fraunce as *Victoria*.

Thomas Nashe, in *Have With You to Saffron Walden*, characterizes Gabriel Harvey as 'such a vaine *Basilisco* and *Captain Crackstone* in all his actions and conversations', and it is easy to see why Nashe paired the two braggarts of comedy. Like Basilisco, Munday's comic hero is a mock-soldier, valiant in speech and craven in action (see especially IV. vi.), and significantly, he is also in love with the heroine of the play. Like Basilisco he is especially proud of his prowess with women, but every woman in the play repudiates him. Like Basilisco with Piston, Crack-stone is overmastered and humiliated by servants. Crack-stone broods about the impropriety of his doing battle with Fedele (1340 ff.) instead of the 'thousandes' of armed foes he is accustomed to combat with, and salves his honour by only pretending to fight. Similarly, Basilisco will not demean himself to contend with Piston, because 'it were a disgrace/To all my chivalrie to combat one so base', and avoids single combat, 'not that I feare, but that I scorne to fight' (II. ii. 89 ff.).

The closeness of both comic figures may be accounted for by convention, of course, whether Italian, native, or classical. Any character study of Basilisco must also emphasize his dependence on the *miles gloriosus* tradition exemplified by Ralph Roister Doister, Thersites, Oldcastle, and Falstaff, and Kyd's influence upon Shakespeare's conception of a braggart soldier has been dealt with on several occasions.[1] But Munday's Crack-stone certainly preceded Kyd's Basilisco, and direct influence seems at least plausible.

Less plausible as a source is the anonymous *Rare Triumphs of Love and Fortune* (1589, possibly acted 1582) which has long been supposed to have suggested to Kyd his frame-story of Fortune, Love, and Death; indeed, Fleay was even moved to attribute *Rare Triumphs* to Kyd himself on the strength of the similarity in design.[2] But beyond the mere idea of allegorical characters (two in *Rare Triumphs*, three in *Soliman*) commenting on the main action, there is no resemblance whatever between the plays. *The Spanish Tragedy* has a framework as similar to that of *Soliman* as has *Rare Triumphs;* and the trinity Love, Death, and Fortune were scarcely unfamiliar to the Elizabethans.[3] Possibly the germ of the dramatic superstructure is also in Wotton: the concluding verses state 'By Fortune, Envie, and by Death/ This couple caughte their bane', and there are numerous instances of characters in the story calling upon one or another such deity. It is possible to suppose that *Rare Triumphs* contributed the frame-arrangement to *Soliman*, but not necessary.

[1] See E. E. Stoll, *Shakespeare Studies* (New York, 1927), pp. 403 ff., 459–60; and general treatments cited by Murray, xxvi–xxvii.

[2] *Biographical Chronicle*, II, 26.

[3] Cf. Petrarch's *Trionfi*, and Watson's Sonnet XLIV (*Poems*, ed. Arber, p. 200) in *Tears of Fancie* (1593).

For the episode of Soliman, Haleb, and Amurath, no direct source is known, although it has been suggested that Kyd had in mind Greene's *Selimus* (1591), where Selimus slays both his brothers, Corcut and Acomet, on different occasions.[1] The names of the respective figures have the same metrical quantity, and in *Selimus* one may also find a 'Hali' and an 'Amurath'. The deaths in *Selimus* have an historical basis, while those in *Soliman* have none; nevertheless, the connexion is rather thin, and we must not preclude the possibility that Kyd simply invented the rather elementary action of I. v., bearing in mind perhaps only the most general and commonplace traditions about the impetuous violence and cruelty of the Turks.

One minor source, indicated by Boas, is important in respect of date: Basilisco (IV. ii. 43) demands of Piston, who unawares has pricked him from behind with a pin:

> Why, sawst thou not how *Cupid*, God of love,
> Not daring looke me in the marshall face,
> Came like a coward stealing after me,
> And with his pointed dart prickt my posteriors?

This is certainly a parody of the dying Tamburlaine (*II Tamburlaine*, [V. iii.] 4459 ff.).

> See where my slave, the uglie monster death,
> Shaking and quivering, pale and wan for feare,
> Stands aiming at me with his murthering dart,
> Who flies away at every glance I give,
> And when I look away, comes stealing on.

It is also possible that Perseda's device for self-immolation, which is not in Wotton, was suggested by Olympia's ruse (itself taken from Ariosto) likewise in *II Tamburlaine*; each heroine escapes the attentions of the anti-hero by tricking him into killing her.

Basilisco's exclamation, 'O coelum, O terra, O maria, Neptune' (IV. ii. 65), was thought by Boas and Murray a general burlesque perhaps on Ovid, but W. P. Mustard pointed out that it is actually a direct quotation from Terence;[2] another Latin tag (V. iii. 16–17) is unidentified, but perhaps a paraphrase or corruption of Justinian.[3]

III. *Date*

The basic limits for *Soliman* are 1578 (the publication of *A Courtlie Controversie*) and 20 November 1592 (the entry of the play

---

[1] 'Shakespeare and *Solyman and Perseda*', *MLR*, LVIII (1963), pp. 484–5.
[2] Mustard, 'Notes', p. 86.
[3] Murray, liii–liv.

for publication). Acting had been inhibited in London and at the Court since 23 June of the same year, and so the performance before the Queen implicit in the last lines of the play (see below) must have taken place before that summer. Between the extreme limits we can narrow the date of *Soliman* somewhat by considering several factors.

To begin with, whether or not we accept that the play is by Kyd, it does bear a recognizable relationship to *The Spanish Tragedy*. Sarrazin originally held[1] that *Soliman* was the 'tragedy' Hieronimo professed to have written 'when in *Tolledo* there I studied', i.e. while Kyd was at school, and that the playlet in the greater tragedy was abridged by Kyd from his own earlier work. Unless, however, we account for such dating factors as the parody of *II Tamburlaine* by positing revision and augmentation, any date before 1587 is precluded; and Boas (lvi–lvii) has argued persuasively that the treatment of Wotton's story, more refined in *Soliman* than in *The Spanish Tragedy*, indicates a later and more mature exploitation of the plot, rather than a primitive effort from which Hieronimo's playlet might be abstracted. We shall argue in Chapter VI that the original 'spanes commodye donne oracioe' was probably an attempt (by Kyd or another) to capitalize on the previous success of *The Spanish Tragedy*, a motive which as well might explain the choice of story in *Soliman*.

A stylistic comparison between the plays suggests that *Soliman* is later, according to the impression of Boas, and the statistical analysis of Wiehl; and Boas also finds a more experienced hand in the metre. These are difficult contentions to substantiate, especially inasmuch as *Soliman* is less carefully finished a work than *The Spanish Tragedy*, but one does gain the impression of a somewhat softer, less enthusiastically formal technique of composition and versification, less deliberate pathos and plangency, less shock value or sensationalism; *Soliman* seems a mellower play. Furthermore, the verbal repetitions from *The Spanish Tragedy* to *Soliman* in almost all cases suggest precedence in *The Spanish Tragedy*, if self-imitation in an author admits of precedence at all; and in a few cases a bit of irony or expansive rhetoric seems simply more advanced in *Soliman* than in *The Spanish Tragedy*, or at least subtler. Brusor in Hieronimo's playlet, for example, is a deep-dyed villain just as he is characterized by Wotton, where in *Soliman*, Brusor has been altered considerably in the direction of sympathy. Would not the more

[1] Sarrazin, pp. 43–45; followed by Arthur Acheson, *Shakespeare, Chapman, and 'Sir Thomas More'* (London, 1931), p. 196.

sympathetic version of Brusor, if it had already existed, have seemed
more appropriate to Kyd for his wronged hero to impersonate?
W. J. Lawrence observes as well that Kyd might not have thought
it necessary to provide a summary of Hieronimo's play-within-play
before its performance if the plot of the playlet were generally
known, through prior dramatization, to a theatre-going audience.[1]

Baldwin's dating arguments[2] are based on three unacceptable
contentions: (1) that Kyd changed the age of Erastus from the
'fifteene' of his source to 'not twentie', so that Edward Alleyn, who
was nearly twenty in 1585-6, might play the part at a Court performance on 27 December 1585, and hence (2) that the play belonged
to the Admiral's Company; (3) that the compliment of the character
Death to the Queen at the end was occasioned by the Parry and
Babington plots against her life in 1584; and (4) that the seven years'
service Kyd entered into with his 'noble lord' precluded play-
writing.

We have already discarded the last-mentioned premise (see
Chapter III); the argument about Erastus's age is absurd (the
English simply did not mature as rapidly as southern peoples), and
there is no evidence whatever for supposing either that *Soliman*
was an Admiral's play or that it was played at Court on the date
named by Baldwin. As for the suggested attempt on Elizabeth's life,
it might just as easily be Tychborne's (1586), about which Kyd
probably had already written a poem (see Chapter VI), or simply a
general compliment unrelated to any specific occasion. Baldwin's
arguments, as usual, are annoyingly arbitrary and correspondingly
dogmatic.

It has, however, been argued and upon occasion credited that the
passing reference to the valour of the Spanish Knight at the tournament of Rhodes (I. iii. 36) would scarcely have passed before the
Queen in the years of and immediately surrounding the Armada—
say 1586-9—and hence that the play was presented at Court either
before or after that period. But the argument is weak, for in reality
the Spanish Knight's valour is little enough to praise. Consider the
pageant of competing knights: the Prince of Cyprus welcomes each
with an epithet or two, and each replies with his 'motto', or *curricu-
lum vitae* in brief. First comes the 'thrise-renowned Englishman,/
Graced by thy country, but ten times more/By thy approved
valour in the field'. He gained his knighthood in Scotland with his

---

[1] 'Plays within Plays', *ES*, XXXIII (1904), 388.
[2] 'On the Chronology of Thomas Kyd's Plays', p. 346.

lance, 'In France . . . tooke the Standard from the King', and bears
scars incurred in Irish wars. Second there is a 'faire Knight of
Fraunce;/well famed . . . for discipline in warre'. He recounts of
himself only a combat at 'single Rapier' with 'a Romane much
renownd,/His weapons point impoysoned for my bane'.[1] The Turk's
'noted word of charge' is characteristically bloody and cruel, glory-
ing in the slaughter and religious conversion of his foes; but with
the Spaniard, we have:

> Cyp. Welcome, *Castilian*, too amongst the rest,
>   For fame doth sound thy valour with the rest.
>   Upon thy first incounter of thy foe,
>   What is thy woord of courage, brave man of Spaine?
> Span. At foureteene yeeres of age was I made Knight,
>   When twenty thousand Spaniards were in field;
>   What time a daring Rutter made a challenge
>   To change a bullet with our swift flight shot;
>   And I, with single heed and levell, hit
>   The haughty challenger, and strooke him dead.

Now, we must realize that Kyd is portraying in this succession of
brags certain national characteristics as they appeared to Elizabethans. The English warrior is still essentially chivalric ('chargde
my Launce') and concerned with taking a standard rather than
annihilating his opposition; he is hardy, scarred, and above all
experienced. The Frenchman is 'faire', and best at duelling with a
light weapon—scarcely a real martialist. The Turk is unpitying,
grandiose, and bloodthirsty; where the Englishman fights for 'my
countries cause', Brusor has been 'chiefe commaunder of an hoast'
which routs the Persians, and stains the African desert with
Moorish blood. But the Spaniard has gained his knighthood with an
extremely dubious action: he has shot, not hacked or hewn, an
opponent—confounding chivalry with assassination, knightly arma-
ments with the 'villainous saltpetre'. The Rutter was 'daring', but
our Spaniard had twenty thousand companions; we are reminded
of the charge 'bravely' attempted by Portuguese Don Pedro against
the Spaniards (*Sp. Tr.*, I. ii. 40) which was repulsed by 'Don
Rogero . . . with our Musketiers'. We may also note that the
Prince of Cyprus commends the Spaniard's valour in somewhat
diffident terms, and by hearsay at that. The bravery given instance
of by the Spaniard himself would hardly be treasonous even in 1588

---

[1] Sarrazin, p. 107, compares Laertes in *Hamlet*.

before the Queen; acting might even turn Cyprus's compliments to pure irony.

Any dating of *Soliman* must consider the vogue of plays about Turkish, Moorish, and Near Eastern wars and warlords which followed hard on the success of *Tamburlaine* (1587). *Soliman* is definitely part of a group of modern history plays, founded partially on romances, which includes *Selimus* (1591). Peele's lost *Mahomet and Hiren the Fair Greek*, *The Battle of Alcazar* (1589), *Alphonsus, King of Aragon* (1587-9), *Tamar Cham* (1588 *et seq.*), and *The Wars of Cyrus* (rev. 1588). We have shown that *Soliman* postdates *II Tamburlaine* (1587-8), and possibly *Selimus*; it is also arguable that Erastus's description of 'the Moore upon his hot Barbarian horse' (I. ii. 56) alludes to the occasion in *The Battle of Alcazar* (V. i. 239) when the Moor 'mounteth on a hot Barbarian horse', but the connexion might also be proverbial.

Of considerable interest are two verbal parallels between *Soliman* and *Edward II* (commonly dated 1592, but possibly earlier):

> It is not meete that one so base as thou
> Shouldst come about the person of a king.
> > (*Soliman*, I. v. 71-72)

> I tell thee tis not meet, that one so false
> Should come about the person of a prince.
> > (*Edward II*, [V. ii.] 2248-9)

And subsequently, from *Soliman*:

> My gratious Lord, when Erastus doth forget this favor
> Then let him live abandond and forlorne.
> > (IV. i. 198-9)

And from *Edward II*:

> And when this favour Isabell forgets,
> Then let her live abandond and forlorne.
> > ([I. iv.] 594-5)

There are a few other less compelling parallels between the plays,[1] but these cited are too close for coincidence; one must be echoing the other. But it is most difficult to establish whose the debt is, in spite of the general assumption that Kyd borrowed from Marlowe. The logic of the conceit 'one so base . . . about the person of a king' is perhaps more consistent than 'one so false' (i.e. it is scarcely 'meet' for any person, slightly or greatly *false*, to attend a king, while there are degrees of 'baseness' which might logically determine the propriety of such access), and one tends to suppose, *in vacuo*,

[1] See Carrère, p. 433.

that *Soliman* originated the couplet and *Edward* altered it. On the other hand, in the 'abandond and forlorne' coincidence, metrical smoothness is on Marlowe's side, and Kyd looks like the imitator. All in all, it would, I think, be injudicious to base any dating argument on the definite precedence of either Marlowe or Kyd in these instances, but if Kyd is the copyist the conventional sequence of these plays is wrong,[1] and if Marlowe is, nothing need be rearranged.

The limits of date for *Soliman*, then, are effectively 1588–92, with the evidence of *II Tamburlaine*, or 1591–2 if *Selimus* is a factor. I have inclined toward the later date chiefly because the few contemporary allusions to the play, and plays appearing to relate in some way to it (*Edward II*, *King John*, Nashe's *Have With You*, *Satiromastix*, *Romeo and Juliet*: see below) are of 1592 or later; but this is a fairly casual opinion.

IV. *Publication, Stage History, and Influence*

Soliman and Perseda was entered for publication by Edward White on 20 November 1592. The first extant edition, however, is undated,[2] printed by White for Edward Allde, and is known in one copy only; conventionally it is assigned the date of the year of entry, 1592.

The undated edition of *Soliman*, like *The Spanish Tragedy*, seems to be what is sometimes termed an 'octavo in fours', or more simply a quarto printed on double-sized paper cut in half: there is a conspicuous torn edge on H4, and the chain lines are vertical.[3] The text is relatively free from corruption, and the copy almost certainly not reportorial; *1592* should form the basis of any modern edition.

White reissued the play in 1599 in a new edition, incorporating a few minor corrections, and dated 1599 in the colophon. Again the imposition was in quarto, but the paper probably double-sized.[4] *1599* is a fairly common book; one of the two copies in the British Museum bears the words 'Newly corrected and amended' on the

---

[1] As in, for example, *Annals of English Drama*, pp. 54, 56.

[2] For the undeniable evidence that the undated edition precedes the 1599 edition, see Boas, lv, and Murray, ix.

[3] Murray, vii, insists on calling this book an octavo, and Boas's description of it as a quarto—which is perfectly correct—'mistaken'. The only distinction between quartos and 'octavos in fours' is in the size of the original paper stock; there is no difference in printing method.

[4] Folger's copy (Murray, ix) has torn edges two to a gathering. Murray incomprehensibly adduces that because there is a spelling variation in the running head on every fourth leaf that the book is therefore again an octavo. The irregularity he notes is evidence, of course, for quarto imposition.

title-page,[1] evidently stamped in by hand after the printing,[2] but this is properly only a point of issue, not edition. The only substantial correction in *1599* is that one line (III. i. 34) which had accidentally been misplaced by the compositor of *1592* between II. ii. 75 and 76 is restored to its intended place;[3] but other alterations of spelling, italicizing, and punctuation in *1599* appear to lack any authority beyond the printer's; the copy for *1599* was evidently *1592*, of which it is essentially a paginary reprint, with identical collation.

We have no record of subsequent printing of *Soliman* before Hawkins's *Origins* of 1773. Harington's collection of plays included 'Solimon and Perseda', probably the 1599 quarto, since the spelling 'Solimon' appears only on the title-page of that edition; *1592* has 'Solyman' on the title-page and 'Soliman' in the running heads and generally in the text. Oxindon possessed 'Tragedy of Soliman & Perseda 1599'. Rogers and Ley list 'Soliman and Persida'; Archer has 'Solyman and Persida T[ragedy]', while in Kirkman it is 'Solimon & Perseda C[omedy]'; likewise Marsh considers it a comedy, '*Solyman* and *Perseda*. c.'[4]

Hawkins took his text from Garrick's copy of the 1599 quarto, and

---

[1] Hazlitt (*Dodsley*, V, 254) says that Philip Bliss's copy (which may be the same) was so designated.

[2] See McKerrow, *Bibliography*, p. 230, discussing this particular instance.

[3] This correction quite possibly was made during the press run of *1592*, but we have no copy to prove so. The line, 'That for retaining one so vertuous' is found at the top of E2ʳ in our one extant copy of *1592*, and correctly placed in *1599* at the bottom of E2ᵛ. But what actually happened was probably that the type fell out of the case from the top of E3ʳ, which occupies the identical position in the outer forme that E2ʳ occupies in the inner (see McKerrow, *Bibliography*, pp. 16–17) and was accidentally replaced in the corresponding position in the other forme. Now if a printer noticed, reading a pull, that the line was out of place, he might remember the episode, and guess what had happened; but because it is easier to fit in the extra type at the leaded bottom of a page than at the crowded top of another set-up page, beneath a running head, he would restore the line to its correct sequence by adding it to the foot of E2ᵛ. Thus the compositor of *1599* would only be following line for line some press-corrected copy of *1592*, in giving the right order to the lines. This would explain how the *1599* compositor happened to catch the error, as it is rather improbable that anyone would adduce the correction at seven years' distance without consulting the original copy again, and the identical appearance of both quartos in most respects argues against that possibility. *Ergo*, the extant example of *1592* is of an early uncorrected state of the printing, and *1599* is set up from a copy of the lost later state, with additional MS. corrections probably by the publisher or printer. Boas's explanation of the confusion (p. 196) is itself somewhat confusing; but Murray (ix) has completely misunderstood both Boas's note and what had happened in the print-shop.

[4] Greg, III, 1312, 1315, 1326, 1336, 1350; IV, 1660.

Hazlitt, who believed that 'there was only one impression, which received no fewer than three title-pages', merely reprinted Hawkins's text. About 1810, however, when the early drama was gaining enough popularity with collectors to inspire such type-facsimile reprints as Triphook's quartos, a type-facsimile of *1599* (without 'corrected and amended' on the title-page) was executed by J. Smeeton, of St. Martin's Lane, London. Smeeton's replica is distinguishable from the original 1599 quarto by its unmistakably post-Caslon type, its poor-quality paper, and a few errors in transcription, but although Smeeton doubtless had no intention of deceiving his or Triphook's clients, some scholars and collectors have confused the genuine quarto with the imitation. One copy of Smeeton's reprint in the British Museum, in which the inconspicuous Smeeton imprint has been trimmed away, was catalogued in the nineteenth century as the 1599 quarto, and, lamentably, Boas chose to regard it as such in the textual notes to his edition of 1901, preferring certain of its spurious variant readings to the true ones in the true quarto.[1] Moreover, the photographic facsimile prepared by John S. Farmer in 1912 perpetuated this ludicrous confusion by reproducing the Smeeton reprint, again the British Museum copy without Smeeton's imprint, as the genuine quarto.[2]

Save for this curious error, which laid open to question the whole range of his bibliographical technique, Boas's edition is workmanlike and serviceable, but a new edition of the play would be most welcome. There is no reprint whatever of 1592. In 1959 *Soliman* was edited as a dissertation at New York University by John J. Murray, and is available xeroxed; but Murray's edition is extremely undependable, both textually and critically.[3]

No auspices for *Soliman* are indicated in the printed copy, although the closing compliment to the Queen (V. v. 37 ff.) has been taken to suggest a Court performance. Baldwin's casual

---

[1] Boas's error was pointed out by, among others, A. W. Pollard, ' "Facsimile" Reprints of Old Books', *The Library*, Fourth Series, VI (1926), 310.

[2] Pointed out by W. W. Greg, 'Mr. Farmer's Facsimiles', *The Athenaeum*, no. 4455 (1913), 316; but Farmer was not claiming, as Murray (xi) states, to be reproducing the undated Grenville copy: Farmer merely mentioned the Grenville copy, and chose the facsimile because it looked the cleanest of the British Museum's examples.

[3] In Murray's edition a considerable quantity of blank verse is printed, for no reason presumably but that it scans a little roughly, as prose (pp. 24, 36, 52, 53, etc.) without any indication of this curious editorial liberty in the textual notes or elsewhere; and apparently no effort was made by Murray to collate more than one of the many copies available of *1599*.

allocation of the play to the Admiral's Men can be ignored, and Murray's contention that the livestock in the play (Basilisco's ass) could not be accommodated on the public stage is nonsense;[1] likewise, W. J. Lawrence's evidence for Inns of Court auspices has only the shadow of corroboration from a non-witness of 1780.[2] We have no considerable knowledge of the original properties of *Soliman*, save the negative testimony of Henslowe, who never mentions the play. That, and Shakespeare's undoubted acquaintance with it, led J. Dover Wilson to propose the Chamberlain's Men as proprietors of *Soliman*;[3] but any number of companies might as well have played it.

Dekker's *Satiromastix* (1601) contains a relevant passage:

> Horace: My name's Hamlet revenge: thou hast been
>   at Parris garden hast not?
> Tucca: Yes Captaine, I ha plaied Zulziman there.

'Zulziman' has invariably been interpreted as a corruption of Soliman (Tucca refers later in the play to 'Sultan Solimane'), and 'Paris Garden' means the Swan Theatre, built in the manor of Paris Garden on the Bankside about 1595.[4] Our only location of a performance, then, if Tucca's allusion is taken literally, would be in the Swan before 1601.

One more false lead is the tale retold as the sixth of the *Merrie Conceited Jests* of George Peele, 'The Jest of *George Peele* at *Bristow*'. In order to raise money, Peele promises the Mayor of Bristol to perform 'a certaine History of the Knight of the Rodes; and withall, how *Bristow* was first founded and by whom, and a briefe of all those that before him [i.e. the mayor] had succeeded in Office in that worshipfull Citie.'[5] The Mayor agrees, George bilks all the playgoers of their money, and lights out for London after performing no more than a gulling prologue. Now, of course, Peele's jest (if actually accomplished) no more demands an extant play of 'the Knight of the Rodes' (which in itself is probably a joke about Peele's

---

[1] See Glynne Wickham, *Early English Stages* (London, 1963), II, part I, p. 316. Banks exhibited his performing horse at the Cross Keys Inn (*Eliz. Stage*, II, 383), and what of the 'hot Barbarian horse' in *The Battle of Alcazar*?

[2] '*Soliman and Perseda*', *MLR*, IX (1914), 524.

[3] *King John*, ed. J. Dover Wilson (Cambridge, 1936), p. liii. Presumably Wilson means later proprietors, as *Soliman* itself predates the formation of the Company.

[4] See Wickham, p. 50; *Eliz. Stage*, II, 411; J. Q. Adams, *Shakespearean Playhouses* (Boston, 1917), pp. 161 ff.

[5] *Merrie Conceited Jests* (London, n.d. [*STC* 19542]), C1r.

familiarity with the English highways) than Sterne's *Tristram Shandy* demands an extant work of Slawkenbergius on noses. But Chambers's misleading note (IV, 47) implies that such a play by Peele actually existed, and Schick earlier, taking the same line, deduced from this that Peele had written *Soliman*.[1] Carrère goes on to affirm that Peele's ghost-title 'conviendrait, sans aucun doute, à la tragédie de *Soliman et Perseda*' (p. 251), and Murray, who has no more consulted the original jest than Carrère has, misquotes Peele (xliii) and declares that 'a play on the subject of *Soliman and Perseda* is evidently alluded to'. If we can draw anything at all from Peele's rag, it would be that Soliman or another lost play on the subject was current enough in the trickster's mind to suggest the subject of his imaginary performance, and hence that Peele's visit to Bristol took place after about 1588.

That *Soliman* never attained the popularity of *The Spanish Tragedy* is evident, both from its scant printing history and the paucity of allusions to it in its own time. Dekker's 'Zulziman' and Nashe's 'Basilisco and Crack-stone' passages have been cited and Dekker's Simon Eyre (*Shoemaker's Holiday*, V. iv. 90–91) says that he knows 'how to speak to a Pope, to Sultan Soliman, to Tamburlaine, an he were here'. But among contemporary dramatists only Shakespeare[2] seems to have been much taken by the play. A clear reference to the clowning of Basilisco and Piston in *King John* (I. i. 234–4) has long been known, and very probably the Prince of Morocco's brag (*Merchant of Venice*, II. i. 24–26) and a line or two elsewhere in the same play betray the influence of *Soliman* as well.[3] Less convincing analogies with *Hamlet* and *Venus and Adonis* have been suggested,[4] but there is perhaps more to be said for a connexion between *Soliman* and *Romeo and Juliet*;[5] all in all, the impression made upon Shakespeare by *Soliman* seems no less than that of Kyd's greater tragedy.

V. *Criticism*

Soliman has received practically no critical treatment. The re-

---

[1] *Archiv für neuere Sprachen*, XV (1893), 176.

[2] Attempts to trace the influence of *Soliman* in the work of Davenant and Settle are unimpressive: See Murray, xli–xlii, and K. Campbell, 'The Sources of Davenant's *The Siege of Rhodes*', *MLN*, XIII (1898), 363.

[3] See S. C. Chew, *The Crescent and the Rose* (Oxford, 1937), p. 254; *The Merchant of Venice* (Arden ed., London, 1927), p. 44.

[4] Murray, xxxvii–xl; A. S. Cook, 'Shakespeare, *Hamlet*, 3. 4. 56', *MLN*, XX (1905), 217.

[5] 'Shakespeare and *Solyman and Perseda*', pp. 481–3.

marks of the early scholars are directed mainly at the problem of authorship, bibliography, and historical significance of the play: Langbaine[1] says only, 'This play, I presume was never acted, neither is it divided into acts.' Hawkins pointed out that 'there is no doubt the author intended each act should close with the Chorus',[2] and divided it accordingly; Hazlitt adds no more than to theorize that *Soliman* was older than *The Spanish Tragedy*.[3] The magisterial Symonds declares that 'It hardly deserves notice, except as showing how the Tragedy of Blood took form',[4] and follows Hazlitt's unwarranted sequence of composition. A. W. Ward,[5] however, thought the play itself at least 'interesting', while concentrating his attention on the authorship (which he allows Kyd) and the influence of the play upon Shakespeare. Willard Farnham finds in *Soliman* 'the same lightly skillful touch (as in *The Spanish Tragedy*) in joining varied incidents of romantic fiction . . . less intrigue and more humour',[6] and Theodore Spencer emphasizes the medieval aspects of Kyd's concepts of death and tragedy.[7] Inevitably one German writer[8] finds *Soliman* so much better a play than *The Spanish Tragedy* that he cannot conceive of Kyd as the author of both.

Even Boas's concern with the quality of the play is subservient to his interest in its authorship, although he feels it 'would be well worthy of Kyd'. Boas goes on, however, (lxi), to censure the 'needless stain thrown on [Erastus's] honour by making him win back the chain from Lucina by the use of false dice', and Perseda's 'hypocritical method of vengeance on [Soliman]', which, 'more repellent far than her stabbing of Lucina, blurs disastrously at the close the fair image of her womanhood'. Today we must find this sort of criticism somewhat dated.

Soliman deserves more serious consideration than this by readers of Elizabethan literature, and at least the currency which a modernized edition would make possible. For, while doubtless *The Spanish Tragedy*, with which *Soliman* inevitably must suffer comparison, remains the superior and historically the more important tragedy there are elements in *Soliman*—the comic scenes, the repartee,

[1] *An Account of the English Dramatick Poets* (London, 1691), p. 550.
[2] Hawkins, *Origins*, II, 197.
[3] *Dodsley*, V, 254.
[4] *Shakespeare's Predecessors*, p. 390.
[5] *A History of English Dramatic Literature* (New York, 1899), I, 309–11.
[6] *The Medieval Heritage of Elizabethan Tragedy* (Oxford, 1963), p. 395.
[7] *Death and Elizabethan Tragedy* (New York, 1960), pp. 85, 182, 233 n.
[8] Arnold Schroer, *Uber Titus Andronicus* (Marburg, 1891), pp. 51–53. (Boas.)

certain isolated lines and passages, a few moments of pathos, and at least two characterizations—in which Kyd goes beyond what he has accomplished in the earlier play, and exhibits a dimension of talent which *The Spanish Tragedy* only hints at. We must read *Soliman* as we read the lesser Shakespeare, prepared to glean from it what is worth gleaning, and to tolerate a fair amount of husk for a handful of grain.

The tragic theme of *Soliman* is, surprisingly, far less successful within the play than the comic ornamentation, and no doubt the flatness of the romantic hero and heroine have gone far toward creating the critical atmosphere we have described. Erastus in particular, like Horatio, is a wooden lover, and his laments for his lost love and homeland do not approach either in rhetorical plangency or in conviction the more moving complaints of Hieronimo; nor is his joy at retrieving both losses handled with great dexterity. As in the rare moments of love and contentment in *The Spanish Tragedy*, Kyd (who seems to find any mood but melancholy a little awkward) reverts to stylized patterns of speech, to Euphuistic compliments, and unconvincing comparisons: e.g., in a moment of presumably untroubled bliss, Perseda's way of expressing her happiness is: 'Our present joyes will be so much the greater/When as we call to minde forpassed greefes/ . . . But if my Love will have olde greefes forgot,/They shall lie buried in *Persedas* brest' (V. i. 13 ff.). We are reminded of Bel-imperia's similar reflection upon 'stormy times', 'pain', and 'the joys that it [i.e. each hour] hath lost' during her supposedly pleasurable assignation with Horatio (II. ii. 6 ff.); and both heroines resort to maritime figures ('a ship at sea . . . may repair what stormy times have worn', and 'the Mariner upon the shore,/ when he hath past the dangerous time of stormes').

In many respects Perseda is like Bel-imperia, but she differs in appearing at least on occasion somewhat softer and more feminine: her outcry against the perfidy of men in general (II. i. 115 ff.) would never pass Bel-imperia's lips. But at a push she is capable of the same vigorous and self-immolating revenge as her Spanish equivalent, and the harshness of her treatment of Lucina (after Basilisco has proved incapable of such cruelty) reveals as dedicated a character in Perseda as Bel-imperia exhibits by stabbing her intended groom. Perhaps Kyd has not sufficiently reconciled for us the pitiable and forlorn girl of the early acts (Boas's 'fair image') with the stoical avenger of the final catastrophe, but after Perseda's summary judgement on Lucina we will not be unduly surprised to see a similarly unpitying fate meted out to her primary antagonist. If Kyd meant us to recognize a process of self-confirmation in Perseda's moral purpose during the play, the scene (IV. i) in which she prefers death to dishonour may serve, beyond its obvious and stereotyped romantic use, to prepare us for further acts of Stoicism; and the 'forpassed greefes' she hints at subsequently may have shaped her character accordingly. But whatever Kyd's intent was in portraying a woman at once delicate, tearful, and sternly vindictive, he has not quite provided dramatic justification for Perseda's turnabout.

Soliman himself is the finest of Kyd's tragic figures in the play, and one must recall that the title of the work is not 'Erastus and Perseda'; *Soliman* is not plotted like *Romeo and Juliet*. Soliman's character is unlike any in *The Spanish Tragedy*, and for that matter unlike Tamburlaine's or any previous tyrant's. Kyd has expanded him from the bare sketch of a love-sick emperor in Wotton to a remarkable amalgam of sensitivity and barbarousness, of brutality and remorse, cruelty and kindness. All his actions follow a pattern of impetuousness followed by regret: he slays his brother Amurath (as well he ought, for Amurath has slain Haleb on slight provocation), but his repentance even for this deed of justice is immediate and convincing:

> Nay, wretched *Solyman*, why didst not thou
> Withould thy hand from heaping bloud on bloud?
> Might I not better spare one joy than both?
> If love of *Haleb* forst me on to wrath,
> Curst be that wrath that is the way to death.
> If justice forst me on, curst be that justice
> That makes the brother Butcher of his brother.

Soliman's self-searching thoughts on wrath and justice raise him above all other characters in intellectual stature, while in his precipitous cruelty and unbridled passions he can sink below even the clowns. Like Hieronimo, he is preoccupied with motives, justice, and even righteousness, but, unlike the wronged father, he is a man of too much action. The tragic dignity, which alternates in Soliman with mere wantonness, is confirmed by the dignity of his speech. On the deaths of his brothers he concludes an evocative soliloquy with a moving couplet:

> Thus, thus let *Soliman* passe on his way,
> Bearing in either hand his heart's decay.

But the course of Soliman's character is to harden, as Perseda correspondingly hardens, while the action progresses: his remorse for Erastus's death is obvious, but instead of accusing himself in so many words, he makes a very inadequate expiation by doing away with most of his accomplices. Similarly, his treatment of Brusor after Perseda's death shows that while his guilt in the mock-trial of Erastus still hangs heavy upon him he is no more willing than earlier to admit that he himself was the prime instigator of the injustice. Brusor, meanwhile, has repented the momentary jealousy which prompted him to suggest Erastus's death to Soliman, and come to a realization of his own responsibility. Lucina is seen 'Butchered dispightfully without the walles' of Rhodes, and Brusor laments:

> Unkinde *Perseda*, couldst thou use her so?
> And yet we usd *Perseda* little better.
>
> (V. iv. 5–6)

Finally, when Soliman, wild to avenge the death of Perseda upon any unoffending object but himself, having slain Basilisco and Piston, demands of Brusor, 'What was *Erastus* in thy opinion?' either Brusor is taken in by the Sultan's subtlety and provides the wrong answer or (more consistently) he has had enough of the whole business and tells the truth: Erastus was fair spoken, wise, courteous, gentle, affable, kind, liberal, and 'all in all, his deeds heroyacall'. Soliman sends him promptly off to the block.

Soliman's end somewhat mitigates the impression we have had of brutality gradually overbalancing kingship and self-knowledge. His long last speech brings the play to a close with a calm acceptance of both death and the deeds he has done; he regrets, but he is not oppressively humble; his demise is, of course, unchristian, but in its Stoicism there is implicit the admiration of the author and the age:

> Ah, Janisaries, now dyes your Emperour,
> Before his age hath seene his mellowed yeares.
> And if you ever loved your Emperour,
> Affright me not with sorrowes and laments:
> And when my soule from body shall depart,
> Trouble me not, but let me passe in peace.
> . . .
> Forgive me, deere *Erastus*, my unkindness.
> I have revenged thy death with many deaths:
> And, sweete *Perseda*, flie not *Soliman*,
> When as my gliding ghost shall follow thee,
> With eager moode, thorow eternall night. . . .

'Revenge' is a somewhat naïve idea, in relation to Erastus, but Kyd may simply have felt obliged to pluck that string once more before the end of the play, if only to confirm Soliman's belief in his own stated motives. The character of a tyrant at once cruel, devious, and likeable—'quick to anger, quick to make amends'—is too complex for a simple resolution in the face of death. Soliman is the most developed and satisfying figure in his own tragedy, and definitely represents a depth of creativity not indicated in *The Spanish Tragedy*, or quite possibly in any earlier English play. For all the glory of Marlowe's language, Tamburlaine is a static mask of a man, and his creator never approaches the human insight, in an otherwise derivative characterization, of Soliman's.

Basilisco, however, the comic hero, is perhaps the most attractive character in the play, and one of the memorable comic characters in all Elizabethan drama. It is inadequate to define him by his antecedents: he goes far beyond the manners of italianate buffoon, native 'vice', or classical *miles gloriosus*. Nor is he a contriving trickster like Captain Crack-stone, nor an oafish blow-hard like Ralph Roister Doister or Sir John Oldcastle; he is portrayed as thin, like Malvolio (I. iii. 214–16), rather than fat, like Falstaff, and his affections are voluntary, not constitutional. He is not stupid. His courtly speech ('saunce dread of our indignation') recalls more Pistol's use of high-flown chivalric language than Falstaff's bombast; but, like Falstaff, in soliloquy he can be realistic enough about himself; yet he is at pains (as in II. ii. 86 ff., V. iii. 93–95) to excuse his own cowardice to himself under the cloak of discretion, and far more self-deluding than Shakespeare's braggart. He is plainly embarrassed when things go badly for him, as in the joust with Erastus, and more anxious to explain away his defeats than most braggart soldiers would be; though his conceit is irrepressible, it takes a number of nasty falls. And, what is most important about Basilisco, in relation to Kyd's characterizational skill, he is a completely consistent comedian in a time and medium which encouraged the sort of irrelevant zaniness Hamlet condemns in clowns. Thus while Basilisco finds himself in any number of absurd situations— with Piston on his back, on top of a 'charger' which is really a mule, sprawled in obeisance to the Turks after his fellow Christians have chosen death over conversion—he never enters into the horse-play. He is not the old give-and-take vaudevillian we find in *The Famous Victories* as Oldcastle, in *Selimus* as Bullithrumble, or in *The Merchant of Venice* as Launcelot Gobbo: he is a complete character, comic in an essentially tragic situation and not merely an excuse for crude sight-gags and slapstick, a pit-pleaser. And his language confirms his identity and singularity. Several of his speeches, including the celebrated *ubi sunt* oration of V. iii and the marvellous Mandevillian narrative of adventures he offers the Prince of Cyprus in I. iii, bear the stamp of fine writing. An occasional understatement or matter-of-fact aside very neatly points up the extravagance of most of his rhetoric:

Sooth to say, the earth is my Countrey, as the aire to the fowle or the marine moisture to the red guild fish: . . . I keepe no table to character my fore-passed conflicts. As I remember, there happened a sore drought in some parts of Belgia, that the jucie grass was seared with the Sunne Gods element: I held it pollicie to put the men children of that climate to the sword, that the mothers teares might releeve the pearched earth. The men died, the women wept, and the grasse grew; els had my Frize-land horse perished, whose losse would have more grieved me than the ruine of the whole Countrey . . . My mercy in conquest is equall with my manhood in fight.

'The men died, the women wept, and the grasse grew' is a magnificent line tucked inconspicuously among inflated conceits, and has the added and striking beauty of surprise. Likewise, when in his *ubi sunt* speech Basilisco modestly recalls:

> I am my selfe strong, but I confesse death to be stronger:
> I am valiant, but mortall, . . .

his simplest truism takes on a kind of significance only the long preparation of pomposity and exaggeration can lend it. Kyd's manipulation of Basilisco's self-consciousness and occasional straightforward confessional style makes him the rich character he is.

Piston is less of a developed personage than Basilisco; his forebears, the *commedia dell' arte* zany and the Plautine clever servant ('God sends fortune to fools. Did you ever see wise men escape as I have done?'), are obvious. He is capable of some seriousness—e.g. in his report of Erastus's death to Perseda, and his last respects to his slain mistress—but he is less the 'trusty Piston' of the source than a foil to Basilisco, necessarily pricking the braggart's bubble when the latter's extravagance exceeds tolerable limits.

Basilisco is an interesting character in the history of English drama, but Kyd's most important achievement in *Soliman*, I believe, is the more general one of bringing about a true confrontation of

comic and tragic themes within mixed scenes. When in III. ii,
Basilisco encounters Lucina and Perseda, both of whom are in
independent mourning for their lost lovers, the braggart jests, 'Why,
Lady, is not *Basilisco* here?/Why, lady, dooth not *Basilisco* live?'
and he goes on to make a crude suggestion about dividing his nights
and days between the two women, Lucina cuts him off with:

> Ah, how unpleasant is mirth to melancholy.

And Perseda adds,

> My heart is full; I cannot laugh at follie.

And both leave Basilisco to ruminate on his *faux pas*. Again, when
Perseda has learned of Lucina's involvement with the plot against
Erastus, she demands: '*Basilisco*, doest thou love me?' and when he
declares he will do anything to prove so, Perseda demands that he
stab Lucina. Now Basilisco 'Takes a dagger and feeles upon the
point of it'; presumably there is a pause, and then he replies:

> The point will mar her skin.

Perseda seizes the dagger and stabs Lucina; and Basilisco offers,
perhaps reluctantly, to dispose of the body. But a deed of considerable horror has been done, and Basilisco's only half-comic evasion
lends more pathos to the act than a dozen pleading lines of Lucina
might have done. Finally, the tardy bravery of Basilisco in the last
catastrophic scene (V. iv. 56–57, 72) concludes, as unreasoning courage must, in death.

The importance of these three confrontations of comedy with
tragedy, I think, may be stressed. We are accustomed to such
moments in Shakespeare—the renunciation of Falstaff, Falstaff and
Hotspur's body,[1] the death of Davy in *Henry V*, the souring of the
joke on Malvolio in *Twelfth Night*—but I doubt if we can find any
example of such a dramatic idea in extant English plays earlier than
Soliman. Any number of early tragedies or histories go about
'mingling kings and clowns', but do any before Kyd bring the two
into the same focus on any single occasion? Does comedy ever
comment on tragedy, or tragedy upon comedy, as Perseda and
Lucina do upon Basilisco's jesting, or Basilisco does on death itself,
and honour? Such a coming together of separately developed comic
and tragic lines create often a new level of pathos: the more 'human'

---

[1] A. W. Ward, *History*, I, 310, suggests that this incident may have been
inspired by Piston's rifling of Ferdinando's corpse.

comic characters are suddenly exposed to the great realities, love, death, and fortune, and the tragic characters, who are preoccupied with great themes, have their own pathos pointed up by the inappropriate foolery of a different kind of creature. The grief of Lucina and Perseda seems more believable after Basilisco makes light of it; their single expressions of annoyance at his raillery do more to objectify their sorrow than all the ornate euphuistic lamenting which preceded it. And Basilisco's helplessness with the dagger brings home both the seriousness of Perseda's act and the essential humaneness of the comic crew, caught up in the web of tragic intrigue which predominates in *Soliman*.

If Kyd was the first to exploit the dramatic potentialities of crossing comedy with tragedy, his innovation deserves the fullest recognition. In the union, or intersection of comic and tragic themes, a whole new sphere of mixed motives and characterological sophistication is opened up; the mere alternation of horse-play with high seriousness—with the comic relief withdrawing as required from the tragic stage—is far superseded by Kyd's more elaborately woven plot lines. In his manipulation of encounters and creation of an interdependence among tragic and comic characters, Kyd has added a new dimension of humanity to the lofty tragic figures, and a corresponding dimension of pathos to the comic. Basilisco is a true forerunner of Falstaff, in more than simple braggadocio and martial pretensions.

CHAPTER VI

TRANSLATIONS, LOST WORKS,
AND APOCRYPHA

I. *Cornelia*

Kyd's translation of Robert Garnier's *Cornélie*, by nature derivative as it was, proved his most celebrated work for nearly two centuries. Charles Crawford has identified twenty-one quotations from the play in *England's Parnassus* (1600),[1] and there are twenty-one more in *Bel-vedere* of the same year.[2] Even before Kyd's death a complimentary evocation, which names neither author, couples *Cornelia* with Shakespeare's *Lucrece*:

> You that haue writ of chaste *Lucretia*,
> Whose death was witness of her spotless life,
> Or pen'd the praise of sad *Cornelia*,
> Whose blameless name hath made her fame so rife,
> As noble Pompeys most renowned wife:
> Hither unto your home direct your eyes,
> Whereas, unthought on, much more matter lies.[3]

The 'home' where more matter lay was Lady Helen Branch, wife of the Lord Mayor, who died on 10 April 1594; the elegist implies that Kyd was alive at the time, which suggests, as is otherwise logical, that the elegy was composed between 10 April and 15 August, the date of Kyd's burial. In the following year W. Covell, in his *Polimanteia*, calls for proper recognition of literary merit, and for a day when 'should not tragicke *Garnier* have his poore *Cornelia* stand naked upon every poste: a work, howsoever not respected, yet excellently done by Th. Kyd'.[4] *Cornelia*, then, was evidently a *succès d'estime*, but not popular; as no doubt the author of the most notorious play on the public stage had intended. Edward Phillips

---

[1] Charles Crawford, ed., *England's Parnassus*, p. 377.

[2] See Charles Crawford, 'Belvedere, or the Garden of the Muses', *ES*, XLIII (1910–11), 206.

[3] Boas, lxxvi.

[4] The allusion was first pointed out by Oldys: see Collier's note in Hazlitt, *Dodsley*, V, 178. *Polimanteia* is frequently attributed to William Clerke, but some copies of *STC* 5883 expand the dedication's 'W.C.' to 'W. Covell'.

writes of Kyd, who 'seems to have been of pretty good esteem for versifying in former times',[1] only that 'There is particularly remembered his tragedy *Cornelia*', and for both Winstanley and Langbaine, *Cornelia* is Kyd's only known work.

In Chapter I we discussed briefly the dedication of *Cornelia*, and the significance of the dedicatee in Kyd's personal history. The translation was entered for publication on 26 January 1594 by Nicholas Ling and John Busby: 'A booke called Cornelia, Thomas Kydd beinge the Authour' (Arber, II, 644). The surviving edition of 1594 has a very plain title-page which does not name the author, but the dedication is subscribed 'T. K.' and at the end of the play appears 'Tho. Kyd'. In the 1595 second edition (actually a reissue of the 1594 sheets with a new title), published after Kyd's death, the dramatist's full name appears on the title-page of an individual book for the first time—and for the last, apparently, before the nineteenth century: 'Written in French, by that excellent Poet Ro: Garnier; and translated into English by Thomas Kid.'

The dedication itself permits us to date the translation with some precision.

Having no leisure (most noble Lady) but such as evermore is traveld with th' afflictions of the minde, then which the world affoords no greater misery, it may bee wondred at by some, how I durst undertake a matter of this moment: which both requireth cunning, rest, and oportunity. . . . Wherein, what grace that excellent GARNIER hath lost by my defaulte, I shall beseech your Honour to repaire with the regarde of those so bitter times and privie broken passions that I endured in the writing it.

And so vouchsafing but the passing of a Winters weeke with desolate *Cornelia*, I will assure your Ladiship my next Sommers better travell with the Tragedy of *Portia*. . . .

Now, this apology points strongly to composition after Kyd's arrest on 12 May 1593. The dedication itself must have been written after 14 December (see Chapter I), and the book came promptly to the press during January of 1594. Boas, however, is simply misreading the last sentence quoted above to adduce that Kyd 'devoted "a winter's week" at the close of 1593 or the beginning of 1594 to the translation' (lxxiv): it is the Countess, not Kyd, who is vouchsafed the 'Winters weeks', a week of reading, presumably, not writing. But the date of composition of *Cornelia* may be limited, with some confidence, to the period in 1593 when Kyd was in and out of prison, in

---

[1] *Theatrum Poetarum*, ed. Egerton Brydges (London, 1800), I, 205–6.

correspondence with Sir John Puckering, and deprived of his patronage—'bitter times' indeed—and his apology for 'what grace that excellent GARNIER hath lost by my defaulte' need not be taken entirely as conventional coyness.

The source of the translation is, of course, Robert Garnier's *Cornélie*, and the inspiration no doubt the earlier translation of Garnier's *Marc Antoine* completed by the Countess of Pembroke on 26 November 1590 and published in 1592.[1] Whether or not Kyd had read Garnier before projecting his own translation or examining Mary Herbert's remains in question;[2] and whether by following the example of nobility Kyd hoped to be taken up by them once again must rest a conjecture. While the translation is not altogether accurate, it is comparatively painstaking, and there is no indication that Kyd regarded it entirely as hackwork for the sole purpose of advancing himself.

[1] There remains a puzzling problem involving, once again, the play *Selimus: Cornelia*, IV. i. 63–65 reads 'I love, I love him deerely. But the love/That men theyr Country and theyr birth-right bears/Exceeds all loves . . .'. This is in turn a close rendering of Garnier's 'Je l'aime cherement, je l'aime; mais le droit/ Qu'on doit à son païs, qu'à sa naissance on doit,/Toute autre amour surmonte . . .'. Now Crawford (*Parnassus*, pp. 399–400) pointed out that three lines in *Selimus* appear to have been borrowed from Kyd's Garnier: 'I love, I love them dearly, but the love/Which I do beare unto my countries good,/Makes me a friend to noble *Selimus* . . .' (*MSR*, 945–7). However, if we accept Kyd's own account of the date of his translation, Crawford's natural inference that *Selimus* was copying from Kyd strikes an awkward snag, for *Selimus* is almost without question pre-1593. It was published without entry 'as it was played by the Queenes Majesties Players', in 1594, a part of the spoils of the break-up of the Queen's Company (*Eliz. Stage*, II, 113–14). Now between 3 February 1594 and April, plague inhibited all performances and between the restoration of playing and 8 May, when 'they broke' (Henslowe) the Queen's Company was managed by Henslowe; *Selimus* does not appear among the plays enacted by them in that period. And before 3 February, and indeed throughout 1593, continuous plague kept the Queen's Company on the road. Furthermore, Greene, who, *pace* Churton Collins, is almost certainly the main author of *Selimus*, died on 3 September 1592; unless *Selimus* was reworked for the 1593 road performances, there seem to be no explanations for the echo, if it is an echo. The remaining possibilities are (1) that Kyd actually translated *Cornélie* earlier than he claims—which I think a far-fetched hypothesis; (2) that the coincidence of words is accidental—which I think possible, but unlikely; (3) that *Selimus* was partly composed or revised by Kyd; and (4) that Greene knew the passage in Garnier, and echoed it independently—which is the least plausible of four alternatives. The whole sequence is most complicated and cloudy, and pending a more detailed investigation of the relationship of *Selimus* to Kyd's known work, I think no more can be asserted; but the possibility of Kyd's involvement in writing *Selimus* is intriguing, and far from preposterous in terms of style.

[2] See Chapter III, and Marion Grubb, 'Kyd's Borrowings from Garnier's *Bradamante*', *MLN*, L (1935), 169–71; and T. W. Baldwin, 'Parallels between *Soliman and Perseda* and Garnier's *Bradamante*', *MLN*, LI (1936), 237–41.

In 1744 Dodsley reprinted, for the first time, the quarto text of *Cornelia*, with some added editorial paraphernalia, and his edition was subsequently corrected and altered by Reed, Collier, and Hazlitt. Hazlitt retained the translation in his edition only because it 'happened that it completes Kyd's dramatic productions, and . . . it formed part of the former edition, which there has been a desire to preserve in its full integrity'.[1] A full old-spelling edition was prepared, in the heyday of German attention to the Elizabethans, by H. Gassner (Munich, 1894), which was quarried from by Boas in his *Works* of 1901; Gassner and, to a considerably greater extent, Boas provide comparisons with the French original, and catalogue Kyd's errors (which are many) and personal augmentations (which are fewer, but not negligible). Witherspoon, in the only extended investigation of Garnier's influence upon Elizabethan writers, calls *Cornelia* 'a paraphrase rather than a translation', and emphasizes 'the great freedom which [Kyd] allowed himself'. The poetic quality of Kyd's *Cornelia* shows no remarkable advance over that of his earlier original tragedies, but the writing is for the most part extremely skilful and meticulous, without being pedantic. Witherspoon characterizes the translation as 'far more spirited and vigorous than Lady Pembroke's, and . . . free from the stiffness which is so noticeable throughout *Antonie*', and praises Kyd's 'ingenuity in reproducing the varied effect of the original by the use of different strophe-forms, each of his choruses having its own peculiar metrical arrangement'. But readers today of Kyd's translations scarcely number with the readers of his original works, and Kyd himself would no doubt have been shocked to observe the turnabout taste has taken since his own epoch. Perhaps in the long run, however, regardless of its importance in relation to Shakespeare, *The Spanish Tragedy* has proved a more enduring work than either *Cornelia* or *Cornélie*, and the loss of 'next Sommers better trauell', a translation of Garnier's *Porcie*, less difficult to bear than that of a *Hamlet* earlier than Shakespeare's.

II. *The Householder's Philosophy*

Nashe's reflection on those who, 'renowncing all possibilities of credit or estimation . . . intermeddle with Italian translations' has been interpreted as an allusion to *The Housholders Philosophie, wherein is perfectly and profitably described, the true oeconomia and forme of housekeeping . . . first written in Italian by that excellent*

[1] Hazlitt, *Dodsley*, V, 176.

orator and poet Signior Torquato Tasso, and now translated by T. K., published at London by Thomas Hacket in 1588. But even if we lay aside the evidence of *Menaphon*, there are reasons to attribute this translation to Thomas Kyd. Boas (lxii-lxiv, and Notes) has very convincingly shown where the translator's additions in *Cornelia* parallel those in *The Householder's Philosophy*, and where *sententiae* in Kyd's known translation seem to derive from Tasso; certain peculiarities of phrasing and vocabulary, lapses of understanding in the original languages, and characteristics of compositional skill and poetic licence are common to both translations. Furthermore, there is no known writer of the period with the initials 'T. K.' whose work more closely resembles the translation than Kyd's,[1] and Meres, in one of his undependable parallels,[2] may be suggesting that Kyd is to be considered the English Tasso, as Watson the English Petrarch. Kyd's authorship of the translation has not been seriously questioned since 1901.

Hacket entered *The Householder's Philosophy* on 6 February 1588, and it was printed for him by John Charlwood in the same year (*STC* 23703). Evidently it was not very popular, for there is a second issue of the edition, of the same year, with a cancel title-page to which the words 'whereunto is anexed a dairie booke for all good huswives' have been added, and in complete copies the separately signed dairy book, evidently the work of Bartholemew or Ka: Dowe, follows the translation; the second issue collates []²×⁴ A–G⁴ [G4 blank]; A–B⁴C², with *The Householder's Philosophy* occupying the leaves through G4. The dairy book itself was entered separately on 9 July 1588, and has its own title-page in the combined edition: what Hacket had done, simply, was to take the unsold sheets of his two 1588 pamphlets and reissue them, with a new title-page, as a small 'nonce collection', presumably during 1588, as the new title preserves the original date and imprint.

Apparently no copy of the dairy book as separately issued has survived, and of the first and separate issue of *The Householder's Philosophy* only one copy is recorded, that in the Bodleian Library.

[1] 'T.K.' is an uncommon set of initials. Only this translation of Tasso and the 'Hendecasyllabon' discussed below employ such initials in the period in question; and the only appropriately named writer of similar pretensions they might also fit is Timothy Kendall, whose *Epigrams* appeared in 1576. But Kendall's literary style is altogether different from Kyd's, and far from compatible with the translation in question.

[2] G. G. Smith, ed., *Elizabethan Critical Essays*, II, 319; see C. S. Lewis, *English Literature in the Sixteenth Century* (Oxford, 1954), p. 430, on the undependability of Meres's parallels.

Of the second issue, there is an imperfect example in the British Museum, lacking the dairy book, and complete copies in the Bodleian, at the Massachusetts Historical Society, and the Huntington Library (uncut). Since 1588 the only reprint has been that of Boas, which is generally satisfactory, save that the 'Catalogue or Index of those things worth the memory contained in this booke' is reprinted with the original leaf-numbers, while the leaf-numbers themselves have not been copied; hence the usefulness of the index is rendered somewhat problematic.

The dedication is 'To the worshipfull and vertuous gentleman Maister Thomas Reade Esquier', and signed 'Your worships most affectionate T. K.' The dedicatee's name is too common to permit even a conjectural identification: there was a groom of the chamber, 'Thos. Read', who was leased a number of properties 'in consideration of service' in 1594, a 'Thos Reade' attached on a commission of rebellion in 1592, a Sir Thomas Reade who was buried in the parish of St. Helen's, Bishopsgate, where Watson may have lived; and a fair sprinkling of the same name in contemporary parish and legal records in London, to say nothing of the country, the Inns of Court, and the universities. Perhaps the most significant thing about the dedication is the very obscurity of its recipient—a comparatively rare phenomenon among contemporary dedications—and its implication that in 1588 Kyd was not altogether dependent on the courtly circle or his own patron for recognition and sustenance. *The Householder's Philosophy*, 'digested thus in haste . . . plaine and unpollished', is clearly work done for money, and both the modest brevity of the dedicatory poem and the choice of an uncelebrated dedicatee suggest that Kyd knew how little he had done and valued his work accordingly.

The printed marginal notes, consisting of explanations of points of geography and natural history, identifications of classical allusions, and one gloss on an Italian phrase, seem to be by the translator, but one must be less confident than Boas (p. 232) that 'the Index also is his addition'.

The original of the translation is Torquato Tasso's dialogue, *Il Padre di Famiglia*, probably written during his long imprisonment, and first published at Venice in 1583. It is notable that the three English writers who, prior to Kyd, show the most knowledge of and influence from Tasso's works, are Kyd's playwright colleague, Thomas Watson (*Amyntas*, based loosely on Tasso's pastoral), and his schoolfellows Thomas Lodge (*Glaucus and Scilla*, as well as shorter poems),[1] and Edmund Spenser. The only English edition of anything by Tasso previous to Kyd's translation was Gentili's Latin version of parts of *Gerusalemme Liberata* (published as *Solymeidos*, 1584, three parts); the earliest full translations of the epic are Carew's of 1594, and the Fairfax version of 1599. By then enough of Tasso's life was known in England to make possible a lost play (1594; rev. by Dekker, 1602), *Tasso's Melancholy*, which probably dealt with the lover's 'madness' for which Tasso was more than once incarcerated.

Given the circumstances of the translation, and the possibility that Kyd was merely doing piece-work for pay, it is questionable how seriously one ought to consider the relation of Tasso's Ciceronian Stoicism to Kyd's way of thinking in his original works. Boas (lxii–lxiii) has pointed only to a preference of 'the wise' for the autumn above all other seasons, in a passage added to Garnier by Kyd (*Cornelia*, II. 132–5), which he believes derived from the householder's remark in Tasso, but Kyd may have found out his seasonal preferences for himself in nature. There is, however, a general quality of temperance and judiciousness exemplified in Tasso's householder which might well have seemed congenial to the translator.

The prose of *The Householder's Philosophy* likewise is beholden to the original, and its refreshing bareness cannot wholly be accounted a result of Kyd's own predilection. But where additions are made to Tasso's text they are in the spirit and style of the translated matter—plain, straightforward, unornamented, and fluent, more conversation than declamation. There is no euphuism or related rhetorical trickery, and the choice among synonyms nearly always seems to be for the simpler word ('make more reckoning of those gaines which are gotte and followed with paine and sweat then those that through deceit, and unconsorted with some labor, have beene and yet are used to be gotton'): Kyd is closer to the chroniclers' direct narrative style than to the exfoliate bellettristic style of Lyly or Sidney or Greene's prose romances. Notwithstanding a certain involution of syntax, which in Kyd derives mainly from a somewhat legalistic overuse of periphrasis and qualifying clauses, *The Householder's Philosophy* is not difficult to read, and the translator has had the good sense for the most part to avoid passive constructions, sometimes employed by the original, in primary clauses. Latinate

---

[1] See Douglas Bush, *Mythology and the Renaissance Tradition in English Poetry* (New York, 1957), p. 84.

words are in frequent use, although sometimes in parallel or redundant construction with their Anglo-Saxon equivalents ('the Chizzel should not be so ponderous and heavie as the Mason may not lift'), but in general Kyd heeds Sir John Cheke's adjuration to keep one's English clear of continental or classical coinages, or to make it obvious, by italics or quotation, when such intrusions are being introduced. The few Latin and Italian tags, and the occasional word of French, duly so designated, are in keeping with such habits of quotation or illustration exhibited by the tragedies. We may also note that the verse-translations in *The Householder's Philosophy* are mostly into 'fourteeners', or poulter-metre, of which we have no other instance in Kyd's undoubted work (although the verse interspersed in prose writings and translations of the period is nearly always in this perhaps already quaint and outmoded form); but one longer passage of verse (p. 281) is in rhymed decasyllabic quatrains, and includes one macaronic rhyme and one Latin couplet.

III. *Lost Works*

It is quite possible that a play nearly as popular as *The Spanish Tragedy*, and of similar if not greater importance in the history of the English drama, but now not extant, was also the work of Thomas Kyd. The tag 'Hamlet revenge!' jocosely used by later playwrights and pamphleteers, is scarcely less common than 'Go by, Jeronimo', and bespeaks the original popularity and perhaps even the post-Shakespearian currency of a pre-Shakespearian *Hamlet*. The evidence for Kyd's authorship of this lost tragedy, to which Nashe alludes, is well known, and has undergone an enormous amount of sifting and reappraisal, especially in relation to the 'bad' quarto of Shakespeare's play and the problem of the provenance of the later German version *Der Bestrafte Brudermord*. The elaborate reconsideration by G. I. Duthie[1] of coincidences in the texts of the *Hamlet* first quarto and *The Spanish Tragedy*, in which evidence formerly used to link Kyd with the lost pre-Shakespearian *Hamlet* is presented as indicating memorial intrusions from *The Spanish Tragedy* into a reported text of *Hamlet*, raises many new questions, not all of which have been dealt with in any satisfactory manner. Carrère and others have conjecturally reconstructed the lost, or *ur-Hamlet*, and adduced from the reconstruction further inferences, necessarily and exponentially conjectural, about Kyd's dramatic technique and role in the development of revenge tragedy. But the

[1] *The Bad Quarto of Hamlet* (Cambridge, 1941).

problem of the lost *Hamlet* is primarily Shakespearian, and attempts to relate it to Kyd depend on so many independent variants and interdependent conjectures and assumptions that the accumulated uncertainty inherent in what is finally said about Kyd comes close to cancelling the value of the observations. We cannot hope, in the space of a few pages, to do justice even to the previous scholarship and the questions generally held to be open, much less proceed toward new answers or a consensus of old ones. Given this impracticality, along with the prospects of a result considerably diminished by (1) the fact that the play is after all lost, and (2) that nothing short of new external evidence can actually prove that Kyd wrote the lost play, I think it best to abandon this aspect of Kyd's canon, popular as it has been, to Shakespearian scholarship. If the study of Kyd's extant work can throw light on the problem for students of Shakespeare's *Hamlet*, the results belong in an estimate of that play and its sources; in the end there is less to be learned about Kyd from Shakespeare than about Shakespeare from Kyd.

By the same token, consideration of a putative *ur-Andronicus*, for which there is little or no external evidence, but a fair amount of internal suggestion, may be dispensed with here. Kyd's responsibility either for a part of the extant play, or for a non-extant earlier version, rests wholly upon speculation, and the basis of the speculation is no more than (1) parallelism in the plots of *Andronicus*, *Hamlet*, and *The Spanish Tragedy*, (2) a few rather puzzling verbal coincidences, which have a non-Shakespearian ring, and (3) a few scraps of evidence, which, however, tend to no single conclusion, that contemporaries linked *Andronicus* with *Jeronimo* when they thought of revenge plays. But again there are too many independent variables, and insufficient reward in conducting an examination of the *Andronicus* problems centred upon Kyd; even if the argument for two versions of the tragedy is admitted, the claims of George Peele on the earlier have about as much to recommend themselves as those of Kyd.

And another lost play has persistently been attributed to Kyd, however, with apparent justification: Henslowe records six performances of 'spanes commodye donne oracioe', or 'doneoracio', 'the comodey of doneoracio', or 'the comodey of Jeronymo', during 1592, and the usual inference has been that 'Henslowe is here mentioning some humorous fore-piece which it was customary to produce by way of introduction to the principal play'.[1] There is no longer

---

[1] Boas, xli.

any serious doubt, however, that the extant *First Part of Jeronimo*, as published in 1605, is not the comedy played for Henslowe. Nevertheless, much of the reasoning about the extant *First Part* has been curiously inadequate. Boas and Chambers detect in Jeronimo's lines (I. i. 25 ff.) about his 'yeare of Jubily', or fiftieth birthday, a direct reference to the Jubilee declared by the Roman Church for 1600, but the argument is extremely thin, and scarcely precludes the possibility of an allusion to a Jubilee in prospect—even at a distance of eight years—or to the Jubilee of 1550, or the stop-gap Jubilees held on occasion between 1550 and 1600. Boas (xlii) notes, too, that 'the constant jests . . . about Jeronimo's diminutive stature are probably suggested by the performance of *The Spanish Tragedy* by the Children of the Chapel in 1604', whereas they seem instead merely to refer to the actual size of the actor (see I. iii. 103, 114; II. iii. 65, 86; III. i. 33 ff., 46), presumably a child, who played the part. Chapel auspices are indeed suggested, for this play in its extant version, by the allusions to Hieronimo's smallness (and see also I. iii. 7, on Lazarotto's small size; but compare III. i. 40 ff.: Balthazar is comparatively tall), and by a probable play on the name of a Chapel actor, William Ostler, in II. iii. 20. The date of the surviving text can be limited by a few literary echoes, particularly in II. iii, a scene which may have been provided by the Children's Company: the whole scene is a semi-parodic imitation of *The Gentleman Usher*, III. ii. (*c.* 1602–4), produced by the Chapel, and I think we may identify echoes of *Julius Caesar* in II. iii. 26, and II. iii. 45. I. iii. 106 appears to echo *Hamlet*, II. ii. 189.

Unquestionably the style of *The First Part* is not Kyd's, and the dating considerations noted above indicate that Kyd could not have written the text as we have it. But I think it is unlikely that anyone fabricated *The First Part* out of thin air,[1] and far more probable that the extant play represents a revision or rewriting of the original 'spanes commodye', and hence that it is fairly close, at least in plot, to the early fore-piece. Given the existence of such a fore-piece, one can hardly believe that whatever hack turned out the version of *The First Part* which survives would not avail himself of it, at least

---

[1] Boas's contention that the old play was strictly unlikely to 'have suddenly appeared by itself in 1605' (xli–xlii) is unconvincing: if the MS turned up, why not print it? And Pavier could scarcely combine *The First Part* in any form with *The Spanish Tragedy* before acquiring the latter property from Edward White in 1599. As to the time lapse between acting and printing, we have only to compare the case of *The Jew of Malta* or *Faustus*: there may, of course, have been earlier editions which perished.

in recollection or report. And if the abortion were, in fact, totally original, would not the publisher, Thomas Pavier, point out that fact as a selling-point? It is simply a more economical hypothesis to assume that the 1605 text is based on a lost version played for Henslowe in 1592.

One can make a further inference about 'spanes commodye', that it was not a genuine 'first part' of a pair of linked plays—like *Tamburlaine* or *Antonio and Mellida*—but rather, even with Henslowe, a comedy (possibly slapstick) predicated on the tragedy. Boas declares that 'in *The Spanish Tragedie* itself there are several allusions which seem to assume a knowledge in the audience of events prior to the opening of the action, and apparently handled in a preliminary piece', but his supporting instances are valueless. The extant *First Part* is manifestly 'after' *The Spanish Tragedy*, even to the extent of duplicating in little a few of the principal events in the tragedy (see especially II. iv. 115 ff.), and if the plot of the *First Part* is based on 'spanes commodye', the earlier version must have been similarly indebted toward the tragedy. A further consideration is that a truly preliminary play would almost necessarily concern Andrea primarily, and end, tragically, in his death, and the capture of Balthazar. Even if the action ended before the war with Portugal, Andrea would have to be the main character; hence, why is it the comedy of 'donne oracioe'? Horatio is the lover of the tragedy proper, but not of the action summarized by Andrea's ghost, and if the fore-piece was the comedy of Horatio, one can explain the situation only as the outcome of an effort to capitalize on the popularity of the tragedy by 'inferring' a comedy concerning the romantic hero of the popular play in happier times. And there is no reason to require that Kyd himself provided the comic 'preliminary' sequel, any more than that Shakespeare need have written *The Tamer Tamed*.

A conjectural reconstruction of the sequence would be: (1) Kyd's *Spanish Tragedy*, (2) 'spanes commodye', by Kyd or anyone else, before 1592, and (3) the revision, probably after 1602, now confidently titled *The First Part of Jeronimo*, and probably performed and/or commissioned by the Children of the Chapel, in line with their policy of reviving the old standards—as apparently they did, without permission, in the case of *The Spanish Tragedy* itself.

IV. *Poems, Fragments, and Apocrypha*

In 1586 appeared a slim pamphlet, printed by John Wolfe, who introduced Machiavelli and Aretino, in Italian, into Elizabethan

England, entitled *Verses of Prayse and Joye written vpon Her Majesties preservation wherevnto is annexed Tychbornes lamentation written in the towre with his owne hand and an avnswere to the same.* The collection consists of five short poems, two in Latin with English translations, on the subject of Queen Elizabeth's successful escape from the Babington, Tychborne, and Salisbury plots against her life; no publisher is named, and it is possible that the pamphlet was privately circulated. One of the poems is the graceful elegy attributed to Tychborne, 'My prime of youth is but a frost of cares', and the 'aunswere' to it is titled, 'Hendecasyllabon T. K. in cygneam cantione Chidiochi Tychborne'. As the only other 'T. K.' of the period with printed poetry to his credit is Timothy Kendall, whose epigrams (1576) are totally dissimilar in style to this curious counter-elegy, one may at least entertain the possibility of attributing the poem so signed to Thomas Kyd. In substance, the poem is nothing but a mechanical reply, image by image, to Tychborne's elegy, and scarcely worth individual appraisal; Boas describes it as 'an adaptation of Tychborne's verses, converting his self-reproaches into fierce invectives', and, earlier (xxv), as 'a specimen of his non-dramatic hack work'. Whether or not, however, the *Hendecasyllabon* is considered Kyd's work, we have no justification for supposing, with Boas, that 'probably T. K. was the writer of the whole tract', Latin elegiacs and all, and the verbal parallels which Boas provides in support of such a contention are merely commonplaces of apostrophe and epithet. We have no other indication of Kyd's involvement in the debilitating enterprise of Court-oriented compliment, save possibly the conclusion of *Soliman and Perseda*, and indeed the passage of verse here ascribed to 'T. K.' is not long or varied enough to admit of much discriminatory analysis in attribution. For want of a better prospect, Kyd may be proposed as the author of *Hendecasyllabon*, and possibly of the remaining unascribed poems, but the proposition is no more than tentative.

Three of the extracts printed by Robert Allott in *England's Parnassus* (1600) naming Kyd as their author are not from *Cornelia*, and have been reprinted by Boas (p. 294), as 'Fragments of lost poems or plays by Kyd'. Of these, the longest, which was elaborately considered by Schick as a possible fragment of a chorus in the pre-Shakespearian *Hamlet*,[1] has been shown to be actually a part of Sylvester's 'Babylon' (before 1594);[2] Allott is far from dependable

---

[1] J. Schick, ed., *The Spanish Tragedy* (London, 1898), xliii; Boas, xxv.
[2] Crawford, ed., *England's Parnassus*, p. 484.

in his attributions, and the remaining unidentified fragments may similarly be called in question. If they are genuinely Kyd's, we have five more lines of undistinguished and sententious verse to add to his canon.

The temptation to distribute the anonymous drama, prose, and poetry of the Elizabethan era among known writers has not omitted to implicate Kyd, and at least eight otherwise unattributed plays and a news-pamphlet have at one time or another been credited to his pen.[1] None of the attributions is particularly convincing, but two (*Arden of Feversham*, and the prose pamphlet, *The Murder of John Brewen*) have been reiterated with some frequency. *John Brewen* is reprinted by Boas among Kyd's *Works* on the strength of a 'contemporary' MS. signature 'Tho. Kydd' added to the foot of the last printed leaf,[2] and another signature on the title-page which Boas later reconsidered, and declared 'that of the printer, John Kyd, and not . . . that of the author, Thomas, which is appended at the end of the pamphlet'.[3] But apparently the Puck of bibliographers, John Payne Collier, had once again been active among the Lambeth books with his watered ink,[4] and this uncharacteristic attribution to the dramatist and poet may now be painlessly extracted from his canon. No internal evidence supports it, and, after editing out Collier's forgery, no external evidence remains. Probably the coincidence of surnames of the publisher and the writer proved too stirring to Collier's vigorous historical imagination to be left unimproved upon, and out of the fabricated signatures has emerged a whole family relationship—John was Thomas's brother—which took in, among others, Sir Sidney Lee and the *DNB*.

At least two scholars have devoted a considerable amount of energy to the problem of *Arden*, but their results have been thoroughly

---

[1] In addition to *Arden*, *John Brewen*, and *Edward III* (mentioned below), Kyd's hand has been sought in *Taming of a Shrew*, *The Rare Triumphs of Love and Fortune*, *King Leire*, in the reportorial early texts of Shakespeare's 2 and 3 *Henry VI* and *Richard III*, and in *Titus Andronicus* (see above); see especially Fleay, *Biographical Chronicle*, II, 26–35, and *Eliz. Stage*, III, 397. Carrère, pp. 436 ff., considers some of these attributions, and summarizes the adequate negative evidence. I have raised the question of Kyd's hand in *Selimus* (p. 169, n. 1 above), but no formal argument is here undertaken.

[2] Boas transcribes the MS words differently on two occasions: 'Kydd' on p. 293, 'Kydde' on cxxv of the 'Corrections and Additions' to the reissue of the *Works*, but without stating which he prefers.

[3] Boas, p. 286. Boas's reconsideration was first printed on a preliminary leaf of the original edition, as a stop-press afterthought.

[4] R. M. Gorrell, 'John Payne Collier and *The Murder of John Brewen*', *MLN*, LVII (1942), 441–4.

unconvincing.[1] Boas's denial of the attribution to Kyd was effort-less and summary, but no new data have since emerged to call it in question. Recently G. Lambrechts[2] has troubled an old ghost by crediting Kyd with the 'Shakespearian' *Edward III*, but the very passages he quotes in parallel belie his arguments, and his reasoning along more general lines is nonsensical.

[1] Crawford and Carrère have led this wing; but with the removal of *John Brewen* from Kyd's definite canon, many of the natural parallels of expression and subject-matter (both *Arden* and *Brewen* concern domestic murders) as well, perhaps, as the original suggestion, go entirely by the board.

[2] '*Edward III*, oeuvre de Thomas Kyd', *Études Anglaises*, XIV (1963), 160–74.

APPENDIX A

Kyd's Letters to Sir John Puckering

The transcript of Letter A follows Tannenbaum's (*The Booke of Sir Thomas Moore*, pp. 108–11), incorporating Baldwin's reading of 'vj yeres', and other material differences with Boas's text. The transcript of Letter B, unsigned, is by W. W. Greg (*English Literary Autographs*, I, XV).

Letter A   MS. *Harl.* 6849, fols. 218–19.

At my last being wth yor L^{p}. to entreate some speaches from yo^{u} in my favor to my Lorde, whoe (though I thinke, he rest not doubtfull of myne inocence) hath yet in his discreeter judgm^{t} feared to offende in his reteyning me, wthout yor hono^{rs} former pryvitie; So is it nowe R. ho: that the denyall of that favo^{r} (to my thought resonable) hath mov'de me to coniecture some suspicion, that yor L^{p} holds me in, concerning *Atheisme*, a deadlie thing wch I was vndeserved chargd wthall, & therfore have I though^{t} it requisite, aswell in duetie to yor L^{p}, & the lawes, as also in the feare of god, & freedom of my conscience, therein to satisfie the world and yo^{u}:

The first and most (thoughe insufficient) surmize that euer [w]as therein might^{t} be raisde of me, grewe thus. When I was first suspected for that libell that concern'd the state, amongst those waste and idle papers (wch I carde not for) & wch vnaskt I did deliuer vp, were founde some fragments of a disputation, toching that opinion, affirmd by Marlowe to be his, and shufled wth some of myne (vnknown to me) by some occasion of o^{r} wrytinge in one chamber twoe yeares synce.

My first acquaintance wth this Marlowe, rose vpon his bearing name to serve my Lo: although his L^{p} never knewe his service, but in writing for his plaie^{rs}, ffor never cold my L. endure his name, or sight, when he had heard of his conditions, nor wold indeed the forme of devyne praiers vsed duelie in his L^{ps} house, haue quadred wth such reprobates.

That I shold loue or be familer frend, wth one so irreligious, were verie rare, when *Tullie* saith *Digni sunt amicitia quib^{s} in ipsis inest causa cur diligantur* wch neither was in him, for p[er]son, quallities, or honestie, besides he was intemp[er]ate & of a cruel hart, the verie contraries to w^{ch}, my greatest enemies will saie by me.

It is not to be nombred amongst the best conditions of men, to taxe or to opbraide the deade *Quia mortui non mordent*, But thus muche haue I (wth yor L^{ps} favo^{r}) dared in the greatest cause, wch is to cleere my self of being thought an *Atheist*, which some will sweare he was.

ffor more assurance that I was not of that vile opinion, Lett it but please yor L^p to enquire of such as he conversd w^thall, that is (as I am geven to vnderstand) w^th *Harriot*, *Warner*, *Royden* and some stationers in Paules churchyard, whom I in no sort can accuse nor will excuse by reson of his companie, of whose consent if I had been, no question but I also shold haue been of their consort, for *ex minimo vestigo artifex agnoscit artificem.*

Of my religion & life I haue alredie geven some instance to the late commission^rs & of my reverend meaning to the state, although p[er]haps my paines and—vndeserved tortures felt by some, wold haue ingendred more impatience when lesse by farr hath dryven so manye *imo extra caulas* wch it shall—never do wth me.

But whatsoeue^r I haue felt R. ho: this is my request not for reward but in regard of my trewe innocence that it wold please yor L^ps so t[o] [. . . . . .] the same & me, as I maie still reteyne the favo^rs of my Lord, whom I haue servd almost theis vj yeres nowe, in credit vntill nowe, & nowe am vtterlie vndon w^thout herein be somewhat donn for my recoverie, ffor I do knowe his L^p holdes yor hono^rs & the state in that dewe reverence, as he wold no waie move the leste suspicion of his loves and cares both towards hir sacred Matie yor L^ps and the lawes whereof when tyme shall serve I shall geue greater instance wch I haue observed.

As for the libel laide vnto my chardg I am resolued wth receyving of ye sacram^t to satisfie yor L^ps & the world that I was neither agent nor consenting thervnto Howbeit if some outcast *Ismael* for want or of his owne dispose to lewdnes, haue wth pretext of duetie or religion, or to reduce himself to that he was not borne vnto by enie waie incensd yor L^ps to suspect me, I shall besech in all humillitie & in the feare of god that it will please yor L^ps but to censure me as I shall prove my self, and to repute them as they ar in deed *Cum totius iniustitiae nulla capitalior sit quam eoru, qui tum cum maximé fallunt id agunt vt viri boni esse videant^r* ffor doubtles even then yor L^ps shal be sure to breake [. . . .] their lewde designes and see into the truthe, when but their lyues that herein haue accused me shalbe examined & rypped vp effectually, soe maie I chaunce w^th *paul* to liue & shake the vyper of my hand into the fier for wch the ignorant suspect me guiltie of the former shipwrack. And thus (for nowe I feare me I growe teadious) assuring yor good L^ps that if I knewe eny whom I cold iustlie accuse of that damnable offence to the awefull Matie of god or of that other mutinous sedition towrd the state I wold as willinglie reveale them as I wold request yor L^ps bette^r thought*es* of me that neuer haue offended yo^u

Yo^r L^ps most humble in all duties

                                              Th. Kydde.

Letter B   MS. *Harl.* 6848, fol. 154.

Pleaseth it yor hono^rable l^p toching marlowes monstruous opinions as J cannot but wth an agreved conscience think on him or them so can J but pticulariz fewe in the respect of them that kept him greater company, Howbeit in discharg of dutie both towrds god yor l^{ps} & the world thus much haue J thoug(*ht* good breiflie to discover in all humblenes ffirst it was his custom when J knewe him first & as J heare saie he contynewd it in table talk or otherwise to iest at the devine scriptures gybe at praie^{rs}, & stryve in argum^t to frustrate & confute what hath byn spoke or wrytt by prophets & such holie meñ/

1 He wold report St John to be o^r savio^r Christes Alexis J cover it wth reverence and trembling that is that Christ did loue him wth an extraordinary loue/

2 That for me to wryte a poem of S^t paules conversion as J was determined he said wold be as if J shold go wryte a book of fast & loose, esteming Paul a Jugler.

3 That the prodigall Childs portion was but fower nobles, he held his purse so neere the bottom in all pictures, and that it either was a iest or els fowr nobles then was thought a great patrimony not thinking it a pable

4 That things esteemed to be donn by devine powe^r might haue a aswell been don by observation of men all wch he wold so sodenlie take slight occasion to slyp out as J & many others in regard of his other rashnes in attempting soden pryvie iniuries to men did ouerslypp though often reprehend him for it & for which god is my witnes aswell by my lords comaundm^t as in hatred of his life & thoughts J left & did refraine his companie/

He wold pswade wth men of quallitie to goe vnto the k of Scotts whether J heare Royden is gon and where if he had liud he told me when J sawe him last he meant to be/

APPENDIX B

Francis Kyd in Chancery

In 1571, when the future dramatist was thirteen and presumably attending Merchant Taylors', Francis Kyd and three other Londoners were involved as co-defendants in a fraud suit in Chancery. The plaintiff, John Dowsson or Dawson, sued to recover possession of a tavern or inn called the Greyhound, formerly the Bell, in the parish of St. Peter's, Cornhill (Proceedings docket, P.R.O. C.2.D.8/45). He asserts that the tenement had passed title illegally, after the decease of a previous owner, John Dalton, via one Walter Meres and subsequently John Bricked or Bricket, to William Abraham and Henry Sutton—one of the most frequent jurors in will-inquisitions—and finally in part to Francis Kyd, who seems to have bought into the enterprise at a slightly later date. Kyd's deposition is filed in common with Sutton's and Abraham's, and the sheet is unfortunately defective and nearly illegible in the short section which concerns him. But it appears that he has personally instigated some sort of action to exclude Dowsson from the premises in dispute, and that Dowsson's suit in Chancery is regarded by the defendents as retaliatory.

On 28 April 1571 the court directed both plaintiff and defendants, naming each, to be ready to 'make answere' 'Mondaye next', or 5 May, under penalty of an adverse decision (P.R.O. C.33.43(1571), fol. 237ᵛ; index vol. 1422). But they do not reappear in the decrees book at the date named, nor at any time in the next year, and one may presume that a settlement was reached out of court.

SELECT LIST OF WORKS EMPLOYED

Acheson, Arthur. *Shakespeare, Chapman and 'Sir Thomas More'*. London, 1931.

Adams, Joseph Quincy. *Shakespearean Playhouses*. Cambridge, Mass., 1917.

Allott, Robert. *England's Parnassus*, ed. Charles Crawford. Oxford, 1913.

Arber, Edward, ed. *An English Garner*. 8 vols. Birmingham, 1877–96.

—*A Transcript of the Registers of the Company of Stationers, 1554–1640*. 5 vols. London, 1875–94.

Bakeless, John. *The Tragicall History of Christopher Marlowe*. Cambridge, Mass., 1942.

Baker, Howard. *Induction to Tragedy*. Baton Rouge, La., 1939.

Baldwin, T. W. 'Nathaniel Field and Robert Wilson', *MLN*, XLI (1926), 32–34.

—'On the Chronology of Thomas Kyd's Plays', *MLN*, XL (1925), 343–9.

—*On the Literary Genetics of Shakespeare's Plays 1592–94*. Urbana, 1959.

—'Parallels between *Soliman and Perseda* and Garnier's *Bradamante*', *MLN*, LI (1936), 237–41.

—'Thomas Kyd's Early Company Connections', *PQ*, VI (1927), 311–13.

Beaumont, Francis, and John Fletcher. *The Works of Francis Beaumont and John Fletcher*, ed. A. H. Bullen *et al*. 4 vols. London, 1904–12.

Bentley, Gerald E. *The Jacobean and Caroline Stage*. 5 vols. Oxford, 1941–56.

—'The Wills of Two Elizabethan Actors', *MP*, XXIX (1931), 110–14.

Biesterfeldt, P. W. *Die Dramatische Technik Thomas Kyds*. Halle, 1936.

Bodenham, John, *Belvedere*. London: Spenser Society, 1875.

Bond, William H. 'The Cornwallis-Lysons Manuscript and the Poems of John Bentley', *Joseph Quincy Adams Memorial Studies* (Washington, 1948), 683–93.

Bowers, Fredson T. *Elizabethan Revenge Tragedy*. Princeton, 1940.

—'Kyd's Pedringano: Sources and Parallels', *Harvard Studies and Notes in Philology and Literature*, XIII (1931), 241–9.

Briggs, W. D. 'On a Document concerning Christopher Marlowe', *SP*, XX (1923), 153–9.

British Records Society. *The Index Library*. Vols. 1–80. London, 1888–1960.

Brooke, C. F. Tucker. *The Life of Marlowe*. London, 1930.

—(ed.). *The Shakespeare Apocrypha*. Oxford, 1908.

Brooke, J. M. S., and A. C. W. Hallen. *The Transcript of the Registers of the United Parishes of S. Mary Woolnoth and S. Mary Woolchurch* . . . *1538–1760*. London, 1886.

Brown, Arthur. 'The Play within a Play: An Elizabethan Dramatic Device', *Essays and Studies*, XIII (1960), 36–48.

Buckley, G. T. 'Who was the Late Arrian?' *MLN*, XLIX (1934), 500–3.

Bush, Douglas. *Mythology and the Renaissance Tradition in English Poetry*. New York, 1957.

Carrère, Félix, *Le Théâtre de Thomas Kyd*. Toulouse, 1951.

Catholic Records Society. *Publications*. Vols. 1–56. London, 1905–64.

Chambers, E. K. *The Elizabethan Stage*. 4 vols. Oxford, 1923.

—*William Shakespeare*. 2 vols. Oxford, 1930.

Chappell, William. *Old English Popular Music*, ed. H. E. Wooldridge. New York, 1961.

Chew, Samuel C. *The Crescent and the Rose*. Oxford, 1937.

Clemen, Wolfgang. *English Tragedy before Shakespeare*, tr. T. S. Dorsch. London, 1961.

Collier, John Payne. *A Bibliographical and Critical Account of the Rarest Books in the English Language*. 2 vols. London, 1865.

—*The History of English Dramatic Poetry to the Time of Shakespeare: and Annals of the Stage to the Restoration*. 3 vols. London, 1831.

Crawford, Charles. 'The Authorship of *Arden of Feversham*', *SJ*, XXXIX (1903), 74–86.

—'Belvedere', *ES*, XLIII (1910–11), 198–228.

—*A Concordance to the Works of Thomas Kyd*. Louvain, 1906–10.

Cunliffe, John W. (ed.). *Early English Classical Tragedies*. Oxford, 1912.

Dekker, Thomas. *The Dramatic Works of Thomas Dekker*, ed. Fredson Bowers. 4 vols. Cambridge, 1953–61.

—*A Knight's Conjuring*, ed. E. F. Rimbault. London, 1842.

—*Non-Dramatic Works*, ed. Alexander Grosart. 5 vols. 1884–6.

Dictionary of National Biography, ed. Leslie Stephen and Sidney Lee. 21 vols. and Supplements. London, 1908–9, etc.

Diesch, Carl Herman. *Die Inszenierung des Deutschen Dramas an der Wende des Sechzehnten un Siebzenten Jahrhunderts*. Leipzig, 1905.

Ditchfield, P. H. *The City Companies of London*. London, 1904.

—*The Story of the City Companies*. Boston, 1926.

Doleschal, Anton. *Der Versbau in Thomas Kyds Dramen*. Steyr, 1892.

Draper, F. W. M. *Four Centuries of Merchant Taylors' School*. London, 1961.

Duff, E. G. *A Century of the English Book Trade, 1457–1557*. London, 1905.

Duffie, G. I. *The Bad Quarto of Hamlet*. Cambridge, 1951.

Eccles, Mark. *Christopher Marlowe in London*. Cambridge, Mass., 1934.

Eliot, T. S. *Essays on Elizabethan Drama*. New York, 1956.

Farnham, Willard. *The Medieval Heritage of Elizabethan Tragedy*. London, 1936; Oxford, 1963.

Feuillerat, Albert. *Documents relating to the Office of the Revels in the Time of Queen Elizabeth.* Louvain, 1908.

Fleay, F. G. *A Biographical Chronicle of the English Drama.* 2 vols. London, 1891.

Foakes, R. A., and R. T. Rickert (eds.). *Henslowe's Diary.* Cambridge, 1961.

Freeman, Arthur. 'New Records of Thomas Kyd and his Family,' *NQ*, CCX (1965), 328–9.

Freeman, Arthur. 'Shakespeare and "Solyman and Perseda",' *MLR*, LVIII (1963), 481–7.

Gibbs, Vicary, G. H. White, *et al. The Complete Peerage.* 13 vols. London, 1910–59.

Giraldi Cintio, Giovanni Battista. *Tragedie.* Venice, 1583.

Goodwin, Gordon. 'Thomas Kyd', *NQ*, 8th ser., V (1894), 305–6.

Greene, Robert. *The Plays and Poems of Robert Greene*, ed. J. Churton Collins. 2 vols. Oxford, 1905.

Greg, W. W. *A Bibliography of the English Printed Drama to the Restoration.* 4 vols. London, 1939–59.

—*English Literary Autographs.* 4 vols. Oxford, 1925.

—(ed.). *Henslowe's Diary.* 2 vols. London, 1904.

—'Mr. Farmer's Facsimiles', *The Athenaeum*, No. 4455 (1913), 316.

—and E. Boswell (eds.). *Records of the Court of the Stationers' Company 1576–1602.* London, 1930.

—'The Works of Thomas Kyd', *MLQ*, IV (1901), 186–90.

Griffiths, Arthur. *The Chronicles of Newgate.* 2 vols. London, 1884.

Grubb, Marion. 'Kyd's Borrowings from Garnier's *Bradamante*', *MLN*, L (1935), 169–71.

Harbage, Alfred. *Annals of English Drama 975–1700*, revised by Samuel Schoenbaum. London, 1964.

Harrison, G. B. *The Elizabethan Journals.* London, 1938.

Hart, Mrs. E. P. *Merchant Taylors' School Register, 1561–1934.* 2 vols. London, 1936.

Hawkins, Thomas (ed.). *The Origin of the English Drama.* 3 vols. Oxford, 1773.

Hazen, A. T. 'Type-Facsimiles', *MP*, XLIV (1947), 209–17.

Hazlitt, W. C. (ed.). *Dodsley's Select Collection of Old English Plays.* 15 vols. London, 1874–6.

Heywood, Thomas. *The Hierarchie of the Blessed Angells.* London, 1635.

Hotson, Leslie. *The Death of Christopher Marlowe.* London, 1925.

Jackson, William A. (ed.). *Records of the Court of the Stationers' Company 1602 to 1640.* London, 1957.

Jensen, Ejner J. 'Kyd's *Spanish Tragedy*: the Play explains itself,' *JEGP*, LXIV (1966), 7–16.

Jonson, Ben. *The Works of Ben Jonson*, ed. C. H. Herford and Percy and Evelyn Simpson. 10 vols. Oxford, 1925–52.

Joseph, B. L. *Elizabethan Acting.* Oxford, 1964.

Keller, Wolfgang. 'The Works of Thomas Kyd', SJ, XXXVIII (1902), 280–2.

Kocher, Paul H. Christopher Marlowe. Chapel Hill, 1946.

Kyd, Thomas. Cornelia, ed. H. Gassner. Munich, 1894.

[—] The Spanish Tragedy (1592). London: Malone Society Reprints, 1948 (1949).

[—] The Spanish Tragedy with Additions 1602. London: Malone Society Reprints, 1925,

—The Spanish Tragedy, ed. Josef Schick. London, 1898.

—Thomas Kyd's Spanish Tragedy . . . Kritischer Text und Apparat, ed. Josef Schick. Berlin, 1901.

—The Spanish Tragedy, ed. Philip Edwards. London, 1959.

—The Works of Thomas Kyd, ed. Frederick S. Boas. Oxford, 1955.

Laird, David. 'Hieronimo's Dilemma,' SP, LXII (1966), 137–46.

Lamb, Charles. Specimens of English Dramatic Poets, ed. I. Gollancz. London, 1893.

Langbaine, Gerard. An Account of the English Dramatick Poets. London, 1691.

Lambrechts, G. 'Edward III Oeuvre de Thomas Kyd', Études Anglaises, XVI (1963), 160–74.

Lawrence, W. J. The Elizabethan Playhouse [First Series]. Stratford-upon-Avon, 1912.

—'Plays within Plays', ES, XXXIII (1904), 384–403.

—'Soliman and Perseda', MLR, IX (1914), 523–5.

Lee, Sidney, A Life of William Shakespeare. New York, 1909.

Leishman, J. B. (ed.). The Three Parnassus Plays. London, 1949.

Levin, Harry. 'An Echo from The Spanish Tragedy', MLN, LXIV (1949), 297–302.

Levin, Michael Henry. ' "Vindicta Mihi!" Meaning, Morality and Motivation in The Spanish Tragedy,' SEL, IV (1965), 307–24.

Lewis, C. S. English Literature in the Sixteenth Century. Oxford, 1954.

Lodge, Edmund. Illustrations of British History, 3rd ed. 3 vols. London, 1838.

Lowndes, William T. The Bibliographer's Manual of English Literature, ed. Henry G. Bohn. 11 vols. London, 1857–64.

Lyly, John. Euphues, ed. Edward Arber. London, 1868.

McIlwraith, A. K. (ed.). Five Elizabethan Tragedies. London, 1938.

McKerrow, R. B. A Dictionary of Printers and Booksellers, 1557–1640. London, 1910.

—An Introduction to Bibliography for Literary Students. Oxford, 1928.

Manly, John M. (ed.). Specimens of the Pre-Shakespearean Drama. 2 vols. Boston, 1897.

Marlowe, Christopher. The Works of Christopher Marlowe, ed. C. F. Tucker Brooke. Oxford, 1910.

Marscheffel, K. Thomas Kyds Tragedien. Weimar, 1880.

Marston, John. *The Plays of John Marston*, ed. H. Harvey Wood. 3 vols. Edinburgh, 1934–9.

Meyer, Edward. *Machiavelli and the English Drama*. Weimar, 1897.

Michael, Otto. *Der Stil in Thomas Kyds Original-Dramen*. Weimar, 1905.

Middleton, Thomas. *The Works of Thomas Middleton*, ed. A. H. Bullen. 8 vols. Boston, 1885–6.

Miksch, Walther. *Die Verfasserschaft des Arden of Feversham*. Breslau, 1907.

Mitchell, Samuel J. 'Rhetoric as a Dramatic Element in the Plays of Thomas Kyd', unpubl. diss., University of Texas, 1951.

Morrison, Paul G. *Index of Printers . . . in STC*. Charlottesville, 1950.

[Munday, Anthony.] *Fidele and Fortunio the Two Italian Gentlemen*. London: Malone Society Reprints, 1909.

Munro, John (ed.). *The Shakespeare Allusion Book*. London, 1909.

Murray, John J. 'The Tragedye of Solyman and Perseda, edited from the Original Texts with Introduction and Notes', unpubl. diss., New York University, 1959.

Murray, John T. *English Dramatic Campanies 1558–1642*. 2 vols. London, 1910.

Mustard, W. P. 'Notes on Thomas Kyd's Works', *PQ*, V (1926), 85–86.

Narcissus, ed. M. L. Lee. London, 1893.

Nares, Robert. *A Glossary or Collection of Words, Phrases, Names and Allusions . . . in the Works of English Authors*, ed. J. O. Halliwell and Thomas Wright. 2 vols. London, 1901.

Nashe, Thomas. *The Works of Thomas Nashe*, ed. Ronald B. McKerrow, corrected reissue ed. F. P. Wilson. 5 vols. Oxford, 1958.

Nelson, Robert J. *Play within a Play*. New Haven, 1958.

Nungezer, Edwin. *A Dictionary of Actors*. New Haven, 1929.

Østerberg, V. *Studier over Hamlet-Teksterne*. Copenhagen, 1920.

Peele, George. *The Life and Works of George Peele*, ed. C. T. Prouty *et al.* Vols. 1–2. New Haven, 1952–61.

—*Merrie Conceited Iests of George Peele*. London: for Henry Bell, n.d. [Type-facsimile by J. Smeeton, *c.* 1810.]

Pendrill, Charles. *Old Parish Life in London*. London, 1937.

Pepys, Samuel. *The Diary of Samuel Pepys*, ed. Henry B. Wheatley. 8 vols. London and Cambridge, 1923.

Phillips, Edward. *Theatrum Poetarum*, ed. Egerton Brydges. 3 vols. London, 1800.

Pollard, A. W. ' "Facsimile" Reprints of Old Books: Preliminary Survey', *The Library*, Fourth Ser., VI (1926), 305–13.

—and G. R. Redgrave, *et al. A Short-Title Catalogue of Books printed . . . 1475–1640*. London, 1926.

Puttenham, George. *The Arte of English Poesie*, ed. Edward Arber. London, 1869.

Robinson, Charles J. *A Register of the Scholars Admitted into Merchant Taylors' School, 1562–1874*. 2 vols. Lewes, 1882.

Routh, James E., Jr. 'Thomas Kyd's Rime Schemes and the Authorship of *Soliman and Perseda* and of *The First Part of Jeronimo*', *MLN*, XX (1905), 49–51.

Sarrazin, Gregor. 'Der Verfasser von *Soliman and Perseda*', *ES*, XV (1891), 250–63.

—*Thomas Kyd und sein Kreis*. Berlin, 1892.

—'*The Works of Thomas Kyd*', *ES*, XXXIII (1903), 113–25.

Schick, Josef. 'Sarrazin's Thomas Kyd', *Archiv*, XC (1893), 176–94.

—'Thomas Kyds Todesjahr', *SJ*, XXXV (1899), 277–80.

Schoenwerth, Rudolf. *Die Niederländischen und Deutschen Bearbeitungen von Thomas Kyd's Spanish Tragedy*. Gräfenhainichen, 1902.

—*Die Niederländischen und Deutschen Bearbeitungen von Thomas Kyd's Spanish Tragedy*. Berlin, 1903.

Schücking, L. L. *Die Zusätze zur 'Spanish Tragedy'*. Leipzig, 1938.

Schwartz, I. A. *The Commedia dell' Arte and its Influence on French Comedy in the Seventeenth Century*. New York, n.d.

Shakespeare, William. *The Complete Works of Shakespeare*, ed. G. L. Kittredge. Boston, 1936.

—*King John*, ed. J. Dover Wilson. Cambridge, 1936.

—*Othello*, ed. J. Dover Wilson. Cambridge, 1957.

—*Titus Andronicus*, ed. J. C. Maxwell. Cambridge, Mass., 1953.

Shirley, James. *The Dramatic Works and Poems of James Shirley . . .*, ed. William Gifford and Alexander Dyce. 6 vols. London, 1833.

Sibley, Gertrude M. *The Lost Plays and Masques 1500–1642*. Ithaca, 1933.

Sisson, C. J. *Lost Plays of Shakespeare's Age*. Cambridge, 1936.

Small, R. A. *The Stage-Quarrel between Ben Jonson and the So-called Poetasters*. Breslau, 1899.

Smet, J. de. *Thomas Kyd, l'Homme et l'Oeuvre*. Brussels, 1925.

Smith, G. Gregory (ed.). *Elizabethan Critical Essays*. 2 vols. Oxford, 1904.

Solimon and Perseda 1599, ed. John S. Farmer. N.p.: Tudor Facsimile Texts, 1912.

Spencer, Theodore. *Death and Elizabethan Tragedy*. Cambridge, Mass., 1936.

Stoll, E. E. *Shakespeare Studies*. New York, 1927.

Stow, John. *A Survey of London (1603)*, ed. C. L. Kingsford. 2 vols. Oxford, 1908.

Stroheker, Friedrich. *Doppelformen und Rhythmus bei Marlowe und Kyd*. Heidelberg, 1913.

Strype, John. *Annals of the Reformation*. 4 vols. London, 1725–31.

Symonds, John Addington. *Shakespeare's Predecessors in the English Drama*. London, 1884.

Tannenbaum, Samuel A. *The Assassination of Christopher Marlowe*. Hamden, Conn., 1928.

—*The Booke of Sir Thomas Moore*. New York, 1927.

—*Thomas Kyd (A Concise Bibliography)*. New York, 1941.

Thorndike, A. H. 'The Works of Thomas Kyd', MLN, XVII (1902), 283–94.

The Tragical Reign of Selimus 1594. London: Malone Society Reprints, 1908.

Venn, John and J. A. Alumni Cantabigiensis, Part I. 4 vols. Cambridge, 1922–7.

Wagner, B. M. 'Thomas Kyd', NQ, CLV (1928), 420.

Ward. A. W. A History of English Dramatic Literature. 3 vols. London, 1899.

Watson, Thomas. Poems, ed. Edward Arber. London, 1870.

Webster, John. The Complete Works of John Webster, ed. F. L. Lucas. 4 vols. London, 1927.

Wickham, Glynne. Early English Stages 1300 to 1660. Volume Two: 1576 to 1660, Part I. London, 1963.

Wiehl, Karl. 'Thomas Kyd und die autorschaft von Soliman and Perseda', ES, XLIV (1912), 343–60.

—Thomas Kyd und sein Vers. Kempten, 1911.

Williams, Franklin B. Index of Dedications and Commendatory Verses in English Books before 1641. London, 1962.

—'Leicester's Ghost', Harvard Studies and Notes in Philology and Literature, XVIII (1935), 271–85.

Witherspoon, Alexander M. The Influence of Robert Garnier on Elizabethan Drama. New Haven, 1924.

INDEX

DATE DUE